Lecture Notes in Computer Science   9961

Commenced Publication in 1973
Founding and Former Series Editors:
Gerhard Goos, Juris Hartmanis, and Jan van Leeuwen

More information about this series at http://www.springer.com/series/7409

Luciano Gamberini · Anna Spagnolli
Giulio Jacucci · Benjamin Blankertz
Jonathan Freeman (Eds.)

Symbiotic Interaction

5th International Workshop, Symbiotic 2016
Padua, Italy, September 29–30, 2016
Revised Selected Papers

 Springer

OPEN

Editors
Luciano Gamberini
University of Padua
Padua
Italy

Anna Spagnolli
University of Padua
Padua
Italy

Giulio Jacucci
University of Helsinki
Helsinki
Finland

Benjamin Blankertz
TU Berlin
Berlin, Berlin
Germany

Jonathan Freeman
Goldsmiths University
London
UK

ISSN 0302-9743   ISSN 1611-3349 (electronic)
Lecture Notes in Computer Science
ISBN 978-3-319-57752-4   ISBN 978-3-319-57753-1 (eBook)
DOI 10.1007/978-3-319-57753-1

Library of Congress Control Number: 2017938156

LNCS Sublibrary: SL3 – Information Systems and Applications, incl. Internet/Web, and HCI

Printed on acid-free paper

This Springer imprint is published by Springer Nature
The registered company is Springer International Publishing AG
The registered company address is: Gewerbestrasse 11, 6330 Cham, Switzerland

Preface

The Symbiotic Workshop is the primary venue for presenting scientific works dealing with the symbiotic relationships between humans and computers and for discussing the nature and implications of such relationships.

This volume collects the papers presented at the 5th International Workshop on Symbiotic Interaction, which was held in Padua (Italy) during September 29–30, 2016. Previous editions of the workshop were held in Padua, London, Helsinki, and Berlin. The proceedings are published this year with an open access license by Springer, to improve their accessibility and dissemination.

The workshop was co-sponsored by the MindSee project (http://mindsee.eu, FP7-ICT n. 611570) and by the Department of General Psychology of the University of Padua and connected to the Open Innovation Days, a three-day national event organized by the University of Padua and the leading Italian economic newspaper *IlSole-24Ore*. It also benefited from the hospitality of Comune di Padova (Padua Municipality) in its historical city hall.

All papers were received in response to a public call and underwent at least two rounds of reviews: In the first round, three members of the scientific committee reviewed each paper double-blind; the 13 accepted papers were then revised by the authors and iteratively checked by the proceedings editors. This led to an acceptance rate of 50%, which is much lower than in the previous editions of this workshop, and to a multiple-step quality check that is the standard for scientific journals more than for conference proceedings. The paper "Prediction of Difficulty Levels in Videogames from Ongoing EEG" by L. Naumann, M. Schultze-Kraft, S. Daehne, and B. Blankertz was awarded best presentation, based on the audience preferences.

In addition to the papers selected through the process described above, the proceedings also include the short abstracts of the presentations by the three keynote speakers (Steve Benford, Hans Gellersen, Sid Kouider), the report of an interdisciplinary panel on the risks of symbiotic systems involving five experts (Mauro Conti, Jonathan Freeman, Giorgia Guerra, David Kirsh, and A. van Wynsberghe), and an introductory note from the two Symbiotic 2016 co-chairs. Some of the posters included in the program were expanded and published in a special issue of the on-line journal *PsychNology* (www.psychnology.org).

We would like to express our gratitude to the colleagues who attended the conference, submitted their work, and reviewed the submissions, for their ideas, attention, and time.

December 2016

Luciano Gamberini
Anna Spagnolli
Benjamin Blankertz
Giulio Jacucci
Jonathan Freeman

Organization

Program Committee

Ilkka Arminen	University of Helsinki, Finland
Fabio Babiloni	University of Rome Sapienza, Italy
Benjamin Blankertz	Technische Universität Berlin, Germany
Marc Cavazza	University of Kent, UK
Mauro Conti	University of Padua, Italy
Manuel Eugster	Aalto University and HIIT, Finland
Stephen Fairclough	Liverpool John Moores University, UK
Jonathan Freeman	Goldsmiths College, University of London, UK
Luciano Gamberini	University of Padua, Italy
Dorota Glowacka	University of Helsinki, Finland
Jaap Ham	Eindhoven University of Technology, The Netherlands
Giulio Jacucci	Helsinki Institute for Information Technology, Finland
David Kirsh	University of California, San Diego, USA
Peter König	University of Osnabrück, Germany
Christian Licoppe	Telecom Paristech, France
Juan C. Moreno	Consejo Superior de Investigaciones Científicas, Spain
Anton Nijholt	University of Twente, The Netherlands
Anna Spagnolli	University of Padova, Italy
Paul Verschure	UPF, ICREA, Spain

Additional Reviewers

Lal, Chhagan
Lazzeretti, Riccardo

Keynote Speakers Abstracts

Rethinking Eye Gaze for Symbiotic Human-Computer Interaction

Hans Gellersen

Lancaster University, Lancaster, UK

Eye tracking has a long history and its use for human-computer interaction predates the ubiquitous computing era. While the technology has been maturing and become affordable for widespread use, there has not been much innovation in the use of eye gaze for interaction. For over 25 years, gaze pointing has remained the prevailing usage paradigm, although it overloads the sensory role of the eyes with a control function. In this talk I will present work that explores new ways of using eye movement for interaction. I will discuss gaze and touch: how hands and eyes can naturally work together; gaze and motion: how the natural gaze-following of moving stimuli enables new types of interface; and gaze and games: how gaze can be social and fun.

Neural Markers of Perceptual Consciousness

Sid Kouider

Ecole Normale Supérieure LSCP, Paris, France

Consciousness is one the most intriguing phenomenon in contemporary science. After a long period of denial, scientists are now actively trying to understand how the brain gives rise to our conscious experience. More specifically, modern brain imaging techniques allows us to uncover the interplay between the conscious and unconscious mind, not only in human adults but also in infants and animals. This lecture describes how scientists are tackling this difficult issue and how much progress has been made so far in determining the neural structures and mechanisms that are responsible for consciousness. I will focus on three main issues. First, I will address recent findings showing that attention and consciousness, classically thought to be equivalent phenomena, are subserved by distinct brain functions. Secondly, I will address how much information can be processed by the brain in the absence of consciousness, by looking at neural responses to stimuli presented either subliminally or during sleep. Finally, I will address how neural signatures of consciousness can be used when verbal report is impossible, in animals, vegetative patients and preverbal infants.

On the Pleasures of Giving Up Control

Steve Benford

University of Nottingham, Nottingham, UK

If there is one thing that rollercoasters teach us it is that giving up control to the machine can be a thrilling experience. I'd like to invite you, the audience, to strap yourselves in and join me on a ride through creative and entertaining examples of relinquishing control to 'the machine'. From the thrills and spills of a breath-controlled bucking bronco, to a meditative brain-controlled movie, to musicians improvising around music recognition systems, I will seek to illustrate the creative possibilities of partial and negotiated control – both of machines and ultimately of our own bodies and thoughts. I will introduce new taxonomies of control as well as the idea of deliberately designing uncomfortable interactions as a route to entertainment, enlightenment and social bonding.

Contents

Towards a Definition of Symbiotic Relations Between Humans and Machines

Luciano Gamberini[✉] and Anna Spagnolli

Department of General Psychology & Human Inspired Technologies Research Centre,
Padua University, Padua, Italy
{luciano.gamberini,anna.spagnolli}@unipd.it

Abstract. What are symbiotic systems? In this short paper, the workshop chairs describe the focus of this workshop and elaborate on the definition of symbiotic human-machine relation.

Keywords: Symbiotic system · Human-computer interaction

Symbiotic relationships are probably most known from biology. In a symbiotic relationship between animals and/or plants, some organism closely interacts with another type of organism to ensure its own survival, so that both end up sharing the same habitat [3]. This biological phenomenon, exemplifying a very tight kind of relationship, is used metaphorically[1] to characterize a growing part of the current human-machine relations, where machines collect users' data that are not even available to the human conscious cognition (e.g. brain signals, social data collected on the web), and then elaborate solutions and make decisions based on such data. Here machines are so interconnected to humans that the term interaction sounds like an understatement [13].

After the pioneering discussion on men-computer [*sic*] symbiosis stimulated in the early 60 by J.C.R. Licklider [9], the reference to symbiotic human-machine interaction appeared again around 2013 in a European Union ICT workprogram stressing that concept[2] and has grown ever since, as is partly documented in the Symbiotic Interaction workshops and proceedings [2, 5]. Surely, in the field of human-computer interaction as well as in philosophy and sociology of technology, the close connection between humans and machines has been emphasized several times: by the concepts of artifacts and embodied cognition, where the propriety of a technology depends on the users' needs and the users' ability depends in turn on the tools s/he is endowed with (e.g., [7]); by the notion of sociotechnical systems, where a technology inevitably includes some symbolic, politic elements as part of the package (e.g., [8]); by the idea of humans as hybrids or cyborgs, which finds real-life incarnations in medical prosthesis and augmentation devices (e.g., [1]). However, the term symbiotic emphasizes a noteworthy change

---

[1] Of course, a metaphor is able to illuminate some aspects of a domain by similarity with some other domain [12], but not all aspects. Where the biological metaphor stops is in referring to two leaving organisms in partnership, since a symbiotic technology is not credited to share the same needs (and rights) as the human being to which it is joined.

[2] http://cordis.europa.eu/fp7/ict/docs/ict-wp2013-10-7-2013-with-cover-issn.pdf.

© The Author(s) 2017
L. Gamberini et al. (Eds.): Symbiotic 2016, LNCS 9961, pp. 1–4, 2017.
DOI: 10.1007/978-3-319-57753-1_1

in the interdependence between humans and machines, pointing to an intimate kind of relation that is made possible by the synergic advances in physiological computing, biometrics, sensing technologies, and machine learning, often combined with the ubiquity of networked devices. Users do not necessarily need to be aware of what is happening while machines help themselves with information, since this process mostly occurs implicitly [6], relying on human biosignals that are out of grasp to the individual user (e.g., [10]) or on billions of traces left by users of networked devices. A symbiotic device does not need to be reprogrammed or fine-tuned: on the contrary, it can learn, sense the context, evolve in close relation with the environment by analyzing the consequences of processes jointly started with humans.

So, although very different in purpose and tradition, all the "symbiotic advances" converge in technological products that tap directly the user to get input information. and evolve their own intelligence on the basis of their performance. The pervasiveness, ubiquity and consequentiality of such devices in everyday life justify their being singled out, monitored and reflected upon. The adoption of a dedicated label for such devices, such as 'symbiotic', is meant to encourage such process.

Elaborating on the description of symbiotic interaction first proposed in 2014 [4], we can identify *symbiotic systems* as those computerized devices that can autonomously fetch information from the users, interpret such information to model the user and then make decisions with the ultimate goal of simplifying the users' task, clarifying possible issues, or refining a service for them (e.g., recommendations); and finally to evolve and become more efficient by learning from previous interaction. To represent this process in terms of human-machine interaction, we can extend Norman's model of action [11] into something similar to what is shown in Fig. 1.

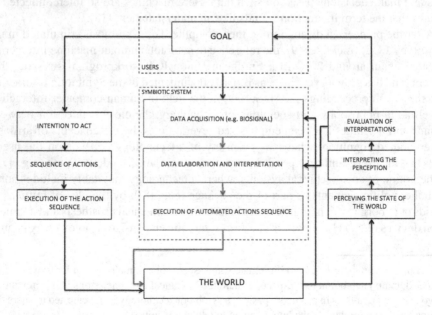

Fig. 1. A modification of Donald Normans action model to include a symbiotic system.

Since this process is meant to release the user from the burden of providing the information necessary to enjoy some improved, tailored service, it is in continuity with HCI principle of usability and intuitiveness. However, this process works so far in the background to become elusive and so peculiar in its interpretation of the users' goals to misjudge them. There is room for reflection then on the risks for users, let alone the clear advantages brought about by symbiotic machines. Advantages will be described by almost all chapters in this book, each one illustrating some applications of symbiotic technology; risks will be highlighted and reflected upon in the next chapter.

Acknowledgments. The present reflections benefit from the work carried out within the EU project MindSee (grant agreement n. 611570).

References

1. Barfield, W.: Cyber-Humans: Our Future with Machines. Springer, Cham (2015)
2. Blankertz, B., Jacucci, G., Gamberini, L., Spagnolli, A., Freeman, J. (eds.): Symbiotic 2015. LNCS, vol. 9359. Springer, Cham (2015). doi:10.1007/978-3-319-24917-9
3. Douglas, A.E.: The symbiotic habit. Princeton University Press (2010)
4. Jacucci, G., Spagnolli, A., Freeman, J., Gamberini, L.: Symbiotic interaction: a critical definition and comparison to other human-computer paradigms. In: Jacucci, G., Gamberini, L., Freeman, J., Spagnolli, A. (eds.) Symbiotic 2014. LNCS, vol. 8820, pp. 3–20. Springer, Cham (2014). doi:10.1007/978-3-319-13500-7_1
5. Jacucci, G., Gamberini, L., Freeman, J., Spagnolli, A. (eds.): Symbiotic 2014. LNCS, vol. 8820. Springer, Cham (2014). doi:10.1007/978-3-319-13500-7
6. Janlert, L.E., Stolterman, E.: The Meaning of Interactivity—Some Proposals for Definitions and Measures. Human–Computer Interaction, pp. 1–36 (2016)
7. Kirsh, D.: Embodied cognition and the magical future of interaction design. ACM Trans. Comput.-Hum. Interact. (TOCHI) 20(1), 3 (2013)
8. Kling, R.: Social analyses of computing: theoretical perspectives in recent empirical research. ACM Comput. Surv. (CSUR) 12(1), 61–110 (1980)
9. Licklider, J.C.: Man-computer symbiosis. IRE Trans. Hum. Factors Electron. 1, 4–11 (1960)
10. Negri, P., Gamberini, L., Cutini, S.: A review of the research on subliminal techniques for implicit interaction in symbiotic systems. In: Jacucci, G., Gamberini, L., Freeman, J., Spagnolli, A. (eds.) Symbiotic 2014. LNCS, vol. 8820, pp. 47–58. Springer, Cham (2014). doi:10.1007/978-3-319-13500-7_4
11. Norman, D.A.: The Design of Everyday Things. Basic Book, New York (1988)
12. Ortony, A.: Metaphor and Thought. Cambridge University Press, Cambridge (1993)
13. Verbeek, P.P.: Beyond interaction: a short introduction to mediation theory. Interactions 22(3), 26–31 (2015)

Adapting the System to Users Based on Implicit Data: Ethical Risks and Possible Solutions

Anna Spagnolli[1(✉)], Mauro Conti[2], Giorgia Guerra[3],
Jonathan Freeman[4], David Kirsh[5], and Aimee van Wynsberghe[6]

[1] Human Inspired Technologies Research Centre and Department
of General Psychology, Padua University, Padua, Italy
anna.spagnolli@unipd.it
[2] Human Inspired Technologies Research Centre and Department
of Mathematics, Padua University, Padua, Italy
mauro.conti@unipd.it
[3] Departmentof Political Science, Law and International Studies,
Padua University, Padua, Italy
giorgia.guerra@unipd.it
[4] Goldsmiths College, University of London, London, UK
J.Freeman@gold.ac.uk
[5] University of California at San Diego, San Diego, USA
kirsh@ucsd.edu
[6] Unversity of Twente, Enschede, Netherlands
a.l.vanwynsberghe@utwente.nl

Abstract. Symbiotic systems are systems that gather personal data *implicitly* provided by the user, derive a *profile/model* of the user from such data and *adjust* their output/service according to their notion of what would be desirable to the user thus modeled. Because of these three characteristics, symbiotic systems represent a step forward towards facilitated, simplified, user-friendly digital devices, or do they? Here we propose three cases describing realistic applications of symbiotic systems that potentially encapsulate some serious risk to their users. Experts of five different domains (i.e., ethics, security, law, human-computer interaction and psychology) dissect each case to identify the risks to the users and derive some possible minimization strategies. This panel aims at contributing to a beneficial development of symbiotic systems as it can be achieved by increasing users' discernment and awareness of their consequences for society and everyday life.

Keywords: Symbiotic system · Implicit data · Ethics · Security · Design · Risks · Information leakage · Privacy · Awareness

1 Introduction

The increasing pervasiveness and refinement of systems that can acquire personal data from users based on the users' own actions on the system - or actions in the environment where the system sensors are positioned - marks a qualitative, discrete change

© The Author(s) 2017
L. Gamberini et al. (Eds.): Symbiotic 2016, LNCS 9961, pp. 5–22, 2017.
DOI: 10.1007/978-3-319-57753-1_2

6   A. Spagnolli et al.

in the way in which the human interaction with technologies articulates. The label
'symbiotic systems' is meant to mark such a change, to make it visible, to single it out
from a continuous line of technological development in physiological computing,
machine learning, and sensing devices.

Symbiotic technologies establish a **symbiotic relationship** with the human users.
They extract information about the users' state, behaviors or preferences, and adapt
their services to the users' profile thereby created. Figure 1 illustrates the rationale of
this process: a human who interprets his/her relation with the environment and acts
consequently is tapped onto by a prosthetic system that can interpret the users' state
and response and can plan interventions on the environment based on a set of built-in
criteria. This model highlights three main characteristics of symbiotic technologies:

- symbiotic technologies **acquire implicit information about the user**, namely data
  that users might not be aware of giving out and whose release and content they
  might not be able to control;
- the implicit information is elaborated so as to create a **model of the user(s)**;
- the system takes over some of the users' **decisions**, according to the user model and
  to what it is programmed to consider as the best way to serve that model of user.

This scheme can foresee several variations: the symbiotic system can get information from many human beings instead of just one, thanks to current network technology and sensors; and the users of the system can be different from the humans
giving out implicit information. These variations notwithstanding, the core of the
system remains centered on the capturing/modeling/deciding process that makes
symbiotic systems able to bypass the user to which they are connected.

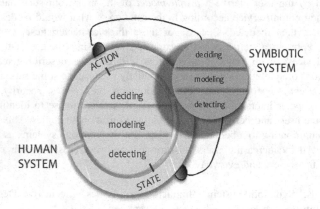

Fig. 1. A schematic representation of the symbiotic system tapping into a human system to
by-pass its detecting/modeling/deciding processes.

On part of the users feeding the system with personal information at low or no cost, the symbiotic relation is a transaction out of which direct or indirect benefits are expected, mostly in the form of having their tasks simplified, their peculiarities acknowledged and their preferences indulged by the system. From this point of view, symbiotic systems bring to the next level the notion of a user-centered system, where the system tailors to the user'state without the user even needing to ask. At the same time, however, the exact notion of what makes a system 'user-centred' is questioned by symbiotic systems, given the possibility that such systems - if incautiously designed - create serious security, ethic, legal and psychological risks to the user. While much debate on the risks of technologies merging with humans focuses on the bodily level of such merge (for example, humans with x-ray sight, robots with realistic emotional responses or networked machines taking control of human society [2]), the merge is already occurring pervasively at a more functional, **information** level. Recently, for instance, concerns have been raised about the ethics risks of merging Virtual Reality analytics and social networks for persuasive purposes [11] or to gather face recognition data in VR peripherals to allegedly customize the users' experience [5]. This chapter reports the reflections on such possible risks made by an interdisciplinary panel of experts gathered during Symbiotic 2016 in Padua. The panel tried to identify concrete ethic risks of current pervasive symbiotic systems from an interdisciplinary perspective, and to have such risks if not solved - at least effectively framed.

To facilitate discussion, three likely everyday life applications of symbiotic systems were presented to the panel's attention, which bore some problematic implications to users and which focused respectively on detecting, modeling and deciding. Each case was examined from five different perspectives: **ethics** (Aimee van Wynsberghe, President of the Foundation for Responsible Robotics and Assistant Professor at the University of Twente, the Netherlands), **information security** (Mauro Conti, University of Padua, Italy), **law** (Giorgia Guerra, University of Padua, Italy), **human-computer interaction** (David Kirsh, University of California, San Diego, US) and **psychology** (Jonathan Freeman, University of London, Goldsmith College, UK perspective). Anna Spagnolli organized and chaired the panel. The examination of each of the three cases is reported in the following sections. The main points are summarized in the final section of this chapter.

2   Case 1, Detecting Users: The Unusual Job Interview

The first case describes the use of symbiotic system where the detection of personal data for uses that are counterproductive to the unaware data owner. Indications about the verisimilarity of such a case are provided by [6, 8, 12, 14] showing that the technology and the preconditions for much of the components of the scenario are already in place.

An *international firm is hiring personnel in the accounting department. At the selection interview, the candidates are asked to use a pc and fill in an electronic form, collecting basic demographic information but also data about previous jobs and a description of the reasons why they think they suit the vacant position. Each candidate is also asked to sign an informed consent allowing the firm to* acquire *the responses to the questionnaire, which will be used for archival reasons as well as to direct the subsequent interview with the human resources manager. The form specifies that the hiring company will use the written responses to the questionnaire as well as data on the pc usage while typing the responses (time, pressure and trajectory of the mouse movements). The questionnaire is mandatory and the firm commits to keep all collected data confidential. None of the candidates is aware that data on typing behavior can be used not just to identify the user but also to detect the probability that s/he is lying.*

2.1 Ethics

RISK: There are multiple risks involved in this case, e.g. lack of informed consent, lack of protection of best interests of the user, risk of deceit, and lack of transparency regarding data collection and data use. I suggest the area of risk involved in case 1 derives from a combination of the above mentioned risks, i.e. the system collects information about a user without informed consent or transparency for a purpose that is detrimental to the user while the benefits from such a collection belong only to the company collecting data through the system. More specifically, this represents a case of treating direct users as a **'means to an end'**, as mere tools to achieve the company's goal, and this would be an ethically questionable position in which to put a user. Once we can justify the use of individuals for this kind of practice – as a means to an end – the list of ethically questionable activities that may be condoned increases exponentially.

SOLUTION: A possible solution could be to mimic the current practices in academic institutes whereby an ethics committee is established to monitor and approve research practices. In so doing, ethical approval has to be obtained for studies to be conducted and to provide guidance on how to do so as well as in order to protect the rights and interests of the participants involved. Outside the academy this could happen on the form of an **Institutional Review Board for companies or an advocacy group**

that transcends the company as a body independent from it (i.e., not in the form of a department in the company itself). Independence is important as a way of striving for objective decisions and avoiding persuasion of ethics decisions.

2.2 Security

RISK: From a security perspective, the problem in case 1 is that the user provides more information than s/he means to. S/he only means to input text in the form, but in fact s/he provides a lot more information while doing so. This process, i.e., trying to use data to infer some other information from it, is known as **information leakage**. There are plenty of other examples of information leakage. For example, analyzing the incoming and outgoing network traffic, the energy consumption patterns and the movement of the phone recorded when using a mobile phone, without having access to content stored on the phone, is sufficient to infer information about the user such as: the application installed on the phone, sex, age range, preferred language, text typed etc. Information leakage is a very real technical possibility, and represents a security risk because such information can be exploited in a malicious way.

SOLUTION: Despite the transaction described in this case represents such an infringement to several policies and users' rights that in some domains it would never been accepted (e.g., in academics), it is nonetheless a very pervasive kind of transaction nowadays. The use of data for extracting more information than it intended to convey by the owner of that data is technically possible and this must make us suspicious that such possibility is actually exploited. It would then be good to find technical means to prevent such leakage to occur in the first place. The best protection in this case would be to **use one's own interface** to use when typing and then avoid typing on other parties' interfaces. And before that I consider it necessary to increase the **awareness** in the user that information leakage is a likely occurrence, so they can ask for using their own interfaces in cases such as the one described in the scenario (as well as for policies, etc.).

2.3 Law

RISK: The data collected here is used for a purpose different from the one for which it was collected; it can be considered as a **deceitful use of data**, and in this specific case this kind of use could create a risk of discriminatory behavior during the recruitment process. The informed consent is insufficient, being not transparent about the use of data. The additional complication is that the collected information, in order to be used, has to be **interpreted**. The reliability information extracted from pc usage is also questionable and still currently under debate. Consequently, this procedure could limit the users' self-determination, since candidates would have behaved differently had they known the actual purpose of the data collection.

SOLUTION: I think the burden for reducing the risk is on the **company**, which is required (especially in the US legal system) to have a more and more "proactive" role by providing more information in the consent form thereby increasing the **transparency** of the process. In particular, the user should be informed that - based on evidence law where "a brick is not a wall" - the interpretation of the information about future use collected in this way (movement of mouse etc.) might not be positively used by the company to inform its recruitment decisions: the reliability of interpreted information has always a margin of questionability that the user needs to be aware of (and the company alike).

2.4   HCI

RISK: From a human-computer interaction perspective, this case represents: (1) **asymmetric value**, where one side stands to gain more than the other side; (2) **asymmetric risk** where one side stands to lose more than the other side; and (3) **asymmetric knowledge** where one side knows what is going on while the other side does not. In a symbiotic relation the two sides are called symbiont and host. The symbiont is the company capturing and analyzing the information and the host is the user unwittingly providing the information. The alleged benefit for the candidate (the 'host') would be to have a chance to obtain the vacant position. Since giving data is mandatory for the application to be considered, it can be construed as forced by the company and of value to them. For the candidate, however, it is not clear that there is any direct benefit for giving out the information. Despite this asymmetry of value this still qualifies as a symbiotic interaction. In biology, symbiotic relations do not need to be mutually beneficial to the parties involved. One can be a parasite on the other.

SOLUTION: One solution is to **change the values in the asymmetry**. This could be achieved by having a policy according to which people have rights over personal information. This requires **defining personal information** and defining the difference between public and private domain. Personal information could be assumed to have a tier structure. When it is clear to the candidate what s/he is giving up – as determined by the tier level of private information – the company could be required to acknowledge that storing and analyzing that information is worth a certain amount. The exchange of information is then seen as a transaction which they have an obligation to pay for in some way. The candidate then would be in a position to make an informed decision whether to give up the information. If the company does not reveal the value or does not offer an appropriate amount in exchange then the candidate has grounds for a lawsuit, since whether s/he knows it or not there was a transaction and it violates the law or recognized policy concerning transactions in such cases.

A society might also decide to set a **cut-off** in such asymmetry, establishing for instance that no parasitic asymmetry is acceptable regardless of cost. That would become a law. Another thing to note is that in addition to the right to know a person might have intrinsic rights over future use. Since the value of a piece of information changes once it is aggregated with the information collected from several individuals it has one value in isolation and a rather greater value when part of the aggregation. If the information is now assigned a value as a function of the value of the aggregation the asymmetry of value is potentially reversed. It might even prove to be so counterproductive to the individual company to purchase information for recruitment purposes since now they would have to pay many individuals, when all they wanted was to select a few candidates. On the other hand, if there is general knowledge to be gained from this sort of data capture then a new business might spring up that provides analytic tools to companies to help them made better hiring decisions. In that case, individual companies would no longer need to capture this data and store. They could make judgments about candidates using existing analyses (sold by the new company) and throw away the data they collect themselves right after they make their decision.

2.5 Psychology

RISK: What in this case strikes from a psychology perspective first of all is a deficiency in informed consent. The case also points to the question of the **timescale** of the use of data: companies collect tons and tons of data which today are not useful, but might turn out to have a high value in the future. Logically the user cannot provide informed consent for the use of their data for a scenario or use case which today is unknown.

SOLUTION: The only approach to solving this risk is to aim for maximum **transparency**: informing users of how their data might be used today (the basis of all informed consent), and also illustrating how it might be used in future. Where future uses of the data are markedly different from those envisaged at the time users consent to their data being collected, it is clear that the data collector should be required to obtain consent for the new use of the data. There are some interesting developments in this space right now, with a number of UK companies developing 'games' as part of selection and recruitment, where behaviors which are monitored during selection process game-play reveal underlying psychological characteristics of the applicant. Whilst these characteristics may be analyzed with the informed consent of the appli-cant today, it is easy to imagine that other relationships between the game-play behavior and other psychological characteristics are discovered in the future. Without seeking new informed consent from the applicant at this point, user's test results should not be analyzed for the newly discovered characteristics.

3 Case 2, Modeling the User: The Tailored Persuasive Message

The second case illustrates a scenario where a symbiotic system is used to Profiling for persuasive purposes. Indications about the realism of such a case are provided by [1, 4, 9], showing how current users' analytics can be exploited for persuasive or manipulative purposes.

"Users of a popular search engine log in to a set of free services connected to the search engine; once they are logged-in, the computer keeps track of all webpages that are visited from the browser where the log in occurs. The search engine stores a great amount of data about users and elaborates profiles about choices and preferences connected to the user and to similar users. In particular, it runs a free game showing several scenes and characters, recording the users positive or negative response to those characters. The search engine also runs and advertising service, which is used during a major election in one European city. The election candidate, who purchases the advertising service for the occasion, uses the stored preferences to automatically personalize the campaign ads and to make his/her portrait as a person looking as similar as possible to the individual elector. It also sends favorable voting forecasts collected from lay citizens whose profile matches the profile of the user, in terms of tastes, sports, family situation etc. Voters are positively impressed by such declarations and feel that the candidate is very close to them. The advertising firm revenue from this campaign is huge, but no money was paid to the search engine users for disclosing their information in the first place."

3.1   Ethics

RISK: Despite the similarities this case shares with the first one, it represents more serious threats for several reasons. In the first case the possibility that the system (of data collection and use) will be exploited for purposes that are negative for the user was questionable; in the present case such negative purposes are certain. Moreover, the negative consequences are far reaching and threaten the values at the very core of a democratic society – protection of human rights as well as undermining the democracy process. I would cluster two different groups of risks: 1. privacy violations and, 2. Human rights violations. For the first cluster, these violations would include: collection of data without informed consent, secondary use of data without consent, use of data for a purpose other than the one specified, possibility to de-anonymize, and lack of transparency. In the philosophical and ethical literature the definition of privacy used to focus on the control one had over one's data; deciding who has access, what it is used for, when it is used, and how much of it is used. Now, the definition of privacy has started to evolve into a concept in which the formation of one's **identity** is the central focus; being able to establish one's identity without having one created for you or becoming just another number. For the second cluster, the threat to human rights exists in the potential to manipulate emotions by targeting preferences and habits of users. This poses a threat to the values of **autonomy and dignity** of individuals. These serious negative consequences change the nature of the scenario; the potential infringement on human rights adds to the threat of the democratic process.

In deciding what to do about competing conceptions of the good life one may focus on the consequences of an action (the **consequentialist approach**) or the duties and principles on which the action is based (the **deontological approach**). Of course it is not so easy to isolate consequences from duties and many ethicists nowadays would go so far as to say that the line dividing one ethical theory from another are blurring; however, it is important in this case to be sure to point that in this case if one can attempts to justify the threat to human rights like autonomy and dignity (by undermining the democratic process) by saying that it could be a "good political candidate that is chosen", then the potential to engage in similar practices in the future with terrible outcomes (e.g. voting for a candidate or policy that is not good) becomes quite real.

SOLUTION: This is a difficult situation to find a solution for as it requires that companies and politicians are honest about their research practices even if it means they lose money. From an ethics perspective it is important to **empower** people to find their own voice to base their decisions on; this is why I would support education to allow people to inform their decision based on deeper knowledge of the issue. This education may come through the media or through an institution. As a solution to preventing these things from happening I would recommend establishing an **advocacy group** or ethics committees that work together to monitor and find solutions that make the symbiotic system process at stake ethical.

3.2 Security

RISK: From an information security point of view this case represents an example of **user profiling.** Currently, most Internet services and social networks collect data from users and try to profile them via the so-called user profiling in order to create target groups which they can target with other services (e.g., advertising) based on their characteristics. When they notify that they might sell such information to third parties, we are talking of buyers in the order of hundreds of companies what will get and use our data. While this information is commonly used in the aggregate form, it could also be exploited maliciously to try and define the profile of a specific user, his/her preferences, location and behavior. In addition the actual term of our decisions about such information is often ambiguous, as is the case when flagging as private an information on certain social media, which will never be private in the same way as we mean it to be.

SOLUTION: Increasing people's **awareness** of the risks involved in releasing data is nowadays necessary since security risks are chiefly underestimated. Such awareness and ability to **imagine possible consequences** should also be projected in the future possible use of the data which is light-mindedly disclosed now. To appreciate the importance of prospective thinking we can consider DNA information sent out to Internet services in exchange for knowing something about ourselves; this equals to disclosing core identity information, information that cannot be changed and that regards not just the individual releasing such information but all his/her relatives and progeny. It is easy to imagine that such information might be used in the future for genetic research applications or discriminations we are not even aware of nowadays and that we should me more jealous of such information than other we protect with much more alacrity.

Regarding possible technical solutions, there are several and they should be better known and more pervasively implemented (the anonymous internet browser system TOR, for example). Awareness, however, is the key solutions since it will not only convince people to prefer safer solutions but also to motivate users, regulators, technicians to ask for such solutions when they are not offered.

3.3 Law

RISK: From a legal point of view this case is about the indirect and unaware use of personal data. More technically, it is an **information security law case**, meaning a distinguished concept from concepts such as privacy and data security. [Many laws that purport to encourage cybersecurity are, in fact, designed with a focus on protecting privacy or encouraging data security]. Unlike privacy and data security, **cybersecurity** is focused not only on the information, but the entire system and network. For this reason, laws that focus only on privacy and data security may not consider all factors necessary to promote cybersecurity.

SOLUTION: **Transparency** and adoption of **best practices**.

On the one hand, the popular search engine where users log in to set free services should inform users of future potential uses of their personal data through the connected advertising service.

On the other hand, there are also some best practices for users that can help to reduce the risk of violation of privacy and unforeseeable use of data:

1. Anonymization: don't collect personal data if you don't need it. Work with anonymous or de-identified data if you can.
2. Disclose only the data you need and required, especially try to minimize the disclosure of sensitive personal data.
3. Encrypt sensitive personal data during transit
4. Check your contract with customers to ensure that you are not agreeing to unreasonable security practice in place.

Also we must consider that different kinds of information would have a different consequence in legal terms: the legal "weight" of human values and rights (e.g. religion; sexual orientation etc.) is different from the legal "weight" of choices and preferences (e.g. kind of theatre preferences; food preferences; sympathy or not for domestic animals etc.). The unaware storage of consumers' information about those different aspects (human rights and human preferences) has, obviously a different legal protection in case of breach. Case number 2 is important because it lets stakeholders thinking about these differences.

3.4 HCI

RISK: I would frame this case similarly to the first case, namely as one of **asymmetry in risk, value and knowledge**. Unlike that case, though, this one adds a complication in terms of human-computer interaction, namely that there is a third party involved, and this party is not the one directly involved in the symbiotic relation. That is, the politician purchasing the service is the third party that benefits from the personal data. Presumably there was a transaction between the symbiont – the party gathering the information and the one who should have paid for it – and the politician.

SOLUTION: The system that manages collection and all transactions – the symbiont and its owners – has an obligation to reveal the value of the information that is being collected. This value concerns the transaction occurring between the system and the user disclosing data but especially between the system owners and the customer using the data collected. One thing is to use the collected information internally and another is to sell it. Can this information be sent to any country whatsoever? For any purpose? Its value depends on what others pay for it. So regulation should shift focus, in this case, from the transaction with the system users to the transactions between the system owner and its customers who buy the collected data. Therefore, the solution would be to develop policy to **regulate transactions whenever collected data are sold**.

Purely from a HCI perspective, transparency can be increased by **re-design**, improving the comprehensibility by clever visualization of the meaning of terms of usage that otherwise is specified in 20 pages of text. The owner of the original information – the information host – ought to also have the right to expect to **re-negotiate** or renew the terms of the transaction once it is apparent the value of the information has changed. Information has a continuously changing value, it is not used once and once forever. Once new value becomes apparent there might be appropriate conditions to ask for a renegotiation. At the same time, acknowledging that some information might not be valuable once it is collected but prove valuable afterwards, it might be foreseen that its value should be paid via **fee-for-use**, namely only when users' data is actually used for some profit or benefit to the system owner.

3.5 Psychology

RISK: I think that in psychological terms this should be understood in terms of **identity and individual differences**, but I wonder how this case - being enabled by a symbiotic technology - differs from typical political campaigning, where politicians commonly adapt their propositions to the audience or the interlocutor.

SOLUTION: In this case, as in the first one, what is critical is to increase transparency. I think that **transparency** in transactions - even commercial ones - should be a leading principle, allowing a better understanding of the value of the transaction. Even more so in a political domain, where democracy is at stake and there is arguably a need for even higher standards of fairness in transactions. And to achieve such transparency, I think that **education** of the citizen and the consumer have a huge role to play (transparency being not possibly in the absence of a user understanding what data a system is acquiring). Also relevant here is that there is a natural pressure for systems to be easy to use (to maximize likelihood of engagement) and it is likely that the user will not realize the importance of transparency of a system until s/he experiences some negative consequence of a lack of transparency.

4   Case 3, Deciding for the User: The AR-Guided Surgical Intervention

The third case illustrates a case where a symbiotic system might lead to the user loosing agency due to automatic responses directly provided by the system. Indications about the realism of such a case are provided by [3, 7, 10].

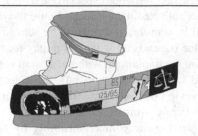

"A hospital has adopted a laparoscopic surgery equipment which is connected to the apparatus acquiring vital signals from the patient under surgery. During the surgical procedure, the physician wears a pair of augmented reality eyeglasses to receive information about vital signals along with data about success probability for each procedure applied to the patient during the surgery, in order to better inform his/her ongoing decisions. This data is recorded for archival reasons by the hospital and can be used in case of a lawsuit against the hospital after surgeries that do not succeed. It is the hospital policy to avoid conflicts between the choice of the physician during the surgical procedure and the data displayed by the machine, the evidence of the patient status recorded by the equipment. Thus in case of the patient reaching a critical condition, the physician is recommended to only rely on the standard procedure and quit any other attempts which is less likely to succeed. Therefore, to a certain extent, the decisions are embedded in the intelligence of the computer elaborating data and making recommendations. Somehow a moral decision is incorporated into the machine."

4.1   Ethics

RISK: To me this represents a prototypical symbiotic relation since parts of the decisional powers are externalized by the physician to the machine based on data it receives. It is a whole system including patients' data, physician's decision and systems' elaboration/recommendations. The most important part of this scenario is the fact that the surgeon is responsible for deciding whether or not he/she will take the advice of the machine. The moment this changes and the surgeon must do what the machine tells it (whether this is an explicit formal policy at the hospital or an implicit one) the scenario changes and the relation is no longer ethically acceptable or desirable. The second scenario is one in which the surgeon's freedom to choose has been limited. This limitation threatens the professionalization of medicine as one would have to be concerned about who is taking decisions and who is liable in case of problems, i.e. if the surgeon does what the machine tells it to do then will the machine be liable if someone goes wrong? Further, will we sue or fire the machine for damages? But responsibility from an ethics point of view is more than liability; it requires a moral agent with intentions who is able to reason through the consequences, understanding the consequences of an action; therefore this cannot be delegated to a machine.

Another potential risk is **deskilling** if the surgeon learns to rely on the technology and its elaboration more than s/he does on his/her own judgment. Moreover, with the use of this new technology the surgeon may not have an instance in which he/she is able to train using conventional methods.

SOLUTION: Using military terms, the surgeon must remain *in* the loop instead of being put *on* the loop. This means that the surgeon should be in control of giving commands and making choices. Part of the **training** with the systems should be to understand how the machine reasons and how to manage disagreements with the machine especially during emergencies. Another part of the training should be to make sure surgeons know how to perform the surgery if/when the machine breaks and the surgeon must rely on his/her own skills without the technology [13].

4.2 Security

RISK: From information security perspective this scenario points on the one hand at the aspects related to data storage in hospitals, and on the other at the possibility that the system is programmed to make decisions, be controlled remotely or being hacked for **malevolent purposes**.

SOLUTION: Solutions from information security perspective for this scenario are common good practices for storage of confidential information and to make computer systems secure: avoiding unauthorized parties to take control of such systems.

4.3 Law

RISK: This case regards the use of extra-clinical tools to support clinical decisions.

In general the gradual shift towards the use of extra-clinical tools to supplement the informed consent process and support clinical decisionsì could present the risk to consider the tool not simply as a decision-support tool but a decision-replacement tool (instead of the patient-physician's decision).

A second important risk is of blurring the principal role of the physician and interfering with his/her **freedom of therapeutic choice** whose responsibility (not simply legal liability) is shared with the patient.

Physicians have long faced tort liability for breach of informed consent if a patient is harmed as a result of the physician's failure to provide the information needed to make an informed medical decision. However, with increased reliance on extra-clinical tools, informed consent mechanisms incur an increased risk of malpractice liability.

The physician who simply relies on eyeglasses without reasoning on the bases of his/her knowledge, under even the most traditional tort principles, will be liable for malpractice. (Failure to engage fully in the informed consent process, even if decision support tools are made available, is a clear breach of the standard of care).

What if the pair of augmented reality eyeglasses gave wrong information? Similar problems where already present in the field of medical guidelines application.

Several scenarios could be traced:

1. the physician follows the eyeglasses indications and is personally persuaded by this choice;
2. the physician follows the eyeglasses indications but personally would have made another choice;
3. the physician does not follow the eyeglasses indications because on the base of his/her knowledge would have made another choice and indeed decides to make such choice.

SOLUTION: It is clear that medical providers who prescribe or use decision support tools may face tort liability if they misuse the tools or provide negligent counseling. This is a simple and relatively uncontroversial expansion of traditional malpractice liability. But the use of decision support tools also poses a secondary problem - namely, that patients may be harmed if the decision aids they use are faulty, misleading, or biased. If the regulatory or certification process aimed at ensuring the quality of decision aids fails, injured patients will look to tort law to provide a remedy. And since current tort doctrine makes it extremely difficult for such claims to succeed, it is time for policymakers and legal scholars to evaluate the costs and benefits of expanding tort liability in these cases.

The risk could be minimized with **a good training and instructions** by the producer on real opportunities offered by the eyeglasses. All information about the real help technology will offer to the patient should be exactly represented to the patient before the surgery in order to share "the potential scenarios".

Apart from this, it is still an open legal question in this field to determine whose responsibility it is to minimize this risk. Producers' will have an important role as well as physicians in transfering to the patient the useful information and sharing potential scenarios prior of the intervention (learned intermediary hand role).

Within the personalized medicine era, these eyeglasses have to be seen as a functional instrument of help in critical situation.

The risk of restricting physician's freedom of choice is inherent and is not avoidable. Perhaps, every physician will have to be aware that the liability for the final decision is due to his/her own choice, so it would be important for him/her to know from the producer the risk of error margin of the high tech product.

It has to be underlined that, because transitioning elements of the consent process into extra-clinical arenas is a dramatic change in the practices of protection medical freedom of choice and informed consent, it necessitates a new kind of conversation about liability. First, although **product liability** law sometimes subjects creators of faulty products to strict liability (that is, liability regardless of fault), decision support tools do not fall within the legal **definition of a "product"** and so are not subject to strict liability. Their **inherent autonomy** is currently under analyses.

Second, in the future it will be crucial to re-analyze issues of **vicarious liability** of the hospital and other involved subjects.

It should be also underlined that if a hospital system requires physicians to use decision aids for particular conditions it will also have a role in the allocation of liabilities, but this element will not be a "safe harbour" for physician who decided.

4.4   HCI

RISK: This case shows that the parties in the symbiotic relation have roles that depend not only on their **knowledge** but also on **external** practices such as the legal attribution of responsibility. The same case appeared years ago concerning expert systems for blood diagnosis, which were about 95% as good as a doctor on a good day. That is way better than most doctors on most days. Yet still hospitals ended up not using them because of the risk of legal suits. In normal cases gross failure leads to a law suit of the doctor. But who do you sue when it is an expert system? And what are the standards that one applies? The risk was that the responsibility for imperfection would have been laid at the foot of the programmer. And that risk might be too high given that the same program would be used in many places. The trouble is that when you think like this you give up reliable expertise (the expert system) to defend a general principle of morality or law. And yet the system is often the best way to proceed.

SOLUTION: Responsibility in this case should be allocated as a function of accountability and ultimately of knowledge. But we want humans in the loop. For instance, if an expert system left the final decision to the physician but also had a facility that would allow the physician to: (a) **delegate the decision** to the system, on a case-by-case basis; or (b) ask the system for its reasons for its suggestion or decisions and to take issue when the reasons are not clear enough, then we manage to keep humans in the loop. The final decision now lies with the physician. And there is the same mechanism used among teams of humans – they talk it out by asking each other for their reasons. The system and doctor now would be a learning team.

4.5   Psychology

RISK: I agree with the other panelists' responses, this case reduces the surgeon's **autonomy** and decreases the surgeon's skills. This reminds of the same issue currently at stake with self-driving cars, where the driver must be able to deactivate the cars' automatic behavior to get in control of the situation.

SOLUTIONS: The system should be transparent, **explaining** itself and then allowing the surgeon to make decisions including the decision to delegate decisions.

5   Synthesis and Conclusions

As mentioned in the introduction, and illustrated in the three cases and related discussion, symbiotic systems bring about a set of information transactions and intervene on the human beings and the environment in ways that are not inherently good or bad, but that at any rate mobilize some interests and values. Symbiotic systems, by which we mean here systems that have the three characteristics mentioned in the introduction (i.e., detecting users' implicit information, modeling the user's state based on such information and making decisions based on such model) can represent a resource to empower the human agent but can also end up serving private goals, manipulate and - ultimately - alienate human beings from their rights. In particular, the risks - as they have been identified during the panel - are of information leakage and malicious user profiling; deceitful use of data and threat to information security; decrease in self-determination, privacy and dignity; deskilling; asymmetry in value, risks and knowledge. The actual position that a given symbiotic system holds in the continuum between beneficial and harmful applications, between protecting the many and serving the few, depends on the **society's ability to set criteria of acceptability for their design and usage and to compel the application of such criteria**. Given the scale and the subdued level at which symbiotic systems operate, it seems urgent that society decides what is a legitimate symbiotic system and finds mechanisms to secure the respect of such decisions. The discussion during the panel highlighted some of these criteria and provisions, which are tentatively summarized in Fig. 2.

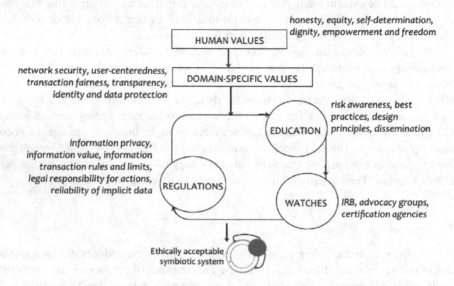

Fig. 2. A framework to collectively take charge of ethically acceptable symbiotic systems

Both the ultimate goals of the system and the ways in which it operates must be legitimate, making sure that it directly pursues, respects or at least does not compromise **society values** such as honesty, equity, self-determination, dignity and freedom. At a less abstract level, these overarching ethic values are achieved by way of **domain-specific values** that decline them into more concrete objectives, such as network security, user-centeredness, transaction fairness, transparency, identity and data protection. These objectives are achieved by way of education, regulation and agents. **Education** is the process to understand the risks of such systems and to learn risk minimization procedures (such as informed consents, enabling of own interfaces to input data in third party's systems, reporting lack of comprehension, design principles). **Regulation** includes the definition of what is a private and public information, how and when the value of a given piece of information is to be (re)defined, what transactions are legitimate, who are the beneficiaries, who is responsible for a decision based on symbiotic systems, and what is the legal value of information derived from implicit data. **Watches** are agencies such as institutional review boards or advocacy groups that specifically monitor ethical risks, certify procedures and represent users' rights by voicing them publicly and promoting regulations and education initiatives.

In conclusion, ethically acceptable symbiotic systems are the results of a collective effort, where the burden of dealing with the risks of releasing personal information is shared with all relevant stakeholders and publicly debated.

Acknowledgments. The present panel was partially funded by the EU project MindSee (grant agreement n. 611570). Individual panelists are responsible for their interventions as they are written here, each one for his/her own area of expertise; the panel organizer is responsible for the introduction and conclusions. We are grateful to Piero Turra for the illustrations of the three cases.

References

1. Acar, G., Eubank, C., Englehardt, S., Juarez, M., Narayanan, A., Diaz, C.: The web never forgets: Persistent tracking mechanisms in the wild. In: Proceedings of the 2014 ACM SIGSAC Conference on Computer and Communications Security, pp. 674–689. ACM (2014)
2. Barfield, W.: The future to merge with AI machines. In: Cyber-Humans, pp. 267–284. Springer, Cham (2015)
3. Baum, S.: Advancing smart glasses as augmented reality tool for surgeons drives Vital Medicals' capital raise. MedCityNews (2015). http://medcitynews.com/2015/02/advancing-smart-glasses-augmented-reality-tool-surgeons-drives-vitals-medicals-capital-raise/
4. Bessi, A., Petroni, F., Del Vicario, M., Zollo, F., Anagnostopoulos, A., Scala, A., Zollo, F., Quattrociocchi, W.: Viral misinformation: the role of homophily and polarization. In: Proceedings of the 24th International Conference on World Wide Web, pp. 355–356. ACM (2015)
5. Brandom, R.: Someone's trying to gut America's strongest biometric privacy law. The verge (2016). http://www.theverge.com/2016/5/27/11794512/facial-recognition-law-illinois-facebook-google-snapchat
6. Burgoon, J.K., Blair, J.P., Qin, T., Nunamaker, J.F.: Detecting deception through linguistic analysis. In: Chen, H., Miranda, R., Zeng, D.D., Demchak, C., Schroeder, J., Madhusudan, T. (eds.) ISI 2003. LNCS, vol. 2665, pp. 91–101. Springer, Heidelberg (2003). doi:10.1007/3-540-44853-5_7
7. Doryab, A., Bardram, J.E.: Designing activity-aware recommender systems for operating rooms. In: Proceedings of the 2011 Workshop on Context-awareness in Retrieval and Recommendation, pp. 43–46. ACM (2011)
8. Granhag, P.A., Vrij, A., Verschuere, B.: Detecting Deception: Current Challenges and Cognitive Approaches. Wiley, Chichester (2015)
9. Kramer, A.D., Guillory, J.E., Hancock, J.T.: Experimental evidence of massive-scale emotional contagion through social networks. Proc. Nat. Acad. Sci. **111**(24), 8788–8790 (2014)
10. Musen, M.A., Middleton, B., Greenes, R.A.: Clinical decision-support systems. In: Shortliffe, E.H., Cimino, J.J. (eds.) Biomedical Informatics, pp. 643–674. Springer, London (2014)

11. O'Brolcháin, F., Jacquemard, T., Monaghan, D., O'Connor, N., Novitzky, P., Gordijn, B.: The convergence of virtual reality and social networks: threats to privacy and autonomy. Sci. Eng. Ethics **22**(1), 1–29 (2016)
12. Sartori, G., Orru, G., Monaro, M.: Detecting deception through kinematic analysis of hand movement. Int. J. Psychophysiology **108**, 16 (2016)
13. van Wynsberghe, A., Gastmans, C.: Telesurgery: an ethical appraisal. J. Med. Ethics **34**(10), e22 (2008)
14. Won, A.S., Perone, B., Friend, M., Bailenson, J.N.: Identifying anxiety through tracked head movements in a virtual classroom. Cyberpsychology Behav. Soc. Networking **19**(6), 380–387 (2016)

Total Immersion: Designing for Affective Symbiosis in a Virtual Reality Game with Haptics, Biosensors, and Emotive Agents

Imtiaj Ahmed[1(✉)], Ville Harjunen[1], Giulio Jacucci[1,2], Niklas Ravaja[1,4,5],
and Michiel M. Spapé[1,3]

[1] Department of Computer Science, Helsinki Institute for Information Technology (HIIT),
Aalto University, Helsinki, Finland
{Imtiaj.Ahmed,Ville.Harjunen,Giulio.Jacucci}@helsinki.fi,
Niklas.Ravaja@aalto.fi
[2] Department of Computer Science, Helsinki Institute for Information Technology (HIIT),
University of Helsinki, Helsinki, Finland
[3] Department of Psychology, Liverpool Hope University, Liverpool, UK
spapem@hope.ac.uk
[4] Helsinki Collegium for Advanced Studies, University of Helsinki, Helsinki, Finland
[5] School of Business, Aalto University, Helsinki, Finland

Abstract. Affective symbiosis for human–computer interaction refers to the dynamic relationship between the user and affective virtual agents. In order to facilitate a true, immersive experience, we believe that it is necessary to adapt the presentation of an affective agent to the user's affective state. Investigating the experience, behavior, and physiological correlates of affective events, such as winning and losing during a competitive game, therefore might be used to adapt the agent's emotional states and system events. An experimental virtual reality game environment was designed as a stepping stone toward a system to demonstrate affective symbiosis. Users were invited to play a game of air hockey with affective agents in virtual reality. We collected the electrocardiography, electrodermal activity, and postural data, as well as self-reports, to investigate how emotional events affected physiology, behavior, and experience. The users were found to be engaged in the competition strongly while only paying limited attention to their adversaries' emotional expressions. We discuss how game events are much stronger causes for affective responses, with the physiological effects of winning and losing becoming more enhanced as the game progresses. We discuss how an affective, symbiotic system could implement both game events and dynamic, affective agents to create a system for total immersion.

Keywords: Affective symbiosis · Virtual reality · Immersion · Haptics · 3D game · Physiology · HCI · Symbiotic interaction

1 Introduction

Human–computer symbiosis is a relationship between a human and computer in a cooperative interactive space in which the computer acts as an organism different from the

© The Author(s) 2017
L. Gamberini et al. (Eds.): Symbiotic 2016, LNCS 9961, pp. 23–37, 2017.
DOI: 10.1007/978-3-319-57753-1_3

human and is not limited to inflexible dependence on predetermined programs [1]. Based on a recent review by Jacucci et al. [2], for a human–computer paradigm, symbiotic interaction is possible to achieve by using technological resources to understand users and to make those resources understandable to users. Computation, sensing technology, and interaction design are key aspects to monitoring and affecting users through the systems output in a closed-loop paradigm. Following the notion of symbiotic interaction in human–computer paradigms outlined by Jacucci et al. [2], we affixed an affective agent or system to form affective symbiosis.

An affective agent, in one respect, can be expressed as the embodied agent or screen-based anthropomorphic entity that can display emotional expressions to affect users emotionally. A number of studies have demonstrated the potential of using affective agents in interaction [3–7]. For example, the use of an embodied agent in an interface can enhance social interaction [8] and improve life-like interaction with agents [5]. Of course, not every situation requires affective agents: Embodied, affective agents in utilitarian contexts can result in negative user emotions (e.g., the Microsoft search puppy). On the other hand, competitive contexts, such as computer games, might employ these agents more appropriately. In these types of systems, it is also much more likely that a relationship among a user, virtual agents, and the system grows and changes over time. Moreover, earlier studies have shown that the competitiveness of the interaction is positively associated with emotional synchrony between human users [9]. In other words, people pay more attention and are more aware of their adversary's emotions as the competitiveness of the interaction increases. In human–computer interaction, this could mean that the agent's affective state becomes more salient for the user when increasing the competitiveness of the game.

However, creating an affective symbiosis between the user and agent requires more than simply integrating emotional expressions into a competitive context. The interaction with the system should be built on a dynamic loop that adapts the system to a user's body, behavior, and experience [10]. In the present study, we took steps toward creating this type of system in a competitive game scenario, expecting that it will enhance engagement and immersion during interaction. At this point, the system's adaptiveness is limited to the adversary's performance, meaning that the performance of the adversary improves directly with the user's performance. We expect that if a user engages in affective symbiosis, (a) the user's behavior and physiological states should be affected strongly by system events, (b) the emotional state of the user should be affected by the emotional state of artificial agents in the system, and (c) engagement with the system should increase as a function of the cumulative degree of interaction. In the present study, we aimed to gain early insights on the relationship between these critical aspects of affective symbiosis. The hope is that identified shortcomings will inform us adequately to enable a full-scale affective symbiosis system in the future.

We implemented an interaction scenario similar to the table-top game of air hockey, featuring virtual reality, haptic feedback, psychophysiological measurements, and affective agents. The virtual agent displayed emotional expressions during play. We also built a haptic glove to display the different forms of tactile feedback during the game events. The air hockey game was selected because it represents a fast-changing competitive context in which the user is facing his/her opponent and is allowed to see his/her adversary's facial expressions without disengaging attention from the game.

In order to investigate the user's engagement in affective symbiosis, we measured the effect of emotional expressions displayed by affective agents. We expected that interaction with the agent could result in two types of emotional relationship, which one might consider, in the context of symbiotic interaction, as either parasitic or mutualistic. From a primarily utilitarian point of view, competition might entail a parasitic emotional effect: a negative expression of one's opponent suggesting a gain and therefore resulting in positive affect. However, many studies have suggested that emotional expressions usually result in mirroring behavior, imitating the agent's expression, which, according to some, might cause associated emotions [11]. In other words, positive emotions expressed by the agents might result in either negative (parasitical affective symbiosis) or positive (mutualistic affective symbiosis) affects in the user.

Because emotions are known to affect users unconsciously on occasion [12], if the system is affectively symbiotic, we expect that the more one interacts with the system, the more one becomes affected by game events. This refers primarily to events that happen to oneself (i.e., one wins or loses). To measure the emotional involvement, we complemented traditional self-report questionnaires with physiological data. To investigate how users implicitly responded to emotional events, we took measures of electrodermal activity (EDA) and heart rate variability (HRV) during the game.

We think that immersion might improve affective symbiosis, because it might create a stronger impression of the importance of the game and events, thus increasing the salience of the agent's emotions. For this reason, we used virtual reality [13] and haptic feedback [14]. The findings of the study will contribute to understandings of some crucial points to consider before developing an affective symbiosis adaptation and/or game model and will direct the possibilities.

2 Related Work

Both systems that adapt to user emotions and affective agents that influence user emotions have been popular topics of research in the field of human–computer interaction (e.g., [15–19]). Work regarding emotionally adapted games has demonstrated how adapting game events to a user's physiological activity can improve the game experience [18]. Kuikkaniemi et al. [19], for instance, used EDA to control the level of difficulty in a first-person shooting game. Results revealed that players who were able to see their biosignal while playing were more immersed and positively affected by the game.

In addition to the adaptive games, affective agents' emotional expressions also have been shown to influence users' emotional states and social behavior [5, 7, 20]. De Melo and colleagues investigated social decision-making between a human and affective virtual agent, demonstrating how users were more willing to cooperate or make concessions if agents were displaying certain emotions [21, 22]. Besides making different decisions, users also have shown to mimic the expressions of affective agents automatically and respond to negative expressions with heightened autonomic arousal [23]. In conclusion, affective agents indeed affect users' emotions and behavior.

Rather than using 2-D screen-based virtual reality, one can use head-mounted displays (HMDs) to achieve better immersion [24] by shutting out the outside world. Recently, advancements in HMD technologies have increased the use of virtual reality and its applications, mostly for gaming purposes [25, 26], to provide the experience of immersion and the enjoyment of full engagement. Though HMDs are used for the visualization of the virtual environment, the realistic feel comes from the feeling of touch and getting a response from the virtual objects [24], which can be achieved through haptic technologies. A haptic feedback technology increases the player's sense of immersion [24] and provides interesting ways to interact with the game [15] while enhancing the entertainment value [27].

To summarize, systems that adapt to a user's emotions and systems in which affective agents influence user emotions have been popular topics of research. However, an immersive system that incorporates adaptive gaming performance into affective expressions requires more research. The present work aims to pave the way toward affective symbiosis by investigating the changes in users' physiology and emotional state in a competitive affective game environment.

3   The Game

An air hockey game (similar to Pong) was designed to investigate the effects of affective agents in an immersive, competitive context. A virtual puck was served from the center left of the air hockey table either toward the agent or the player, alternatively. Both the player and agent blocked the puck using a virtual mallet. There were slots on either end of the air hockey table that served as goal bars. The angle of the puck-serving direction was randomly generated between 15° to 75° angles toward either the agent or the player.

3.1   Player Interaction

We used Leap Motion, a tiny device used to sense a user's hand and finger motions using infrared cameras in an interactive 3-D space, to track the user's right-hand movements. This device was positioned underneath a glass table and enabled sight of the player's hand in virtual reality. A transparent plastic sheet was used to help move the user's right hand freely on the glass table. The default hand model, provided as part of Leap Motion's Unity3D package (www.leapmotion.com), was used to enable interaction in virtual reality. In virtual reality, a user could grip the virtual mallet and move it to face the moving puck. A player's left-hand index, middle, and ring fingers rested on the arrow keys of a PC keyboard and were used to provide answers to the self-reported items shown during gameplay (Fig. 3).

3.2 Agent Interaction

The agent faced the puck using a set of hand-movement animations. Twelve agents' hand-movement animations were designed to reach 12 predefined target points on the game table (see Fig. 1). While the puck moved toward the agent, the agent tried to find the closest target point according to the puck's movement direction, and the agent played the corresponding hand movement animation to bounce the puck. To make the game competitive based on player performance, we designed three levels of difficulty: *easy*, *medium*, and *hard* (Fig. 1). The adaptation of the competing model depended on the player's performance so that players could gradually improve their skill along with the agent and continually enjoy the competition.

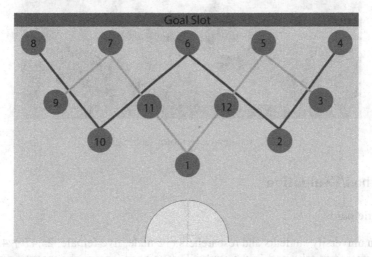

Fig. 1. Competing models. Yellow lines represent the medium model and its selected target points. Red lines represent the easy model. All target points were selected for the hard model. (Color figure online)

3.3 Tactile Feedback

A recent work by Ahmed et al. [28] showed that differences in haptic technologies affect how simulated touch in virtual reality is perceived. They found that haptic exciters provided a more intense signal than the commonly used C2 vibrotactile actuators. However, mechanical actuators were found to make the touch feel more natural. This motivated us to use both a haptic exciter and a mechanical device to provide tactile feedback for different game events. We designed a glove (Fig. 2) using a piece of cotton fabric. We attached a micro servo motor (9 g, speed 0, 10 s/60, torque 1.3 kg/cm at 4.8 V) on top of the glove. Three elastic strips of tape were attached to the glove and connected by a thread to the horn of the servo motor. The servo motor rotated up to 180° (c), thereby pulling the thread, creating tension on the elastic tape (b), and applying pressure to the user's hand. This mimicked the sensation of a player gripping the mallet. Two audio haptic exciters (Tectonic's 14 mm, 8 O TEAX14C02-8, www.tectonicelements.com/audio-exciters) were placed on top of the glove

(a) to produce vibration on the user's hand while the user bounces the puck. Because the skin on a human hand is sensitive to vibrations over 20 Hz and a square wave is perceived to be more intense than the commonly used sine wave [29], we selected a 35 Hz square wave of 50 ms vibration as the puck-bouncing feedback.

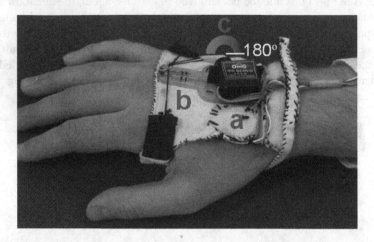

Fig. 2. Exciter-servo motor tactile glove.

4   Method/Evaluation

4.1   Participants

Seventeen university students and researchers (12 male, five female, 25.47 ± 4.4 years old) volunteered to take part in the study. They signed informed consent agreements prior to the start of the experiment and, afterward, received a movie ticket for their time.

4.2   Test Setup

The Unity 3-D game engine (version 4.5.4, www.unity3d.com) was used to implement the experimental system, providing the game scenario and questionnaires visually in virtual reality via the HMD, recording user responses, and communicating with the physiological apparatus. Virtual reality was enabled using the Oculus Rift VR HMD (Oculus Rift Developer Kit 2, Resolution 960 × 1080 per eye, Refresh Rate 75 Hz, 100° nominal field of view). The player's head movements were tracked at 1000 Hz using a three-axis accelerometer, gyroscope, magnetometer, and external positional tracker (www.oculusvr.com).

Affective agents in virtual reality were designed by combining a face model and a body model. The face model used was the original one provided by Faceshift (www.faceshift.com), and the body was designed using the FUSE design tool provided by Mixamo (www.mixamo.com). The texture of the face and body were edited in order to build three different-looking agents. The agent displayed three emotional expressions

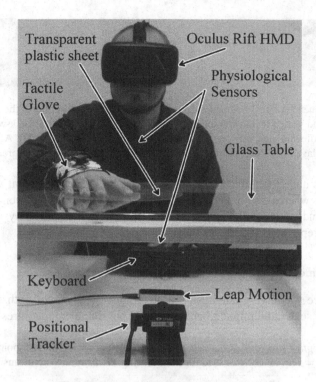

Fig. 3. Test setup and player interaction.

(happiness, anger, neutral control condition). These were recorded prior to the study by capturing a live presentation by a professional actress using Faceshift algorithms. Each expression animation lasted 4 s, ending with neutral expression. Prior to the experiment, a pilot study was conducted in which a sample of human participants was used to classify the expressions based on categories of six basic emotions (disgust, fear, sadness, anger, happiness, and neutral). Expressions of anger, happiness, and neutrality were then selected for the final paradigm based on their relatively higher recognition accuracy (happy: $95 \pm 14\%$, neutral: $90 \pm 14\%$, angry: $90 \pm 23\%$).

4.3 Procedure and Design

As illustrated in Fig. 4, at the beginning of the game, the player grabbed the mallet. The haptic glove applied tension to the user's hand to mimic gripping the mallet physically. The agent's facial expression was presented as a common starting point for every trial. The same facial animation was played throughout the entire trial. After 3 s, the puck was served toward either the agent or player in alternating order. A short vibration through the glove was displayed on the dorsal of the player's hand while the player bounced the puck. The trial lasted until a goal was scored, after which the scores were updated. After 1 s, a short questionnaire (see Sect. 4.4) was presented.

Fig. 4. Trial sequences. Users grabbed a virtual mallet (A). At the beginning of the trial, the agent was displayed and started to show emotional expression (B). After 3 s, the puck was served (C) and the vibrotactile stimulus was presented as the user bounced the puck (D). After each goal, scores were displayed (E). After each block, a self-reported questionnaire was presented (F).

Participants undertook nine blocks of seven trials. The virtual agent was changed between blocks whereas the order of agents was counterbalanced between participants. Trials were randomized fully across the 63 possibilities obtained by orthogonally crossing the 3 repetitions × 3 agents (angry, happy, neutral) × 7 serves.

4.4   Measurements

User experience was investigated using a quantitative analysis of both explicit self-reported Likert scales and implicit behavioral and physiological measures.

Table 1. *Descriptive statistics of self-reported questionnaire (N = 17).* A 5-point Likert scale (1 = not at all, 5 = very much) was used for item scoring. *Note:* values are means ± SEs

Questionnaire item	Emotion		
	Neutral	Angry	Happy
I felt frustrated	2.29 (±0.20)	2.19 (±0.23)	2.02 (±0.16)
I felt influenced by the agent's mood	2.03 (±0.14)	2.54 (±0.19)	2.81 (±0.19)
I felt tense	2.83 (±0.18)	2.79 (±0.19)	2.50 (±0.19)
I found it boring	2.19 (±0.22)	2.27 (±0.26)	2.07 (±0.19)
I had to put a lot of effort into the game	2.79 (±0.22)	2.81 (±0.27)	2.76 (±0.24)
I thought it was fun	3.58 (±0.22)	3.57 (±0.26)	3.85 (±0.21)
I deeply concentrated on the game	2.09 (±0.17)	2.54 (±0.19)	2.81 (±0.19)
I was good at it	3.28 (±0.19)	3.37 (±0.17)	3.46 (±0.19)
The agent caught my attention	2.48 (±0.17)	3.05 (±0.14)	3.45 (±0.16)

Note: Values indicate mean values on Likert scale from 1 to 5 ± standard errors

Self-reported Data. Self-reported data on emotional interdependence, co-presence, game experience, and emotion-classification items were collected. Scales of emotional interdependence, co-presence, and game experience were single-item measures obtained from the social presence module of the game experience questionnaire (FUGA, [30]). Items are shown in Table 1. Participants filled out the questionnaires using their other (i.e., non-virtual) hand, resting on the arrow keys of a PC keyboard. The questionnaires used 5-point Likert-style scales, while the emotion classification used a three-alternative forced choice.

Implicit Measures. The users' electrocardiography (ECG), EDA and right-handed biaxial accelerometer (ACC) were recorded using a Brain Products QuickAmp biosignal amplifier at a sample rate of 1,000 Hz (Fig. 5). ACC data were transformed to movement speed by taking the root mean square of the first derivative over both axes (i.e., the Euclidean distance traveled per ms). Physiological sensors to measure EDA were placed on the index and middle fingers of the left hand, and to measure ECG were placed on the chest. EDA commonly is used as an emotional arousal indicator [31] or to describe the intensity of an experience. Electronically, it represents the potential difference between two areas of the skin. Two key measurements of the EDA are tonic (low frequency baseline conductivity level indicates slow changes in arousal) and phasic (higher frequency indicates rapid changes in arousal). The average, raw EDA was taken as a tonic measure of autonomic activity. Furthermore, the measure was transformed to reflect phasic arousal related to non-specific events [31] by applying a continuous, local, positive peak (of at least 0.5 μS) detection algorithm and calculating the rate of skin-conductivity responses per second. Finally, the latency (in ms) between heartbeats, or inter-beat interval (IBI), was used to calculate the average IBI (inversely related to heart rate).

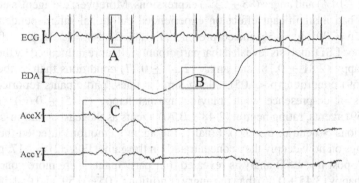

Fig. 5. Ten seconds of raw heart rate (ECG), EDA, and 2-D accelerator (ACCX and ACCY) data during gameplay. Red boxes show events of interest: (A) single heart-beat used for calculating heart rate variability, (B) phasic EDA response used for calculating skin conductivity response rate, and (C) movement across X and Y used for calculating movement speed. (Color figure online)

5   Results

5.1   Emotion Recognition, Game Experience, and Presence Measures

Participants' judgments concerning emotions, game experience, emotional interdependence, and co-presence were investigated using one-way repeated measure ANOVAs

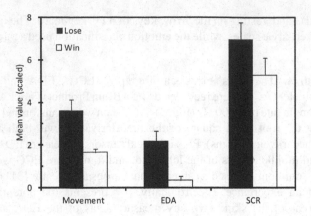

Fig. 6. Effect of losing or winning on the first 3 s of movement speed, EDA/10, and skin conductivity response rate (SCR*10).

(RMANOVAs) with the agent's emotional expression (neutral vs. angry vs. happy) as a factor. The agent's emotional expressions were judged correctly in 91% of cases. Furthermore, some of the expressions were recognized significantly better than others, $F(1.36, 21.82) = 4.34$, $p = .04$. A post hoc LSD (Least Significant Difference) analysis revealed significantly higher recognition rates ($p < .05$) for happy (100%) compared to neutral ($88 \pm 14\%$) and angry ($85 \pm 23\%$) expressions. Moreover, the agent's emotional expression had a significant effect on experienced emotional interdependence, $F(2, 32) = 9.01$, $p = .001$, $\eta^2 = .36$, and co-presence, $F(1.43, 22.84) = 15.31$, $p < .001$, $\eta^2 = .49$. A post hoc LSD analysis revealed that participants felt more influenced by the agent's mood in happy (2.81 ± 0.78) and angry (2.54 ± 0.77) conditions than in the neutral (2.04 ± 0.59) condition ($p < .05$). Along similar lines, participants reported higher experiences of co-presence while playing against happy (3.45 ± 0.66) vs. angry (3.05 ± 0.59) agents, rating neutral (2.48 ± 0.70) agents as the least attention-capturing (both emotions > neutral, $p < .05$). Finally, the agent's emotions affected the participant's ratings on how deeply they concentrated on the game, $F(2, 32) = 7.17$, $p = .003$, $\eta^2 = .31$. A post hoc LSD analysis revealed that participants were more concentrated during the happy (3.45 ± 0.66) than the angry condition (3.05 ± 0.59) and that the neutral expression (2.48 ± 0.70) was associated with poorest concentration ($p < .01$).

5.2 Experience of Game Events: Behavior and Physiology

Trials were included in the analysis only if both the agent and user successfully blocked or bounced the puck at least once. Seventeen users were tested, although the accelerator recordings were missing for one. Data for this user were omitted from movement-related analyses.

In order to find out whether the agent's emotion had a general effect on behavioral and physiological responses, RMANOVAs were conducted with the agent's emotion as factor and performance, movement, tonic EDA, average heart rate, HRV (standard deviation of the IBI), and skin conductance response rate as measures. Tonic EDA was found to be affected by the agent's emotional expression significantly, F(2, 32) = 4.59, p = .03, but no effect was observed for any other measure, $p > 0.1$. Angry agents increased tonic EDA (883 µS) relative to neutral (829 µS) and happy (802 µS) conditions.

Next, we investigated how winning or losing affected the behavioral (movement data) and physiological (EDA, SCR, IBI) response. RMANOVAs were conducted on measures taken in the first 3 s after the game event of winning or losing with performance (win vs. loss) as factor. Performance significantly affected EDA, F(1, 16) = 15.20, p = .001, SCR(1, 16) = 17.92, p = .001, and movement, F(1, 15) = 20.15, p < .001. Losing increased EDA, SCR, and the amount of movement.

Finally, we explored emotional investment as the game progressed. We used the average SCR measure evoked by successfully blocking (bouncing) the puck across time. As shown in Fig. 7, the more often the puck was blocked (N bounced), that is, the further the game progressed, the higher the SCR related to the event itself. In other words, the more the user became excited by the event of blocking, the more the game progressed. Interestingly, this upward trend also was visible when the SCR was measured in response to the agent's, rather than the user's, blocking. Thus, this shows that the user is emotionally involved with both the game and the agent and that this emotional engagement evolves over time, suggesting affecting symbiosis (Fig. 7).

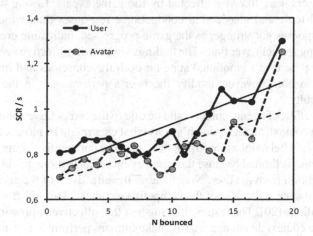

Fig. 7. Skin conductance response rate (SCR/s) related to blocking the puck as the game progresses.

6 Discussion and Conclusion

The emergence of interest in human–computer symbiosis and affective communication calls for examinations into the possibilities of affective symbiosis in the human–computer paradigm. Here, we developed a competitive VR game environment working as a stepping stone toward a system that allows affective symbiosis. Previously, symbiotic interaction has been considered a beneficial aspect of collaborative interaction. However, recent findings from human–human gaming have demonstrated that affective linkage between users is crucial in competitive contexts [9]. Developing a similar affective linkage in a human–computer paradigm would require new sources of information, such as biosignals, and a system that is able to adapt the game events to such information. In the present study, we built a simple, behaviorally adaptive, competitive environment in order to investigate how the affective agent's emotional expressions affected the user's emotions and game performance.

The results of the present study showed that the agent's expressions affected emotional interdependence and co-presence, indicating that the adversary's happy and angry rather than neutral expressions caught users' attention and affected their conscious emotional state. Moreover, users reported concentrating more on the game when the agent expressed happiness. However, neither the difficulty of the game nor other game-related experiences were influenced by the agent's emotion. Thus, the results suggest that the computer agent's affective expressions modified the user's attention and emotional experience but did not change the degree to which the user found the game difficult or entertaining.

Additionally, the implicit measures supported this conclusion. Users' tonic EDA level was higher when their adversaries were angry, whereas users' game performance was not influenced by the agent's emotion. EDA and other implicit measures also revealed that users were likewise affected by the game events. Losing was related to more amplified tonic and phasic skin conductance responses than winning. Finally, users' EDA responses got stronger as the game progressed, indicating greater personal investment or engagement over time. The findings suggest that affective agents and game events influence the user's emotional state on both the conscious and implicit levels. These effects do not, however, modify the user's performance in the game or its perceived difficulty.

The limited effect of agents' affect could be due to the competitive nature of the task. In a negotiation context, another person's nonverbal cues might be more salient and thus influence the user's behavior more [6]. In turn, in more competitive contexts, the influence of social cues is limited because the game events change more quickly and require continuous attention from the user. Nonetheless, the affectivity of the agent influenced users' emotional state regardless of the competitive context. This effect was consistent with earlier findings [20]. The results thus suggest that affective expressions presented in a competitive context do not necessarily make humans perform better in the game but improves the overall social experience.

The findings of this study will help us understand users' experiences while interacting with affective adversaries in an immersive competitive environment. The results also can be used to build an affectively adaptive system that integrates users' behaviors to their emotional responses when calculating further game events. More knowledge of agents' adaptive emotional responses and their effect on the user is required. In the future, one could, for instance, investigate whether varying the agents' affective state according to game events would intensify the effect of the agent's emotions on the user's emotions and behavior.

Acknowledgements. This work was supported by the Academy of Finland. Project number 268999 (HapCom).

References

1. Licklider, J.C.: Man-computer symbiosis. IRE Trans. Hum. Factors Electron. **1**, 4–11 (1960)
2. Jacucci, G., Spagnolli, A., Freeman, J., Gamberini, L.: Symbiotic interaction: a critical definition and comparison to other human-computer paradigms. In: Jacucci, G., Gamberini, L., Freeman, J., Spagnolli, A. (eds.) Symbiotic 2014. LNCS, vol. 8820, pp. 3–20. Springer, Cham (2014). doi:10.1007/978-3-319-13500-7_1
3. Isbister, K.: Better Game Characters by Design: A Psychological Approach. Elsevier/Morgan Kaufmann, Amsterdam/Boston (2006)
4. Burleson, W., Picard, R.W.: Gender-specific approaches to developing emotionally intelligent learning companions. IEEE Intell. Syst. **22**, 62–69 (2007)
5. Dietz, R., Lang, A.: Affective agents: effects of agent affect on arousal, attention, liking and learning. In: Proceedings of the Third International Cognitive Technology Conference, San Francisco (1999)
6. Melo, C.M., Carnevale, P., Gratch, J.: The influence of emotions in embodied agents on human decision-making. In: Allbeck, J., Badler, N., Bickmore, T., Pelachaud, C., Safonova, A. (eds.) IVA 2010. LNCS (LNAI), vol. 6356, pp. 357–370. Springer, Heidelberg (2010). doi: 10.1007/978-3-642-15892-6_38
7. Choi, A., Melo, C.D., Woo, W., Gratch, J.: Affective engagement to emotional facial expressions of embodied social agents in a decision-making game. Comput. Animat. Virtual Worlds. **23**, 331–342 (2012)
8. Yee, N., Bailenson, J.N., Rickertsen, K.: A meta-analysis of the impact of the inclusion and realism of human-like faces on user experiences in interfaces. In: Proceedings of the SIGCHI Conference on Human Factors in Computing Systems, pp. 1–10. ACM (2007)
9. Spapé, M.M., Kivikangas, J.M., Järvelä, S., Kosunen, I., Jacucci, G., Ravaja, N.: Keep your opponents close: social context affects EEG and fEMG linkage in a turn-based computer game. PLoS ONE **8**, e78795 (2013)
10. Fairclough, S.: A closed-loop perspective on symbiotic human-computer interaction. In: Blankertz, B., Jacucci, G., Gamberini, L., Spagnolli, A., Freeman, J. (eds.) Symbiotic 2015. LNCS, vol. 9359, pp. 57–67. Springer, Cham (2015). doi:10.1007/978-3-319-24917-9_6
11. Strack, F., Martin, L.L., Stepper, S.: Inhibiting and facilitating conditions of the human smile: a nonobtrusive test of the facial feedback hypothesis. J. Pers. Soc. Psychol. **54**, 768 (1988)
12. Dimberg, U., Thunberg, M., Elmehed, K.: Unconscious facial reactions to emotional facial expressions. Psychol. Sci. **11**, 86–89 (2000)
13. Riva, G., Mantovani, F., Capideville, C.S., Preziosa, A., Morganti, F., Villani, D., Gaggioli, A., Botella, C., Alcañiz, M.: Affective interactions using virtual reality: the link between presence and emotions. Cyberpsychol. Behav. **10**, 45–56 (2007)
14. Andrews, S., Mora, J., Lang, J., Lee, W.S.: Hapticast: a physically-based 3D game with haptic feedback. In: Proceedings of the International Conference on the Future of Game Design and Technology (Future Play) (October 2006)
15. Moghim, M., Stone, R., Rotshtein, P., Cooke, N.: Adaptive virtual environments: a physiological feedback HCI system concept. In: 2015 7th Computer Science and Electronic Engineering Conference (CEEC), pp. 123–128. IEEE (2015)
16. Edlinger, G., Holzner, C., Guger, C., Groenegress, C., Slater, M.: Brain-computer interfaces for goal orientated control of a virtual smart home environment. In: 4th International IEEE/EMBS Conference on Neural Engineering (NER 2009), pp. 463–465. IEEE (2009)
17. Lalor, E., Kelly, S.P., Finucane, C., Burke, R., Reilly, R.B., McDarby, G.: Brain computer interface based on the steady-state VEP for immersive gaming control. Biomed. Tech. **49**, 63–64 (2004)

18. Saari, T., Turpeinen, M., Kuikkaniemi, K., Kosunen, I., Ravaja, N.: Emotionally adapted games – an example of a first person shooter. In: Jacko, J.A. (ed.) HCI 2009. LNCS, vol. 5613, pp. 406–415. Springer, Heidelberg (2009). doi:10.1007/978-3-642-02583-9_45

19. Kuikkaniemi, K., Laitinen, T., Turpeinen, M., Saari, T., Kosunen, I., Ravaja, N.: The influence of implicit and explicit biofeedback in first-person shooter games. In: Proceedings of the SIGCHI Conference on Human Factors in Computing Systems, pp. 859–868. ACM (2010)

20. Beale, R., Creed, C.: Affective interaction: how emotional agents affect users. Int. J. Hum. Comput Stud. **67**, 755–776 (2009)

21. de Melo, C.M., Carnevale, P., Gratch, J.: The effect of expression of anger and happiness in computer agents on negotiations with humans. In: The 10th International Conference on Autonomous Agents and Multiagent Systems, vol. 3, pp. 937–944. International Foundation for Autonomous Agents and Multiagent Systems (2011)

22. de Melo, C.M., Carnevale, P., Gratch, J.: The impact of emotion displays in embodied agents on emergence of cooperation with people. Presence Teleoperators Virtual Environ. **20**, 449–465 (2011)

23. Weyers, P., Mühlberger, A., Hefele, C., Pauli, P.: Electromyographic responses to static and dynamic avatar emotional facial expressions. Psychophysiology **43**, 450–453 (2006)

24. Sziebig, G., Rudas, I., Demiralp, M., Mastorakis, N.: Achieving total immersion: technology trends behind augmented reality - a survey. In: WSEAS International Conference, Proceedings. Mathematics and Computers in Science and Engineering (WSEAS) (2009)

25. Firth, N.: First wave of virtual reality games will let you live the dream. New Sci. **218**, 19–20 (2013)

26. Kushner, D.: Virtual reality's moment. IEEE Spectr. **51**, 34–37 (2014)

27. Morris, D., Joshi, N., Salisbury, K.: Haptic battle pong: high-degree-of-freedom haptics in a multiplayer gaming environment. In: Experimental Gameplay Workshop, GDC. Citeseer (2004)

28. Ahmed, I., Harjunen, V., Jacucci, G., Hoggan, E., Ravaja, N., Spapé, M.M.: Reach out and touch me: effects of four distinct haptic technologies on affective touch in virtual reality. In: Proceedings of the 2016 ACM on International Conference on Multimodal Interaction. ACM (2016)

29. Van Erp, J.B.: Guidelines for the use of vibro-tactile displays in human computer interaction. In: Proceedings of Eurohaptics, pp. 18–22 (2002)

30. Poels, K., de Kort, Y.A.W., Ijsselsteijn, W.A.: FUGA-the fun of gaming: measuring the human experience of media enjoyment. Deliverable D3. 3: Game Experience Questionnaire. FUGA Proj. (2008)

31. Leiner, D., Fahr, A., Früh, H.: EDA positive change: a simple algorithm for electrodermal activity to measure general audience arousal during media exposure. Commun. Methods Meas. **6**, 237–250 (2012)

Analysis of the Human-Computer Interaction on the Example of Image-Based CAPTCHA by Association Rule Mining

Darko Brodić[1]([⊠]) and Alessia Amelio[2]

[1] University of Belgrade, Technical Faculty in Bor, V.J. 12, 19210 Bor, Serbia
dbrodic@tfbor.bg.ac.rs
[2] DIMES University of Calabria, Via P. Bucci Cube 44, 87036 Rende, CS, Italy
aamelio@dimes.unical.it

Abstract. The paper analyzes the interaction between humans and computers in terms of response time in solving the image-based CAPT-CHA. In particular, the analysis focuses on the attitude of the different Internet users in easily solving four different types of image-based CAPTCHAs which include facial expressions such as: animated character, old woman, surprised face, worried face. To pursue this goal, an experiment is realized involving 100 Internet users in solving the four types of CAPTCHAs, differentiated by age, Internet experience, and education level. The response times are collected for each user. Then, association rules are extracted from user data, for evaluating the dependence of the response time in solving the CAPTCHA from age, education level and experience in Internet usage by statistical analysis. The results implicitly capture the users' psychological states showing in what states the users are more sensitive. It reveals to be a novelty and a meaningful analysis in the state-of-the-art.

Keywords: Image-based CAPTCHA · Statistical analysis · Association Rules · Human-Computer Interaction · Cognitive psychology

1 Introduction

HCI (Human Computer Interaction) studies the interaction between humans, i.e. computer users and computers as well as the major phenomena surrounding them. Essentially, HCI concerns development, evaluation and implementation of computer systems that are interactive in their core. The interactive design is linked with the feelings, words and their expressions. It represents usability elements that are firmly connected to the user-interface and human factors. Hence, it is deeply involved with the computer science, artificial intelligence and cognitive psychology. From all aforementioned, HCI includes the elements of understanding the computer user needs as well as the usability elements. To be efficient it should be fluent, cognitive, expressive and communicative.

Usability is the main concept in HCI. It is linked with the following elements: (i) easy to learn, (ii) easy to remember how to use, (iii) effective to use, and (iv)

© The Author(s) 2017
L. Gamberini et al. (Eds.): Symbiotic 2016, LNCS 9961, pp. 38–51, 2017.
DOI: 10.1007/978-3-319-57753-1_4

efficient to use. From this point of view, the puzzles such as CAPTCHA, which humans can easily solve, i.e. decrypt in contrast to the computers, represent an element of HCI. CAPTCHA is an acronym for Completely Automated Public Turing test to tell Computers and Humans Apart. It represents a test program with a task. If the user gives the right answer to the task asked by the program, then the program classifies it as a human, i.e. computer user [10]. Hence, it is created to differentiate the computer users from bots (computer program) in order to effectively login into a certain website. The aim of CAPTCHA is to stop the attacks made by bots. Hence, its main function is to: (i) protect web sites, applications, interfaces and services such as Google, Yahoo or similar, (ii) prevent spam in blogs, and (iii) protect email addresses [9].

CAPTCHA involves three different elements: (i) usability, (ii) security, and (iii) practicality [3]. Usability is linked with the process of solving the CAPTCHA by the computer users. It measures the efficiency of solving the CAPTCHA as well as the response time the computer user needs to solve the CAPTCHA. However, it is sometimes linked with the user's acceptance of the CAPTCHA, too. Security is deeply connected to the difficulty of finding solutions to CAPTCHA by computer. Practicality refers to the easiness of the programmers realization of CAPTCHA.

In this study, the image-based type of CAPTCHA will be considered. Among all types of CAPTCHA, the image-based ones are the most related to the elements of HCI, because they are linked to cognitive psychology. Also, the tested CAPTCHA samples are deeply connected to facial expressions, whose solving is influenced by human factors [6]. The main goal of this paper is exploring the usability elements such as user response time, usage, and preferences related to the image-based CAPTCHA which includes the facial expressions. We used four different image-based CAPTCHAs for testing purposes. Each of them consists of five different images and only one is related to the solution of CAPTCHA. In the experiment, the given CAPTCHAs are tested on a population of 100 different Internet users. The tested Internet users are differentiated by the given attributes: (i) age, (ii) Internet experience, and (iii) educational level. Specifically, we investigate (i) users' response time relating to the usability aspects of the CAPTCHA, and (ii) usage statistics connected to the response time of efficiently solving image-based CAPTCHA which includes elements of facial expression. To process tested data, the association rules are used. In this way, the user response time to efficiently solve certain CAPTCHA is analyzed by the association rule method. The obtained results will show the natural dependence and relationship between different variables which are of importance to the way of solving the CAPTCHA. Also, this approach identifies the influence of facial expression to efficiently solve the image-based CAPTCHA. Hence, it is invaluable for choosing a certain type of CAPTCHA to be accustomed to a certain group of Internet users. At the end, it improves the knowledge about the symbiotic system, because it gives information about to what human states the users are more sensitive, determining a speed response in solving the CAPTCHA.

The paper is organized as follows. Section 2 describes the image-based CAPT-CHA. Section 3 clarifies the data mining elements like association rules, which will be used as the main evaluation tool. Section 4 describes the elements of the experiment. Section 5 presents the results and gives the discussion. Section 6 draws conclusions.

2   CAPTCHA

All CAPTCHAs can be divided into the following groups: (i) text-based CAPT-CHA, (ii) video-based CAPTCHA, (iii) audio-based CAPTCHA, and (iv) image-based CAPTCHA. Text-based CAPTCHA is the most commonly used CAPT-CHA. It usually includes distorted text with different background. To solve this type of CAPTCHA, the distorted characters should be correctly recognized. It is easy to generate, but easily exposed to vulnerable attacks by bot due to efficient Optical Character Recognition (OCR) software. Video-based CAPTCHA uses video to create a puzzle to be solved. YouTube videos are typically used as a basis. To be solved, a CAPTCHA user is asked to tag videos with descriptive keywords. The users can reach an efficiency of solving CAPTCHA up to 90%. Audio-based CAPTCHA usually plays a set of characters or words. The users should recognize and type them in the designated area. This type of CAPTCHA is critically exposed to bot attacks due to rapid development in the speech recognition. The attack rate can reach up to 70%. Image-based CAPTCHA is usually considered as the most advanced and safest one. This type of CAPTCHA requires users to find a desired image inside a list of images. Because it is based on image details, it represents a very difficult task for bots. Furthermore, this type of CAPTCHA can easily integrate HCI elements connected to cognitive psychology. Figure 1 shows some image-based CAPTCHA types.

Fig. 1. Image-based CAPTCHA types

Existing image-based CAPTCHAs generally rely on image classification. In that way, the users see a series of images, which have to be identified as well as the relationship between them. Identifying the facial expression is a task accustomed to the humans [6]. Hence, it is easy to be solved by humans, but an impossible task for bots. Accordingly, integrating such HCI elements in an image-based CAPTCHA can create a very successful CAPTCHA in terms of security, usability as well as practicality.

3   Association Rule Mining

Association Rules (ARs) are the most intuitive tool to find the frequent sets of feature values and to understand the co-occurrence of these values in a dataset [1]. We start by defining the set of items representing all values n features can assume as $T = T_1 \cup T_2 \cup, ..., \cup T_n$, where $T_i = \{t_i^1, t_i^2, ..., t_i^x\}$ is the set of x items which are the possible values of feature i. Accordingly, a transaction I in our case is a subset of n items from T, such that each item is a value of a distinct feature. This means that $\forall t_i^j, t_k^h \in I$, $i \neq k$, and j and h are two possible values respectively of feature i and k. From the aforementioned, an Association Rule (AR) is defined as an implication $W \Rightarrow Z$, characterized by *support* and *confidence*, where W and Z represent disjoint sets of items, called respectively antecedent and consequent. Support quantifies the frequency of $W \cup Z$ in the transactions inside the dataset. It is related to the statistical significance of AR. Confidence measures the frequency of $W \cup Z$, given the transactions containing W. It evaluates the conditional probability of Z given W.

The main goal is the extraction of the ARs whose support value is $\geq$ *minsupport* and whose confidence value is $\geq$ *minconfidence*, by adopting the well-known *Apriori* algorithm [2]. It is composed of two main phases: (i) finding all the sets of items with frequency $\geq$ *minsupport* in the dataset; (ii) determining the ARs from obtained sets of items, taking into account the *minconfidence* threshold. The concept underlying the algorithm is based on the *anti-monotonicity* property: if a set of items is infrequent, also every its superset will be. Accordingly, unfrequent sets of items are eliminated in each iteration from the algorithm. First of all, the algorithm finds the sets of items of size k whose frequency is $\geq$ *minsupport*. Then, the sets of items are enlarged to size $k + 1$, by inserting the only sets of items of size 1 and frequency $\geq$ *minsupport*. These two phases are iterated from $k = 1$ to a given value of k, such that sets of items of size $k + 1$ with frequency $\geq$ *minsupport* cannot be detected further. Secondly, rules are created from each frequent set of items F. It is performed by detecting all the subsets $f \subset F$ such that confidence value of $f \to F - f$ is $\geq$ *minconfidence*.

Another interesting measure to evaluate the ARs has been introduced in [5], and it is called *lift*. Lift quantifies the number of times W and Z co-occur more often than expected if they were statistically independent [7]. If the lift assumes a value of 1, then W and Z are independent. On the contrary, if the lift assumes a value greater than 1, W and Z will co-occur more often than expected. It indicates that the occurrence of W has a positive effect on the occurrence of Z.

4   Experiment

Our experiment measures the usability elements of the proposed image-based CAPTCHAs, which incorporate facial expression elements. In that sense, the time needed to efficiently solve a certain CAPTCHA is measured. Each CAPT-CHA includes five images representing a certain facial expression. One of the images presents the asked facial expression among the other four images which are not. Hence, the users should choose the right image among the five given under consideration. The main goal is to measure and differentiate the influence of facial expressions to efficiently solve the image-based CAPTCHA linked with cognitive elements. We propose four CAPTCHAs representing the following facial expressions: (i) animated character, (ii) old woman, (iii) surprised face, and (iv) worried face. Figure 2 shows the proposed CAPTCHAs.

Fig. 2. Image-based CAPTCHAs incorporating facial expressions: animated character, old woman, surprised face and worried face

4.1 Participants

An experiment is conducted on a population sample of 100 Internet users. The first half of them is composed of women, and the other half is composed of men. The age of participants is from 18 to 52 years. They have a secondary or higher education level. The population sample includes students, engineers, officials, but also unemployed people. Participants have an Internet experience of at least one up to nine years. All users have joined the experiment voluntarily, knowing that their data would be made publicly available for study purposes, but without publishing their names (anonymous poll). The interview of each participant was conducted personally, by asking to solve the image-based CAPTCHAs. In particular, each Internet user is required to solve the 4 different types of the aforementioned image-based CAPTCHAs. For each user, the response times (in seconds) for finding the solution to the CAPTCHAs are registered. Hence, participants are differentiated by their: (i) age, (b) educational level, and (iii) working experience on the Internet. Also, they are characterized by a certain response time in solving the image-based CAPTCHAs.

4.2 Dataset Creation

At the end, a dataset including 7 features (age, education level, number of years of internet usage, response time in solving the animated character, old woman, surprised face, and worried face CAPTCHAs) is created, for a total of

100 instances of 7 features each. The feature corresponding to the age of the Internet users is linearly divided into two groups, which are below 35 years and above 35 years. The education level feature can assume also two values, which are the higher education and the secondary education levels. About the number of years of Internet usage, this feature has integer values from 0 to $+\infty$. In particular, in the dataset it varies from 1 to 9. Consequently, it is discretized by employing an Equal-Width Discretization [8], obtaining 3 different ranges, named as high Internet usage (> 6 years), middle Internet usage (from 4 to 6 years), and low Internet usage (< 4 years). The features corresponding to the response time in solving the 4 different types of image-based CAPTCHA have decimal values varying from 0.0 to $+\infty$. A test has been conducted for discretization of these features with multiple methods, including Equal-Width Discretization. It demonstrated that most of the methods fail in this task because they obtain a poor discretization. On the contrary, discretization by adopting the K-Medians clustering algorithm [4], whose advantage is finding the natural groups of data based on their characteristics, performed successfully, identifying 3 different ranges. The aim of the K-Medians is to determine K ranges from the values of the features, by minimizing a function J. It measures the total sum of L_1 norm between each value in a certain range and its centroid, which is its median value. We run the K-Medians algorithm 10 times with $K = 3$ and selected the set of ranges with the lowest value of J as the optimal solution. Hence, K-Medians found 3 ranges corresponding to low response time ($<$ 12.34 s), middle response time (from 12.34 s to 27.30 s), and high response time (> 27.30 s). Table 1 reports the feature values, eventually discretized.

Table 1. Possible values and corresponding ranges for each feature of the dataset

Features	Values	Interval
Age	Below 35	-
	Above 35	-
Education level	Higher education	-
	Secondary education	-
Number of years of internet usage	High Internet usage	> 6 years
	Middle Internet usage	$4 - 6$ years
	Low Internet usage	< 4 years
Response time in solving animated character CAPTCHA	High response time	> 27.30 s
	Middle response time	12.34 s $- 27.30$ s
	Low response time	< 12.34 s
Response time in solving old woman CAPTCHA	High response time	> 27.30 s
	Middle response time	12.34 s $- 27.30$ s
	Low response time	< 12.34 s
Response time in solving surprised face CAPTCHA	High response time	> 27.30 s
	Middle response time	12.34 s $- 27.30$ s
	Low response time	< 12.34 s
Response time in solving worried face CAPTCHA	High response time	> 27.30 s
	Middle response time	12.34 s $- 27.30$ s
	Low response time	< 12.34 s

4.3   Association Rules Extraction

The obtained dataset is subjected to the *Apriori* algorithm for detection of the ARs, by which we investigate on the association among the different feature values. Specifically, we find sets of frequently co-occurring feature values and that are related to a given response time in solving the 4 types of image-based CAPTCHA. Also, by tuning the *minconfidence* and *minsupport* to appropriate values, we are able to evaluate the strength of such a relationship. It determines a psychological analysis of the HCI, because we are able to understand (i) to which human conditions (age, education level, number of years of internet usage) is more likely the image-based CAPTCHA to be easily solved, and (ii) what type of image-based CAPTCHA is easier to be solved by a human subject. It is an interesting psychological analysis, if we think that each type of image-based CAPTCHA corresponds to a given condition or "state of mind" (worried, surprised, etc.), to which human subjects could be more or less sensitive. For this reason, the analysis is split into 4 parts, each corresponding to detect the ARs for a given type of image-based CAPTCHA. This means that we extract all the ARs by adopting the *Apriori* algorithm. Then, we filter them by selecting those ARs having only the response time feature value of a certain type of image-based CAPTCHA as consequent. Finally, we group the ARs based on the response time of the different types of image-based CAPTCHA, and evaluate them separately.

In our case, n is equal to 7 features. All the possible values of each of them are reported in Table 1. An example of transaction I, corresponding to a row of the dataset, with eventually discretized feature values, is given in Table 2.

Table 2. Example of transaction I (row of the dataset)

Age	Educ. level	Num. years Int. usage	Time anim. char.	Time old wom.	Time surpr. face	Time worr. face
Above 35	Sec. educ	Middle int. usage	Middle resp. time	Middle resp. time	Middle resp. time	Low resp. time

Also, an example of AR defined on this transaction is given below:

(Educ. level)   (Num. years Internet usage)   (Resp. time worried face)

$$\textit{secondary educ., middle Internet usage} \rightarrow \textit{low response time} \qquad (1)$$

The antecedent W of the AR is {*secondary educ., middle Internet usage*}, while the consequent Z is {*low response time*}. We can observe that $W \cup Z$, which is {*secondary educ., middle Internet usage, low response time*}, is found inside the transaction in Table 2. The meaning of this AR is that a secondary education level and a middle experience in Internet usage are enough to easily solve the worried face CAPTCHA.

5 Results and Discussion

Feature discretization, extraction and post-processing of the ARs have been performed in MATLAB R2012a on a notebook quad-core at 2.2 GHz, 16 GB RAM and UNIX operating system.

Tables 3, 4, 5 and 6 show the ARs, sorted by antecedent, detected from the dataset by the *Apriori* algorithm, whose consequent is the response time in solving the 4 different types of CAPTCHA. For each AR, we report the antecedent W, the consequent Z, the support, the confidence and the lift values. In order to extract ARs of interest, we fix the *minsupport* and *minconfidence* respectively to 5% and to 50%. The differences between the tables corresponding to missing ARs with the same antecedent are denoted as '-'. It is worth noting that the lift is always greater than 1. It indicates that the extracted ARs are statistically meaningful and that the antecedent and consequent are always positively correlated.

Table 3. Sorted association rules extracted from the dataset, for which the consequent is the response time in solving animated character CAPTCHA

Antecedent	Consequent	Supp.	Conf.	Lift
Below 35	Low resp. time	0.50	1.00	1.47
Below 35, Higher educ.	Low resp. time	0.24	1.00	1.47
Below 35 Secondary educ.	Low resp. time	0.26	1.00	1.47
Below 35, Low internet usage	Low resp. time	0.12	1.00	1.47
Below 35, Middle internet usage	Low resp. time	0.26	1.00	1.47
Below 35, High internet usage	Low resp. time	0.12	1.00	1.47
Below 35, Higher educ., Middle internet usage	Low resp. time	0.15	1.00	1.47
Below 35, Higher educ., High internet usage	Low resp. time	0.09	1.00	1.47
Below 35, Secondary educ., Low internet usage	Low resp. time	0.12	1.00	1.47
Below 35, Secondary educ., Middle internet usage	Low resp. time	0.11	1.00	1.47
High internet usage	Low resp. time	0.15	0.88	1.30
Higher educ., High internet usage	Low resp. time	0.12	0.86	1.26
Above 35, Secondary educ., Middle internet usage	Middle resp. time	0.08	0.73	2.51
Above 35, Middle internet usage	Middle resp. time	0.20	0.71	2.46
Above 35, Higher educ., Middle internet usage	Middle resp. time	0.12	0.71	2.43
Higher educ.	Low resp. time	0.33	0.69	1.01
Above 35, Higher educ.	Middle resp. time	0.15	0.63	2.15
Above 35	Middle resp. time	0.29	0.58	2.00
Above 35, Secondary educ.	Middle resp. time	0.14	0.54	1.86

In particular, we can observe that animated character CAPTCHA is the easiest to be solved among the 4 types of CAPTCHA (see Table 3). It is mainly because in general the ARs with a low response time exhibit higher support and

Table 4. Sorted association rules extracted from the dataset, for which the consequent is the response time in solving the old woman CAPTCHA

Antecedent	Consequent	Supp.	Conf.	Lift
Below 35	Low resp. time	0.49	0.98	1.31
Below 35, Higher educ.	Low resp. time	0.24	1.00	1.33
Below 35, Secondary educ.	Low resp. time	0.25	0.96	1.28
Below 35, Low internet usage	Low resp. time	0.11	0.92	1.22
Below 35, Middle internet usage	Low resp. time	0.26	1.00	1.33
Below 35, High internet usage	Low resp. time	0.12	1.00	1.33
Below 35, Higher educ., Middle internet usage	Low resp. time	0.15	1.00	1.33
Below 35, Higher educ., High internet usage	Low resp. time	0.09	1.00	1.33
Below 35, Secondary educ., Low internet usage	Low resp. time	0.11	0.92	1.22
Below 35, Secondary educ., Middle internet usage	Low resp. time	0.11	1.00	1.33
High internet usage	Low resp. time	0.16	0.94	1.25
Higher educ., High internet usage	Low resp. time	0.13	0.93	1.24
above 35, Secondary educ., Middle internet usage	Middle resp. time	0.06	0.55	2.37
–	–			
–	–			
Higher educ.	Low resp. time	0.40	0.83	1.11
–	–			
–	–			
Above 35, Secondary educ.	Middle resp. time	0.14	0.54	2.34
Higher educ., Middle internet usage	Low resp. time	0.26	0.81	1.08
Middle internet usage	Low resp. time	0.42	0.78	1.04
Above 35, Secondary educ., Low internet usage	Middle resp. time	0.08	0.53	2.32
Above 35, Low internet usage	Middle resp. time	0.09	0.53	2.30

confidence values than in the other types of CAPTCHA. It indicates that a low response time is likely to occur more often than in the other types of CAPTCHA. In fact, users below 35 years are associated to a low response time, also independently from the education level, which has no meaningful impact in solving this CAPTCHA, and from the level of internet usage, with a support of 0.50, a confidence of 1.00 and a lift of 1.47. The second more difficult type of CAPTCHA to solve is the old woman one (see Table 4). In fact, the pattern for the users below 35 years is maintained with similar but slightly lower values of support and confidence with respect to animated character CAPTCHA. Because in general the support and confidence values of the rules whose consequent is the low response time are smaller in the case of old woman than in the case of animated character, we will have a smaller probability to determine a low response time in solving the CAPTCHA. On the other hand, the ARs extracted for old woman CAPTCHA present the highest number of differences with respect to the other types of CAPTCHA (see the four missing rules denoted as '-' in Table 4). The

Table 5. Sorted association rules extracted from the dataset, for which the consequent is the response time in solving surprised face CAPTCHA

Antecedent	Consequent	Supp.	Conf.	Lift
Below 35	Low resp. time	0.44	0.88	1.49
Below 35, Higher educ.	Low resp. time	0.20	0.83	1.41
Below 35, Secondary educ.	Low resp. time	0.24	0.92	1.56
Below 35, Low internet usage	Low resp. time	0.10	0.83	1.41
Below 35, Middle internet usage	Low resp. time	0.23	0.88	1.50
Below 35, High internet usage	Low resp. time	0.11	0.92	1.55
Above 35, Higher educ., Middle internet usage	Middle resp. time	0.15	0.88	2.32
Below 35, Higher educ., High internet usage	Low resp. time	0.08	0.89	1.51
Below 35, Secondary educ., Low internet usage	Low resp. time	0.10	0.83	1.41
Below 35, Secondary educ., Middle internet usage	Low resp. time	0.11	1.00	1.69
High internet usage	Low resp. time	0.13	0.76	1.30
Higher educ., High internet usage	Low resp. time	0.10	0.71	1.22
Above 35, Secondary educ., Middle internet usage	Middle resp. time	0.06	0.55	1.43
Above 35, Middle internet usage	Middle resp. time	0.21	0.75	1.97
Below 35, Higher educ., Middle internet usage	Low resp. time	0.12	0.80	1.35
Higher educ.	Middle resp. time	0.24	0.50	1.31
Above 35, Higher educ.	Middle resp. time	0.20	0.83	2.19
Above 35	Middle resp. time	0.32	0.64	1.68
–	–			
Secondary educ., Middle internet usage	Low resp. time	0.16	0.73	1.23
Secondary educ.	Low resp. time	0.35	0.67	1.14
Secondary educ., Low internet usage	Low resp. time	0.16	0.59	1.00
Higher educ., Middle internet usage	Middle resp. time	0.18	0.56	1.48

third type of CAPTCHA, more difficult to be solved, is the surprised face one (see Table 5), having the same pattern for users below 35 years, but corresponding lower support and confidence values, indicating that the correlation between users below 35 years and low response time is weaker than before. Also, a higher education level is sufficient to obtain a low response time in animated character, while it is able to solve the surprised face CAPTCHA only in a middle response time. The last type of CAPTCHA presenting the highest difficulty level is the worried face one (see Table 6). We can observe that the extracted ARs for this CAPTCHA are very similar to the ARs extracted for surprised face CAPTCHA. In particular, the pattern for the users below 35 years is also visible, but with support and confidence values less than in the surprised face CAPTCHA, and in general in all the other types of CAPTCHA. It indicates that a smaller percentage of transactions contain the co-occurrence of users below 35 years and low response time. This means that users below 35 years are less correlated to a low response time in solving this CAPTCHA. In general, the differences in

Table 6. Sorted association rules extracted from the dataset, for which the consequent is the response time in solving worried face CAPTCHA

Antecedent	Consequent	Supp.	Conf.	Lift
Below 35	Low resp. time	0.38	0.76	1.43
Above 35, Higher educ.	Middle resp. time	0.21	0.88	1.99
Below 35, Secondary educ.	Low resp. time	0.23	0.88	1.67
Below 35, Low internet usage	Low resp. time	0.09	0.75	1.41
Below 35, Middle internet usage	Low resp. time	0.19	0.73	1.38
Below 35, High internet usage	Low resp. time	0.10	0.83	1.57
Above 35, Higher educ., Middle internet usage	Middle resp. time	0.16	0.94	2.14
Below 35, Higher educ., High internet usage	Low resp. time	0.07	0.78	1.47
Below 35, Secondary educ., Low internet usage	Low resp. time	0.09	0.75	1.41
Below 35, Secondary educ., Middle internet usage	Low resp. time	0.11	1.00	1.89
High internet usage	Low resp. time	0.12	0.71	1.33
Higher educ., High internet usage	Low resp. time	0.09	0.64	1.21
Above 35, Secondary educ., Middle internet usage	Low resp. time	0.06	0.55	1.03
Above 35, Middle internet usage	Middle resp. time	0.21	0.75	1.70
Below 35, Higher educ., Middle internet usage,	Low resp. time	0.08	0.53	1.01
Higher educ.	Middle resp. time	0.30	0.63	1.42
Below 35, Higher educ.	Low resp. time	0.15	0.63	1.18
Above 35	Middle resp. time	0.32	0.64	1.45
–	–			
Secondary educ., Middle internet usage	Low resp. time	0.17	0.77	1.46
Higher educ., Middle internet usage	Middle resp. time	0.23	0.72	1.63
Secondary educ.	Low resp. time	0.35	0.67	1.27
Secondary educ., Low internet usage	Low resp. time	0.15	0.56	1.05
Middle internet usage	Middle resp. time	0.28	0.52	1.18

the 4 types of CAPTCHA represent distinctive characteristics of each type of CAPTCHA that is mandatory to deeply analyze.

Specifically, looking at Table 3, we can observe that users above 35 years and with a middle internet usage are associated to a middle response time in solving the animated character CAPTCHA, also independently from the education level. This pattern is not present for the old woman CAPTCHA (see Table 4), for which users above 35 years and with a middle internet usage are associated to a middle response time only in the case of secondary education level. Furthermore, in animated character CAPTCHA, we find that users above 35 years are related to a middle response time, also independently from education level (hence, also with higher education level) and number of years of Internet usage. On the contrary, for old woman CAPTCHA (see Table 4), the strongest rule in terms of support, confidence and lift (respectively of 0.14, 0.54 and 2.34) involving the users above 35 years indicates that users above 35 years are able to solve the CAPTCHA in a middle time if they have a secondary education level. Again, looking at Table 5 of surprised face CAPTCHA, another difference can be observed with animated character CAPTCHA. In particular, it is required a higher education level to the users above 35 years to solve this CAPTCHA in a middle time. On the contrary, for the animated character CAPTCHA, the users above 35 years are able to solve it in a middle time also when they have a secondary education level. In the case of worried face CAPTCHA in Table 6, we observe a meaningful difference with animated character CAPTCHA for the users above 35 years. In fact, in the case of animated character CAPTCHA, the users above 35 years are associated to a middle response time even if they have a secondary education level, while, in the case of worried face, if they have a higher education level, with similar values of support, confidence and lift. A last difference is visible between the ARs of the surprised face CAPTCHA and those of the worried face CAPTCHA. In fact, in the second ones, a middle internet usage is related to a middle response time in solving that CAPTCHA, with a support of 0.28, a confidence of 0.52 and a lift of 1.18. Differently, this rule is not present for the surprised face CAPTCHA.

Finally, we can make the following observations: (i) Internet users below 35 years have a good attitude in solving the image-based CAPTCHA; (ii) the easiest type of image-based CAPTCHA to be solved is the animated character one, followed by old woman, surprised face and the more complex worried face ones; (iii) the users above 35 years are able to solve the animated character CAPTCHA in a moderate time; (iv) the users above 35 years have an attitude to solve the old woman CAPTCHA in a moderate time if they have a secondary education level; (v) it is required a higher education level to the users above 35 years to solve the surprised face and the worried face CAPTCHAs in a moderate time.

6   Conclusions

The paper analyzed the human response to the facial expressions given in specific image-based CAPTCHA. Hence, it explored the computer users' response time (reaction rate) to the given CAPTCHA according to cognitive psychology linked with facial expression recognition. The obtained results were statistically processed by the ARs. The analysis by ARs revealed interesting co-occurrences of feature values and their association with a given response time to solve the facial expression image-based CAPTCHA. Although the results were quite similar, the AR methodology proved to be powerful to differentiate subtle variations between processed values. In that way, the results showed that computer users can more easily recognize CAPTCHAs that incorporate animated characters. Also, the facial expressions such as surprised or worried face are the most difficult to recognize and differentiate. It is worth noting that recognition of the old woman among the other images was characterized by different elements to be influenced to than the images presented in other analyzed CAPTCHAs. The obtained results and further research in the given area can help in finding the most appropriate CAPTCHA for a wider range of Internet users. Also, the knowledge about the symbiotic system is improved by showing in what human states the users are more sensitive.

In this context, ARs have not been properly used for prediction, but for unsupervised detection of the natural dependencies and relationships between feature values and response times. Hence, future work will be focused on tree-based methods for prediction of the response time by supervised learning. Analysis will be further enriched by providing a larger dataset and a literature review of cognitive science on how people differentiated by age or educational level react to different image stimuli. It will be useful to formalize hypotheses on the expected correlations between the response time and the other features.

Acknowledgments. The authors are grateful to the participants for publicly providing their data. This work was partially supported by the Grant of the Ministry of Education, Science and Technological Development of the Republic Serbia, as a part of the project TR33037.

References

1. Agrawal, R., Imieliński, T., Swami, A.: Mining association rules between sets of items in large databases. In: Proceedings of the ACM SIGMOD International Conference on Management of Data - SIGMOD, pp. 207–216 (1993)
2. Agrawal, R., Srikant, R.: Fast algorithms for mining association rules in large databases. In: Proceedings of the 20th International Conference on Very Large Data Bases, VLDB, pp. 487–499 (1994)
3. Baecher, P., Fischlin, M., Gordon, L., Langenberg, R., Lutzow, M., Schroder, D.: CAPTCHAs: the good, the bad and the ugly. In: Frieling, F.C. (ed.) Sicherheit. LNI, vol. 170, pp. 353–365. GI (2010)
4. Bradley, P.S., Mangasarian, O.L., Street, W.N.: Clustering via concave minimization. In: Advances in Neural Information Processing Systems 1996, pp. 368–374. MIT Press (1997)
5. Brin, S., Motwani, R., Ullman, J.D., Tsur, S.: Dynamic itemset counting and implication rules for market basket data. In: Proceedings of the ACM SIGMOD International Conference on Management of Data - SIGMOD, pp. 265–276 (1997)
6. Erickson, K., Schulkin, J.: Facial expressions of emotion: a cognitive neuroscience perspective. Brain Cogn. **52**(1), 52–60 (2003)
7. Hahsler, M.: A probabilistic comparison of commonly used interest measures for association rules (2015). http://michael.hahsler.net/research/association_rules/measures.html
8. Sullivan, D.G.: Data Mining V: Preparing the Data. http://cs-people.bu.edu/dgs/courses/cs105/lectures/data_mining_preparation.pdf
9. The CAPTCHA test. http://en.wikipedia.org/wiki/CAPTCHA
10. Von Ahn, L., Blum, M., Langford, J.: Telling humans and computers apart automatically. Commun. ACM **47**(2), 47–60 (2004)

The "NeuroDante Project": Neurometric Measurements of Participant's Reaction to Literary Auditory Stimuli from Dante's "Divina Commedia"

Giulia Cartocci[1(✉)], Anton Giulio Maglione[1], Enrica Modica[1], Dario Rossi[1], Paolo Canettieri[2], Mariella Combi[2], Roberto Rea[2], Luca Gatti[2], Carmen Silvia Perrotta[1], Francesca Babiloni[1], Roberto Verdirosa[1], Roberta Bernaudo[1], Elena Lerose[1], and Fabio Babiloni[1]

[1] Department of Molecular Medicine, University of Rome Sapienza, Rome, Italy
giulia.cartocci@uniroma1.it
[2] Department of European, American and Intercultural Studies, University of Rome Sapienza, Rome, Italy

Abstract. This work is a pilot study that used neurometric indexes during the listening of selected pieces of Dante's "Divina Commedia" in 20 participants. Half of them had a literary formation (Humanist; university students of literature) while the other half of is attending other university courses (Not Humanist). The study applied the electroencephalographic (EEG) rhythms variations, the heart rate (HR) and galvanic skin response (GSR) during the listening of the excerpts. The neurometric indexes here employed were the Approach Withdrawal (AW), the Cerebral Effort (CE) and the Emotional indexes (EI). Results for the comparisons of the estimated AW, CE and EI related to the perception of the *canticas* showed as the Humanist group reported higher AW and EI values when compared to the Not Humanist sample ($p < 0.03$ and $p < 0.01$, respectively). Results suggest that the perception of the aesthetic experience is significantly modulated by the previous specific knowledge experienced by the participants. Finally, results of this kind of research could find application in the implementation of software and devices based on symbiotic relation with the perspective reader or listener of a literature opera, in order to personalize and maximize the fruition of them.

Keywords: Approach Withdrawal · Cerebral Effort · EEG · Alpha · Theta · Electrodermal Activity · HR · GSR · Emotion · Russell's circumplex model of affects

1 Introduction

Reading and listening stories is a very peculiar human activity. In fact, other animal species on earth have not engaged (as far as we know) in such task. On a more basic level, a lot of knowledge has been accumulated in these last three decades of neuroscientific studies on the perception and appreciation of visual stimuli and the "internal" factors able to shape such perception [1]. Moreover, a lot of knowledge has been also obtained on the evaluation of the cerebral activity related to the judgment of syntactic

L. Gamberini et al. (Eds.): Symbiotic 2016, LNCS 9961, pp. 52–64, 2017.
DOI: 10.1007/978-3-319-57753-1_5

and grammatical violations on speech listening [2]. However, a recent research path moves from the measurements and the relative understanding of the basic characteristic of the sensory perception towards the more complex way in which we, as specie, perceive and enjoy the reading and listening of stories [3]. In this attempt, researchers have started to measures cerebral and emotional activities manipulating some factors that could alter or increase the pleasure in the story perception [4, 5]. Furthermore, the knowledge of the features modulating the emotional involvement in the reader could be also implemented in designing e-books [6], also potentially based on a symbiotic inter-action with the user. Additionally, the neurophysiological approach could provide meas-urable information on the emotional content of a text, as evidenced by the lowering of the heart rate and the variation of the breathing and the electroencephalographic (EEG) alpha rhythm asymmetry [7].

In this scenario, neuroaesthetics is an emerging disciplines investigating the biolog-ical underpinnings of aesthetic experiences, and since its formal birth in 90s by Semir Zeki (for a review [8]) it constitutes a field receiving growing interest by the scientific community. Although traditional topic of neuroaesthetic investigation are visual art and music [9, 10], an enlargement in the horizon of artistic items to be investigated is begin-ning and literature and poetry are experiencing a renewed scientific interest from the neuroaesthetics perspective [3]. That is, the question we would like address here is "Which biological underpinnings make classical authors cognitively and emotionally engaging?". Two aspects of poetry may contribute to the emotional responses it may elicit: its lexical content and its structural features (i.e., poetic form). Meter and rhyme constitute the key features in poetry [11], additionally they have been found to be significant contributors to the aesthetic and emotional perception of poetry [4], but it is difficult to investigate the contribution of the content "per se" due to the needing to compare different kinds of texts. A possibility to overcome this limitation is offered by the famous Italian XIV century poem the "Divina Commedia" by Dante Alighieri (1265–1321). The book is characterized by a repetitive and constant structure, as it is composed by three parts (canticas: Inferno –Hell–, Purgatorio –Purgatory- and Paradiso –Para-dise-), each part is composed by thirty-three cantos, for an average length of 142 verses. The verse scheme used, "terza rima", is hendecasyllabic (lines of eleven syllables), with the lines composing tercets relying to the rhyme scheme xyx yzy z. Each cantica, despite the conservation of the metric structure is characterized by a different content. The reader follows Dante's journey through Hell, Purgatory and Paradise, where the poet respec-tively meets damned souls, then souls expiating their sins and finally enjoys the vision of God. Studying the reaction to the exposure to stanzas belonging to each of the three canticas would enable to test the effect of the content of the excerpts, maintaining the meter and the rhyme scheme constant. Furthermore, the comparison among different canticas would enable to assess the effect of a potentially differential previous knowledge of the peculiar cantica.

In this work, we described the results of a pilot study that used neurometric indexes during the listening of a selected pieces of the Divina Commedia in a reduced sample of voluntary participants. Noteworthy, half of the participants had a literary formation in their advanced studies (Humanist; they are students of literature at the University) while the other half of the sample are attending other university courses (Not Humanist).

The study applied the gathering of the electroencephalographic rhythms variations, as well as the heart rate (HR) and galvanic skin response (GSR) during the listening of the excerpts. The neurometric indexes here employed were the Approach-Withdrawal (AW) [12], the Effort (CE) [13] and the Emotional indexes (EI) [14]. It is worth noticing that different research teams previously validated those indexes in literature. Results are related to the comparisons of the estimated AW, CE and EI related to the perception of the analyzed canticas in the sample population.

2 Methods

In the present study, 20 healthy participants (mean age Humanist 24.9 and Not Humanist 26.2 years old) have been enrolled on a voluntary base and not receiving any compensation from taking part in the research. Participants were university students at Sapienza University of Rome, half of them attending humanistic courses and the second half scientific courses. All participants were given of detailed information on the study and signed an informed consent.

The experiment was performed in accord to the principles outlined in the Declaration of Helsinki of 1975, as revised in 2000, and it was approved by the University ethical committee. Participants were sitting on a comfortable chair and instructed to listen to the auditory stimuli. The three target stimuli were randomly played among, so producing different trains of auditory stimuli. The train was preceded and followed by sentences in Italian language that belongs to a standardized set of sentences used normally for audiometric purposes in clinic (Audiometria Vocale. Cutugno, Prosser, Turrini). Such sequence of short phrases lasted 1 min of length and has been used as the baseline in this experimental setup. The target stimuli belonged to excerpts from the reading of the Dante Alighieri's Divina Commedia. The excerpts texts were read by an Italian professional actor, so to ensure the quality of the elocution. The three selected emblematic pieces have been chosen by experts in Italian literature (academic professors and researchers) and each belonged to one of the three canticas of the poem: Inferno (Hell), Purgatorio (Purgatory) and Paradiso (Paradise) respectively. The neurometric indexes employed in the study were the Approach-Withdrawal (AW) [14], the Effort (CE) [15] and the Emotional indexes (EI) [16].

2.1 Behavioral Assessment

At the end of the listening session, participants underwent a short recognition test. Participants were asked whether they recognized the audio pieces and to say what they thought to have listened. These behavioral data were collected and analyzed.

2.2 EEG Recordings and Signal Processing

The EEG activity was recorded by means of a portable 24-channel system (BEmicro, EBneuro, Italy). Nineteen electrodes were used in this experiment according to the 10–20 international system. The impedances were kept below 10 kΩ and the signals have been acquired at a sampling rate of 256 Hz. To detect and remove components due to eye movements, blinks, and muscular artefacts, over the EEG traces were applied a notch filter (50 Hz), lowpass filtered (lp = 30 Hz) and the Independent Component Analysis (ICA). For each participant, the Individual Alpha Frequency (IAF) has been calculated in order to define the frequency bands of interest according to the method suggested in the scientific literature [15]. The Global Field Power (GFP) has been calculated for each frontal channel and for each participant. Several studies in literature (e.g. [12, 16, 17]) describe the frontal cortex as an area of interest for the analysis of the approach or withdrawal attitude [12, 18, 19] and the cerebral effort [15, 20] in response to a wide range of stimuli. In particular there are evidences indicating a link between dorso-lateral prefrontal cortex (PFC) area and approach motivation [21, 22]. Concerning approach motivation, the PFC has been found to be systematically related [23] to approach-motivated states, as well as the nucleus accumbens (ACC). The same authors also found systematic relations between avoidance-motivated states and the amygdala and the ACC. Thus, there is increasing evidence that emotional states related to approach and avoidance involve localisable brain circuits [24, 25].

It must be noted that the data here analyzed are relative to the scalp level, and a one-to-one correspondence between the frontal scalp recorded EEG and the cortical activity of the prefrontal areas cannot be precisely determined. The formula defining the Approach Withdrawal (AW) index is the following:

$$AW = GFPa\_right - GFPa\_left \qquad (1)$$

where the GFPa_right and GFPa_left stand for the GFP calculated among right (Fp2, F4, F8) and left (F7, F3, Fp1) electrodes, in the alpha band. Electrode's labeling follows the International 10–20 Positioning system. The estimated cerebral AW index has been computed for each second and then averaged for all the duration of the auditory stimuli proposed to the participants. The AW index was then standardized according to the baseline EEG activity acquired at the beginning and at the end of the experiment. Positive AW values mean an approach motivation toward the stimulus expressed by the participant, while negative AW values a withdrawal tendency.

To evaluate the cerebral effort frontal electrodes in theta band (Fp2, F4, F8, Fz,F7, F3, Fp1) have been used. The GFP from such frontal electrodes have been successively estimated. Then the cerebral effort index (CE) data have been standardized according to the baseline EEG activity acquired at the beginning and at the end of the experiment. Higher level of CE imply higher level of task difficulty [13, 26].

2.3   HR and GSR Recordings and Signal Processing

Electrodermal Activity (EDA) and Heart Rate (HR) were recorded by means of a NeXus-10 (Mindmedia, The Netherlands) system with a sampling rate of 128 Hz. Disposable electrodes provided by the Mindmedia company were applied to the participant's wrist to collect cardiac activity. To obtain the HR signal the Pan-Tompkins algorithm [27] has been employed. Skin conductance was acquired by the constant voltage method (0.5 V). The electrodes were attached, on non-dominant hand, to the palmar side of the middle phalanges of the second and third fingers of the participant, following published procedures [28]. The tonic component of the skin conductance (Skin Conductance Level, SCL) was obtained using LEDAlab software [29]. In the attempt to match SCL and HR signals we referred to the circumplex model of affect plane [30, 31], where the coordinates of a point in the space are defined by the HR (horizontal axis) to describe the valence and by the SCL (vertical axis) to describe the arousal phenomena (see [32] for a review). In order to obtain a monodimensional variable, the emotional state of a participant has been described by the Emotional Index (EI), as defined in previous studies [14]. The interpretation of the EI implies that the higher the value the more positive the emotion experienced by the participant and vice versa.

2.4   Statistical Analysis

Statistical analysis has been performed on the biometric results obtained during the exposure to the three *canticas* by repeated measures analysis of variance (ANOVA) for all the considered biometric indices (AW, CE and EI). Factors considered in the ANOVA were: (i) BACKGROUND, with 2 levels (Humanistic and Not Humanistic); (ii) CANTICA, with 3 levels (Inferno, Purgatorio e Paradiso). Duncan's post hoc test has been used to investigate the significant interactions resulting from ANOVA test. Fisher's exact test has been used for the analysis of the behavioral data concerning the recognition of the *canticas*. Logistic regression analysis has been performed between values reported for each index (AW, CE and EI) and the behaviorally declared recognition of each cantica by the participants [33].

3   Results

3.1   Behavioral Results

The Humanist group reported a higher average number of participants who correctly recognized the different *canticas*. Approximately the 90% of the Humanist group verbally recognized the *canticas* in comparison to the 40% of the Not Humanists (Fisher's exact test p = 0.06).

3.2   Approach Withdrawal Index

The effect of the factor BACKGROUND didn't reach the statistical significance alone (F = 2.65, p = 0.12), as well as the effect of the CANTICA (F = 1.01, p = 0.37) (Fig. 1). The AW index showed a statistical significant effect of the interaction between the factors BACKGROUND and CANTICA (F = 3.74, p = 0.03) (Fig. 2).

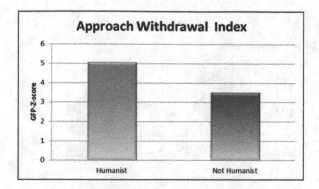

Fig. 1. Approach Withdrawal Index mean values for the Divina Commedia canticas over-all in the Humanist and Not Humanist groups.

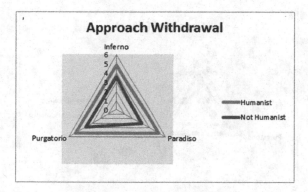

Fig. 2. Approach Withdrawal Index mean values for the different Divina Commedia canticas in the Humanist and Not Humanist groups.

Results of the logistic regression performed between AW values and verbally declared recognition scores showed a statistical significance (p = 0.04). Furthermore, the logistic regression analysis between AW values reported for each cantica and verbally declared behavioral recognition highlighted a statistical significance for Paradiso (p = 0.04), while Purgatorio and Inferno didn't show any significance (p = 0.12 and p = 0.92 respectively).

3.3 Cerebral Effort

The factor BACKGROUND (Fig. 3) didn't show a statistically significant difference between Humanist and Not Humanist (F = 2.71, p = 0.12), as long as the factor CANTICA (F = 0.82, p = 0.44). The CE values (Fig. 4) showed a statistically significant effect of the interaction between the factors BACKGROUND and the kind of CANTICA (F = 3.30, p = 0.05).

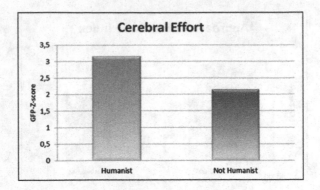

Fig. 3. Effort Index mean values for the Divina Commedia canticas over-all in the Humanist and Not Humanist groups. On the axis GFP Z-score unit is displayed.

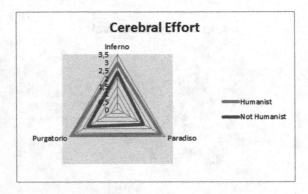

Fig. 4. Effort Index mean values for the different Divina Commedia canticas in the Humanist and Not Humanist groups. On the axis GFP Z-score unit is displayed.

The logistic regression analysis performed between CE values and verbally declared recognition scores showed a statistical significance ($p = 0.02$). In addition, the logistic regression analysis between CE values reported for each cantica and verbally declared behavioral recognition highlighted a statistical significance for Paradiso ($p = 0.02$), while Purgatorio and Inferno didn't show any significance ($p = 0.45$ and $p = 0.34$ respectively).

3.4 Emotional Index

A statistically significant effect was reported for the factor CANTICA ($F = 17.38$, $p < 0.01$), while the BACKGROUND factor did not show a statistical significance (0.84, $p = 0.37$) (Fig. 5). Furthermore, the EI index (Fig. 6) showed a statistical significant effect of the interaction between the factors BACKGROUND and the CANTICA ($F = 7.47$, $p < 0.01$). Post hoc comparison showed a higher emotional reaction to Inferno and Paradiso canticas in comparison to the Purgatorio ($p < 0.01$) in the Humanist group, while in the Not Humanist group the Inferno reported higher values in comparison to both Paradiso and Purgatorio ($p < 0.01$, $p = 0.04$ respectively). When the comparison of the Inferno cantica has been performed between the two groups no statistical significant differences were shown ($p = 0.18$). Conversely, statistical significant differences have been reported for Paradiso and Purgatorio comparisons between the groups ($p < 0.01$ and $p = 0.01$ respectively).

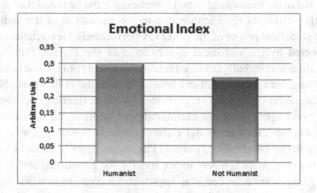

Fig. 5. Emotional Index mean values for the Divina Commedia canticas over-all in the Humanist and Not Humanist groups.

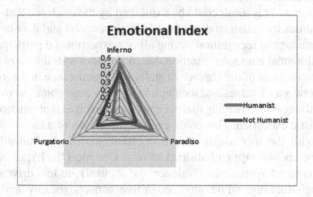

Fig. 6. Emotional Index mean values for the different Divina Commedia canticas in the Humanist and Not Humanist groups. On the axis an arbitrary unit related to the emotional index, whose range is between −1(very sad) to 1(very happy) is displayed.

Results of the logistic regression performed between EI values and verbally declared recognition scores didn't show a statistical significance ($p = 0.64$). Finally, the logistic regression analysis between EI values reported for each cantica and verbally declared behavioral recognition highlighted a statistical significance for Paradiso ($p = 0.02$) and Purgatorio ($p = 0.04$), while Inferno didn't show any significance ($p = 0.30$).

4 Discussion

Results from this pilot study showed that the Humanist group reported higher AW values for the canticas in comparison to the Not Humanist group and this evidence could be related to the higher knowledge of these texts in comparison to the other experimental group, as reflected in the behavioral data. However, it must be noted that such difference did not reach the statistical significance due to the limitation of the sample size here employed (low statistical power of the ANOVA performed). Nevertheless this evidence could be supported by the statistical significance of the logistic regression analysis between AW values and verbally declared recognition scores of the canticas. To partially discuss this finding, we reported that in literature Leder and colleagues [34] theorized a descriptive information-processing stage model for the aesthetic experience, consisting of 5 stages: perception, explicit classification, implicit classification, cognitive mastering and evaluation. The model differentiates between aesthetic emotion and aesthetic judgments as two types of output. This hypothesis is in accord with our data when considering results for the AW index and for the Emotional Index. In particular, the Humanist group showed a cerebral approach motivation towards the canticas in general, but a more selective emotional involvement for two of them: both Inferno and Paradiso in comparison to the Purgatorio. Additionally, except for the Inferno, there was a statistical significant difference in the EI for Paradiso and Purgatorio between the two experimental groups. This result could be explained by the evidence that Inferno is the most studied cantica by Italian students (also in high schools) and the one that reported the highest percentage of recognition among all our experimental participants, so don't producing a differential emotional reaction due to previous specific knowledge. On the other hand, as a comment of the absence of statistical significance in the logistic regression analysis between EI values and recognition scores could come the evidence found by Leder and colleagues [35] saying that the emotional reaction is attenuated by attention to style and artistic execution. This could explain the reason of a lack of increase of EI values along with the increase in the recognition scores. Additionally, evidences deriving from behavioral rating of abstract artworks, support the hypothesis that affective components of art appreciation (valence and arousal) are less driven by expertise acquired through training, while more cognitive aspects (beauty and wanting) of aesthetic experience depend on viewer characteristics such as art expertise [36].

Concerning the cerebral effort, probably the canticas were more cognitively involving for the Humanist group, since their previous knowledge of them. That could stimulate the transferring of information subserving the processing of the content and the application of art-specific classifications [37]. The present result could find confirmation in the statistical significance highlighted in the logistic regression analysis between CE values and verbally declared recognition scores of the cantica. In other words, Humanist group generated more effort in following the proposed canticas, because such canticas were in an ancient language when compared to their actual natural language. The opposite could be hypothesized for the not Humanist group, that probably faced difficulties in follow the Dante's ancient language of the two not popular excerpts (from Purgatorio and Paradiso) that they have not studied in the high schools or at the university. This difficulty in turn partially switch off the effort in such group to follow the narration and release cognitive faculties from the listening, causing a decrease of the measured cognitive efforts in such group. As already pointed out, the excerpt from the Inferno is very popular in Italy and all the participants involved already know in greater part the words and the meaning involved in such part.

5 Conclusion

In general, the collected data suggest a difference for the cerebral and emotional perceptions of the aesthetic experience related to the Divina Commedia listening on the base of the previous cultural background for the two investigated groups. This result could be explained by the evidence that aesthetic experience is a function of previous knowledge [38]. In this framework, experts and non-experts rely on different cues to evaluate artworks in terms of liking and comprehension [35, 39]. The present results, obtained by a pilot study, need further investigation on an enlarged sample so to provide indications on the literature and poetry aesthetic experience in experts and non-experts. Recent studies showed the employment of the neurofeedback using a real-time PFC alpha asymmetry, as an index of subjective empathy and positive disposition toward the character, in order to modify the development of a drama [40]. In addition, seeking for the personalization of the experience, a similar approach has been used presenting cultural heritage material, with the aim of developing an adapting provision of information in order to sustain the interest of the visitor [41]. Finally, as a future perspective the present study approach to the literature perception could be implemented in the building of personalized narrative experiences, based on the detection by a symbiotic system participant's response from both the cognitive and emotional nature.

Acknowledgment. Thanks to the Cinecittà Experimental Cinematography Centre (Centro Sperimentale di Cinematografia di Cinecittà), to its director Adriano De Santis and to the actor Roberto Antonelli who gave voice to the Divina Commedia canticas.

The present study was partially funded by "Ricerca di Ateneo" grant from University of Rome Sapienza.

References

1. Freeman, J.B., Johnson, K.L.: More than meets the eye: split-second social perception. Trends Cogn. Sci. **20**, 362–374 (2016). doi:10.1016/j.tics.2016.03.003
2. Caffarra, S., Molinaro, N., Davidson, D., Carreiras, M.: Second language syntactic processing revealed through event-related potentials: an empirical review. Neurosci. Biobehav. Rev. **51**, 31–47 (2015). doi:10.1016/j.neubiorev.2015.01.010
3. Jacobs, A.M.: Neurocognitive poetics: methods and models for investigating the neuronal and cognitive-affective bases of literature reception. Front. Hum. Neurosci. **9**, 186 (2015). doi:10.3389/fnhum.2015.00186
4. Obermeier, C., Menninghaus, W., von Koppenfels, M., Raettig, T., Schmidt-Kassow, M., Otterbein, S., Kotz, S.A.: Aesthetic and emotional effects of meter and rhyme in poetry. Front. Psychol. **4**, 10 (2013). doi:10.3389/fpsyg.2013.00010

5. Obermeier, C., Kotz, S.A., Jessen, S., Raettig, T., von Koppenfels, M., Menninghaus, W.: Aesthetic appreciation of poetry correlates with ease of processing in event-related potentials. Cogn. Affect Behav. Neurosci. **16**, 362–373 (2015). doi:10.3758/s13415-015-0396-x
6. van Erp, J.B., Hogervorst, M.A., van der Werf, Y.D.: Toward physiological indices of emotional state driving future ebook interactivity. PeerJ Comput. Sci. **2**, e60 (2016)
7. Brouwer, A.-M., Hogervorst, M., Reuderink, B., van der Werf, Y., van Erp, J.: Physiological signals distinguish between reading emotional and non-emotional sections in a novel. Brain-Computer Interfaces **2**, 76–89 (2015). doi:10.1080/2326263X.2015.1100037
8. Chatterjee, A., Vartanian, O.: Neuroaesthetics. Trends Cogn. Sci. **18**, 370–375 (2014). doi: 10.1016/j.tics.2014.03.003
9. Ishizu, T., Zeki, S.: Toward a brain-based theory of beauty. PLoS ONE **6**, e21852 (2011). doi: 10.1371/journal.pone.0021852
10. Zatorre, R.J., Salimpoor, V.N.: From perception to pleasure: music and its neural substrates. Proc. Nat. Acad. Sci. U.S.A. **110**(Suppl 2), 10430–10437 (2013). doi:10.1073/pnas. 1301228110
11. Jakobson, R.: Closing statement: linguistics and poetics. In: Style in Language, pp. 350–377 (1960)
12. Davidson, R.J.: What does the prefrontal cortex 'do' in affect: perspectives on frontal EEG asymmetry research. Biol. Psychol. **67**(1–2), 219–234 (2004)
13. Wisniewski, M.G., Thompson, E.R., Iyer, N., Estepp, J.R., Goder-Reiser, M.N., Sullivan, S.C.: Frontal midline θ power as an index of listening effort. NeuroReport **26**, 94–99 (2015). doi:10.1097/WNR.0000000000000306
14. Vecchiato, G., Maglione, A.G., Cherubino, P., Wasikowska, B., Wawrzyniak, A., Latuszynska, A., Latuszynska, M., Nermend, K., Graziani, I., Leucci, M.R., Trettel, A., Babiloni, F.: Neurophysiological tools to investigate consumer's gender differences during the observation of TV commercials. Comput. Math. Meth. Med. **2014**, 12 (2014)
15. Klimesch, W.: EEG alpha and theta oscillations reflect cognitive and memory performance: a review and analysis. Brain Res. Rev. **29**(2–3), 169–195 (1999)
16. Cherubino, P., et al.: Neuroelectrical indexes for the study of the efficacy of TV advertising stimuli. In: Nermend, K., Łatuszyńska, M. (eds.) Selected Issues in Experimental Economics. SPBE, pp. 355–371. Springer, Cham (2016). doi:10.1007/978-3-319-28419-4_22
17. Maglione, A.G., Scorpecci, A., Malerba, P., Marsella, P., Giannantonio, S., Colosimo, A., Babiloni, F., Vecchiato, G.: Alpha EEG frontal asymmetries during audiovisual perception in cochlear implant users. A study with bilateral and unilateral young users. Methods Inf. Med. **54**(6), 500–504 (2015)
18. Flumeri, G., et al.: EEG frontal asymmetry related to pleasantness of olfactory stimuli in young subjects. In: Nermend, K., Łatuszyńska, M. (eds.) Selected Issues in Experimental Economics. SPBE, pp. 373–381. Springer, Cham (2016). doi:10.1007/978-3-319-28419-4_23
19. Chang, Y.-H., Lee, Y.-Y., Liang, K.-C., Chen, I.-P., Tsai, C.-G., Hsieh, S.: Experiencing affective music in eyes-closed and eyes-open states: an electroencephalography study. Front. Psychol. **6** (2015). doi:10.3389/fpsyg.2015.01160
20. Gevins, A., Smith, M.E.: Neurophysiological measures of cognitive workload during human-computer interaction. Theor. Issues Ergon. Sci. **4**, 113–131 (2003). doi: 10.1080/14639220210159717
21. Spielberg, J.M., Miller, G.A., Warren, S.L., Engels, A.S., Crocker, L.D., Banich, M.T., Sutton, B.P., Heller, W.: A brain network instantiating approach and avoidance motivation. Psychophysiology **49**, 1200–1214 (2012). doi:10.1111/j.1469-8986.2012.01443.x

22. Berkman, E.T., Lieberman, M.D.: Approaching the bad and avoiding the good: lateral prefrontal cortical asymmetry distinguishes between action and valence. J. Cogn. Neurosci. **22**, 1970–1979 (2010). doi:10.1162/jocn.2009.21317

23. Wager, T.D., Phan, K.L., Liberzon, I., Taylor, S.F.: Valence, gender, and lateralization of functional brain anatomy in emotion: a meta-analysis of findings from neuroimaging. Neuroimage **19**, 513–531 (2003)

24. Barrett, L.F., Wager, T.D.: The structure of emotion evidence from neuroimaging studies. Curr. Dir. Psychol. Sci. **15**, 79–83 (2006)

25. Wager, T.D., Barrett, L.F., Bliss-Moreau, E., Lindquist, K., Duncan, S., Kober, H., Joseph, J., Davidson, M., Mize, J.: The neuroimaging of emotion. In: The Handbook of Emotion, vol. 3, pp. 249–271 (2008)

26. Cartocci, G., Modica, E., Rossi, D., Maglione, A.G., Venuti, I., Rossi, G., Corsi, E., Babiloni, F.: A pilot study on the neurometric evaluation of "Effective" and "Ineffective" antismoking public service announcements. In: Conference Proceedings of IEEE Engineering in Medicine and Biology Society (2015, in press)

27. Pan, J., Tompkins, W.J.: A real-time QRS detection algorithm. IEEE Trans. Biomed. Eng. BME **32**, 230–236 (1985). doi:10.1109/TBME.1985.325532

28. Boucsein, W., Fowles, D.C., Grimnes, S., Ben-Shakhar, G., Roth, W.T., Dawson, M.E., Filion, D.L.: Society for psychophysiological research Ad Hoc committee on electrodermal measures. Publication recommendations for electrodermal measurements. Psychophysiology **49**, 1017–1034 (2012). doi:10.1111/j.1469-8986.2012.01384.x

29. Benedek, M., Kaernbach, C.: A continuous measure of phasic electrodermal activity. J. Neurosci. Methods **190**, 80–91 (2010). doi:10.1016/j.jneumeth.2010.04.028

30. Russell, J.A., Barrett, L.F.: Core affect, prototypical emotional episodes, and other things called emotion: dissecting the elephant. J. Pers. Soc. Psychol. **76**, 805–819 (1999). doi:10.1037/0022-3514.76.5.805

31. Posner, J., Russell, J.A., Peterson, B.S.: The circumplex model of affect: an integrative approach to affective neuroscience, cognitive development, and psychopathology. Dev. Psychopathol. **17**, 715–734 (2005). doi:10.1017/S0954579405050340

32. Mauss, I.B., Robinson, M.D.: Measures of emotion: a review. Cogn. Emot. **23**, 209–237 (2009). doi:10.1080/02699930802204677

33. Zar, J.H.: Biostatistical Analysis, 4th edn., vol. 1, 389–394. Prentice Hall, Upper Saddle River (1999)

34. Leder, H., Belke, B., Oeberst, A., Augustin, D.: A model of aesthetic appreciation and aesthetic judgments. Br. J. Psychol. **95**, 489–508 (2004). doi:10.1348/0007126042369811

35. Leder, H., Gerger, G., Brieber, D., Schwarz, N.: What makes an art expert? Emotion and evaluation in art appreciation. Cogn. Emot. **28**, 1137–1147 (2014). doi:10.1080/02699931.2013.870132

36. van Paasschen, J., Bacci, F., Melcher, D.P.: The influence of art expertise and training on emotion and preference ratings for representational and abstract artworks. PLoS ONE **10**, e0134241 (2015). doi:10.1371/journal.pone.0134241

37. Hsieh, L.-T., Ranganath, C.: Frontal midline theta oscillations during working memory maintenance and episodic encoding and retrieval. Neuroimage **85**, 721 (2014). doi:10.1016/j.neuroimage.2013.08.003

38. Consoli, G.: From beauty to knowledge: a new frame for the neuropsychological approach to aesthetics. Front. Hum. Neurosci. **9**, 290 (2015). doi:10.3389/fnhum.2015.00290

39. Bohrn, I.C., Altmann, U., Lubrich, O., Menninghaus, W., Jacobs, A.M.: When we like what we know – a parametric fMRI analysis of beauty and familiarity. Brain Lang. **124**, 1–8 (2013). doi:10.1016/j.bandl.2012.10.003

40. Gilroy, S.W., Porteous, J., Charles, F., Cavazza, M., Soreq, E., Raz, G., Ikar, L., Or-Borichov, A., Ben-Arie, U., Klovatch, I., et al.: A brain-computer interface to a plan-based narrative. In: IJCAI, pp. 1997–2005. Citeseer (2013). ISBN: 978-1-57735-633-2
41. Karran, A.J., Fairclough, S.H., Gilleade, K.: A Framework for psychophysiological classification within a cultural heritage context using interest. ACM Trans. Comput. Hum. Interact. **21**, 34:1–34:19 (2015). doi:10.1145/2687925

A Biosymtic (Biosymbiotic Robotic) Approach to Human Development and Evolution

Marta Ferraz[(✉)]

Faculdade de Ciências e Tecnologia/Nova Universidade de Lisboa, Media Ground,
Almada, Portugal
atomicdesigners@gmail.com

Abstract. We demonstrate that the current Child-Computer Interaction paradigm is not potentiating human development to its fullest. It is linked to several physical and mental health problems and appears not to be maximizing children's cognitive development and performance. To potentiate children's physical and mental health (including cognitive development and performance) we conceived a new approach to human development and evolution. This approach proposes a particular synergy between the developing human body, computing machines and natural environments. It emphasizes that children should be encouraged to interact with challenging physical environments offering multiple possibilities for sensory stimulation and increasing physical and mental stress to the organism. We created and tested a new set of robotic devices to operationalize our approach – Biosymtic (Biosymbiotic Robotic) devices.

Keywords: Child-Computer Interaction · Human development and evolution · Physical and mental health · Cognition · Biosymtic · Natural environments

1 Introduction

Hominids evolved while moving in order to survive. Hunter-gatherer children were very active, constantly interacting with challenging natural environments - information processing occurred in a multisensory world. They were nomadic, had to elude predators, walked and ran long distances to forage [25]. Conversely, modern children spend most of their time in artificially controlled environments (ACE; indoors), interacting with screen-based computer devices (SBCDs), stimulating mostly the visual and auditory senses and instilling sedentary behavior [27, 36]. The Digital Age was accompanied by a strong decline in physical activity (PA) in modern children. This decline sparked multiple physical and mental health issues [25]. Furthermore, it seems that whole-body interaction [30] in natural environments [13] still benefits children's cognitive function (e.g., conceptual knowledge, attention and memory functions) compared to sedentary interaction indoors.

The following section describes the physical and mental health issues linked to the use of SBCDs in ACE and real-world settings (including why cognitive development/performance are not being optimized). Our approach is described in Sect. 2 - a solution based on the employment of Biosymtic devices. Conclusions are then presented in Sect. 3.

L. Gamberini et al. (Eds.): Symbiotic 2016, LNCS 9961, pp. 65–76, 2017.
DOI: 10.1007/978-3-319-57753-1_6

1.1 Sedentary and Whole-Body Motion Screen-Based Computer Devices in Artificially Controlled Environments and Mobile Screen-Based Computer Devices in Real-World Settings

Sedentary SBCDs encourage children to experience visual-auditory information-gathering scenarios. Children typically engage SBCDs via user interfaces requiring hand–eye coordination skills (HECS; e.g., mouse/keyboard; multi-touch). HECS (e.g., tap, drag, slide) allow controlling virtual environments on a two-dimensional (2D) display. Interaction with sedentary SBCDs is linked to improvements in children's cognitive function, e.g., attentional control, selective attention and creativity [18, 19]. However, researchers have shown sedentary SBCDs to be linked with a diversity of physical and mental health complications in children.

Overuse of sedentary SBCDs is associated with obesity, aggressive behaviors, anxiety, increased risk of depression, hyperactivity, attention problems, sleep disorders, attachment and obsessive-compulsive disorders, hand-arm vibration syndrome, bodily discomfort, reduction of physical and emotional awareness, poor fitness, photosensitive epilepsy, visual problems and motion sickness [1, 8, 11, 39].

We also suggest that sedentary SBCDs, in ACE, may fail to maximize children's cognitive development and cognitive performance.

Aerobic-based PA and physical exercise (PE), at moderate-intense levels, tend to optimize cognitive function (e.g., attention and memory functions, including academic achievement) and cognitive structure (e.g., increasing hippocampal and basal ganglia volumes - improving cognitive control/response resolution) in children (post-activity benefits), compared to sedentary conditions [7, 21]. Furthermore, while frequently interacting with sedentary SBCDs, in ACE, children get exposed to restricted sensorimotor experiences - restricting the perceptual process (identification, interpretation and organization of sensory information) to auditory and visual events. The child loses the possibility of interacting with a variety of sensory information that natural physical environments (NPE) have to offer - stimulating the visual, auditory, chemical, cutaneous, proprioceptive and vestibular senses [6].

Embodied Cognition research demonstrates that sensorimotor experiences with requirements beyond fine motor skills (demanding small muscular groups and precise actions) tend to improve children's cognitive development/performance. For example, the development of gross motor skills (demanding large muscular groups and less precise actions) improves the development of cognitive function and optimizes academic achievement [34]; gesturing reduces mental effort and facilitates memory retrieval during problem solving [17]. We observed that whole-body interaction in natural environments benefits children's cognitive function (attention and memory functions) compared to sedentary interaction indoors (as we will later describe).

In addition, depriving the child from interaction with multisensory environments may delay or eliminate her ability to integrate multiple sources of sensory information throughout development (difficulty in generating coherent percepts from the physical world and difficulty acting in it) [6, 24].

Whole-body motion (WBM) devices provide enhanced sensorimotor experiences compared to sedentary SBCDs. However, it seems that WBM devices are not promoting children's physical and mental health and may fail to maximize their cognitive development/performance.

WBM interfaces make use of whole-body movements in ACE to control virtual information on computer devices, e.g., visual and audio data control can be accomplished through the use of gesture-based and/or sensor-based interfaces [33]. Computer games requiring physical effort are characterized as exergames or active video games (AVGs) and include WBM interfaces [32].

Active Healthy Kids Canada conducted a meta-analysis of the long-term effects of AVGs on children's health and behavior (age 3 to 17 years). This analysis comprised 1367 published papers dated from 2006 to 2012, including 1992 participants from 8 countries. It concluded that AVGs are not promoting the 60 min of moderate to vigorous PA (MVPA) necessary to benefit children's physical and mental health. There was also a lack of evidence suggesting long-term spontaneous adherence to AVGs [23]. Other studies have supported these findings [3].

Because WBM devices, in ACE, are not promoting MVPA levels, they may also be failing to benefit children's cognitive function/structure. WBM devices, in ACE, restrict sensorimotor experiences. While moving, children are encouraged to center attention on a 2D display, depriving them from a variety of motor experiences (proprioceptive and vestibular stimuli) available in three-dimensional space (limiting possibilities to coordinate lower and upper limbs, head and eyes in the physical world). Sensor-based interfaces typically integrate similar materials and textures (e.g., plastic or rubber), limiting tactile experiences. There is also a lack of stimuli variation to the nerve network at the bottom of the feet, as ACE tend to lack textural diversity. Multisensory experiences tend to improve children's cognitive development/performance.

Furthermore, while interacting with SBCDs and WBM devices, in ACE, face-to-face and body-to-body interaction (physical contact) appears to be impaired by the continuous focus on a 2D display - weakening the channels of bodily communication. Children who lack human physical contact are more prone to develop anxiety, depression and aggressive behaviors [31].

Children who frequently interact computer devices, in ACE, may also lose benefits from natural ultraviolet radiation (B UVB) - vitamin D for blood level normalization, increased bone mineral density and autoimmune disease prevention. Significant vitamin D deficits may cause bone deformities and fractures [35]. ACE reduce children's contact with germs, diminishing stress on their immune system, which requires contact with germs to properly mature. ACE are associated with a diminished production of antibodies that protect children from life-threatening pathogens [25]. Lack of exposure to natural bright light may also compromise the development of the visual system [37].

SBCDs have been connected to real world settings - Pervasive Computing, e.g., through the use mobile computing devices (MCDs). However, we suggest that these devices may be associated with physical health problems in children and may not be maximizing their cognitive performance. Pervasive Computing unobtrusively connects users and digital worlds [29], e.g., encouraging children to move in the physical space while using MCDs [10, 15].

Prolonged interaction with SBCDs placed lower or higher than the child's gaze is linked to posture issues - burdening upper limbs and neck [12]. MCDs encouraging the child to continuously center attention on a 2D display (placed lower than their gaze) may also strain upper limbs and neck. Humans evolved to move in space by maintaining an efficient body posture: neck straight in an upright position [25]. We alert for possible postural problems linked to the use MCDs encouraging movement while focusing on a 2D display. In addition, by hand holding these devices, children restrict upper limb motor actions (limiting interaction with the physical world).

MCDs typically induce split-attention effect – alternating attention from the device to the physical world. Conversely, external information sources, combined in space and synchronized in time, tend to optimize perceptual integration and improve learning [26, 41]. Hence, MCDs may fail to maximize cognitive performance.

2   A Biosymtic (Biosymbiotic Robotic) Approach to Human Development and Evolution

Our approach proposes a particular combination between the human body, computing machines (CMs) and NPE in order to potentiate children's physical and mental health - including cognitive development/performance.

2.1   Potentiating Children's Cognitive Development – Perceptual Abilities - Through Computing Machines

We suggest two formats of interaction with CMs in order to potentiate the development of perceptual abilities in children:

• Whole-body motion interfaces that allow for multiple possibilities of bodily action in the NPE (the human body as an interface)

Throughout development, children's ability to direct behavior and generate coherent percepts from the environment benefits from multisensory experiences in the physical world – linked to the development of higher-order cognition, e.g., attention, memory and inhibition [6, 24, 42]. Hence, to optimize the development of perceptual abilities, CMs should encourage children to be exposed to multiple bodily action possibilities in multisensory environments. CMs should be combined with WBM interfaces: the child is encouraged to perform a variety of movements (e.g., running, jumping, throwing) to interact with virtual information on CMs, while experiencing the NPE.

• Whole-body motion interfaces that extend the possibilities of bodily action in the NPE (extending physical interfaces)

"Affordances" represent environmental possibilities for action. Perception is a process extended to the structural characteristics of the body and the environment where action evolves [16]. Species perceive the physical world according to their body structures, e.g., a chair suggests "seating" for most humans, a crocodile will probably not notice it [4, 9]. Changes in the structural features of the human body while maturing, and corresponding action possibilities, influence perception – how children identify, interpret and organize environmental sensory information [42]. We suggest that by structurally augmenting the human body, through extending physical interfaces offering new action possibilities (new body structure layout), the child may generate perceptual representations of the environment throughout development, beyond those of the standard human body. We defined this augmentation as "Motoric-Metamorphosis" - a transformation through which the child may generate novel ways of representing and understanding the environment.

CMs should encourage children to experience new action possibilities in enhanced sensory environments (NPE): the child is encouraged to perform new types of bodily action through extending physical interfaces (e.g., moving horizontally in a vertical position, grabbing an object with three arms), which in turn, control virtual information on CMs, while experiencing the NPE.

2.2 Potentiating Children's Cognitive Performance Through Computing Machines – Combining Computing Devices with Human Biology

We suggest an adequate combination between CMs and the human anatomical structure (sensory organs) to avoid postural problems and split-attention effects in children. For example, visual virtual information should be directly aligned with the visual system (e.g., see-through head-mounted displays). The combination between virtual information and the human body should also enable free body movement in the physical world - to freely interact with multiple sources of sensory information (multisensory experiences tend to improve children's cognitive function). We describe this combination as "Virtual-Sensorimotor Alignment" (VSMA).

2.3 Potentiating Children's Physical and Mental Health Through Computing Machines

Children should do at least 60 min of daily MVPA to benefit physical and mental health [46]. As previously mentioned, MVPA optimizes children's cognitive function/structure.

A high heart rate (HR) frequency correlates with high levels of PA [2]. HR frequency may vary due to emotional states or excitement levels [38]. Children's HR values increase in situations of excitability or fear: may increase 20–40 beats per minute (BPM) above the actual resting value [28]. PA in hot or humid climates tends to increase HR values (15 to 20 BPM higher than in neutral climates). HR values also tend to be higher if the produced mechanical work includes gross motor skills [38]. The use of equipment and larger spatial areas increases children's PA levels [44].

Hence, to increase PA levels, children should be encouraged to perform activities in large spatial areas, such as NPE, offering climatic variation (to increase HR values). As the use of equipment may increase PA, children should also be encouraged to interact with a variety of physical tools (user interfaces) fostering the use of gross motor skills. Because children's HR values may also increase in situations of excitability or fear, video game play may be an optimal solution to produce this effect. In fact, children refer to video games as engaging mainly due to the opportunity of experiencing challenging fantasy worlds [20].

CMs should promote body-to-body and face-to-face interaction to avoid anxiety, depression and aggressive behaviors and improve bodily communication in children (achieved via VSMA). CMs should also encourage interaction with NPE, as natural bright light improves the development of the visual system. NPE are associated with vitamin D synthesis; stress to the immune system; reduce stress levels and aggressive behaviors and improve children's cognition (restore attention levels) [22].

2.4 Biosymtic (Biosymbiotic Robotic) Devices

Our approach is operationalized through a new form of robotic devices, termed Biosymtic (Biosymbiotic Robotic) devices. The central goal of a Biosymtic device (BSD) is to potentiate children's physical and mental health (including cognitive development/performance), while helping them connect with challenging natural environments offering multiple possibilities for sensory stimulation and stressing the multiple systems of the organism [e.g., skeletomuscular, cardiovascular, immune, endocrine and nervous systems (including mental and emotional arousal)].

A BSD is characterized as an artificial system (ranging from physical robots to virtual software agents) displaying automatic control functions while (two modes):

(1) Directly connected to a human organism (human-integrated automatic control);
(2) Disconnected from a human organism (working as an autonomous robot).

In mode 1, a BSD encourages a child to be physically active in NPE through automatic feedback control mechanisms – included in the system's hardware and/or software programs (e.g., video games). A BSD encourages the child to achieve a certain physiological state (e.g., MVPA) in order to improve physical and mental health. Physiological data is always used to persuade a covert response in the child: physical action (an example will be later detailed).

In mode 2, a BSD builds autonomous functions through interaction with a human. We termed this process Bio-Kinesthetic Programming (BKP). BKP is an approach to Robot Programming by Demonstration aiming to help a robot build autonomous functions through human guidance techniques, such as whole-body interaction (e.g., the child's locomotion works as an example to be replicated by the device during autonomous navigation) and physiological states transfer (e.g., the robot learns to manage its power sources according to the child's metabolism), while physically and mentally benefiting the human organism. Hence, a BSD and a human form a symbiosis: the association, or close union, between organisms in mutual benefit [5].

A BSD may also encourage a child to perform PA in a NPE without external control of physiological states - encouraging exploratory play. That is, a child may interact freely with software programs allowing exploratory action in the NPE. These programs allow access to physiological, motion and environmental data, in real-time, e.g., through visual and auditory information (e.g., HR, brain activity; motor performance; humidity, temperature). While accessing a variety of data, the child is encouraged to explore/regulate her body processes in relation to environmental ones. For example, she may draw inferences about the relations between motion, HR and temperature/humidity in the environment (e.g., HR increasing in humid and hot climates for similar motor performance); relations between particular contexts (e.g., mountainous areas; forested areas) and brain states (e.g., alertness, distraction).

We developed and tested two Biosymtic devices to assess the premises of our approach: "Cratus" and "Albert".

The BSD "Cratus" mimics a Roman gladiator/inventor. The physical structure of this device consists of a head connected to a torso, with a wheel mechanism on its base. It also includes a computer processor, on the center back of the torso, that outputs visual and audio information (aligned with the child's visual system - VSMA). System inputs (to control virtual information, e.g., put a video game avatar into action) are made through whole-body motion, e.g., the child may push, pull, rotate and throw the apparatus while running, jumping or trotting. The child may also skate while using this system – feet placed on top of the wheelbase (Motoric-Metamorphosis). The system includes wireless sensors to capture motion data (e.g., accelerometer; moving the system on the terrain translates as virtual locomotion of the game avatar). The system also captures physiological data – e.g., communicates wirelessly with a HR biosensor placed on the child's chest (see Fig. 1).

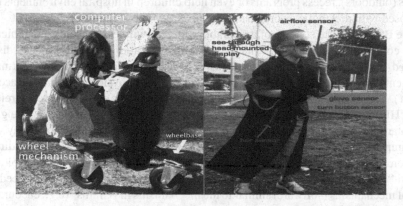

Fig. 1. Left. "Cratus". A child pushes "Cratus" to put a game avatar into motion (visualized on the computer processor); Right. "Albert". A child blowing air into an airflow sensor to put a game avatar into motion (visualized on a see-through head-mounted display).

"Cratus" includes automatic feedback control mechanisms (software) that encourage certain physiological states, e.g., MVPA while playing video games. In the latter, a software actuator controls changes in the displacement speed of the game avatar to encourage MVPA. For instance, if the child engages in low levels of PA (sedentary, measured via HR sensor), while interacting with "Cratus" (e.g., pushing it), the system increases the inertial forces applied to the avatar - the child needs to move faster to reach MVPA. The system also includes a verbal actuator producing audio output. If, for instance, the child engages in low levels of PA, the verbal actuator emits specific feedback, e.g., "Run faster!" or "Give me more power!".

In one cross-sectional study ("Increasing Children's Physical Activity Levels Through Biosymtic Robotic Devices") - presented in [14] - we evaluated the effects of "Cratus" on the PA levels of a group of 20 typically developing children aged 6 to 8 (9 male and 11 female). Children interacted freely with "Cratus" in a natural forested land-scape - playing a video game encouraging MVPA. Children's expectations and opinions regarding the device were also assessed. Results indicated that interacting with "Cratus", in a NPE, instilled vigorous PA levels. Children mentioned they were highly motivated to interact with "Cratus".

The latter results demonstrate that "Cratus", and the NPE, seem a promising solution to promote physical and mental health in children aged 6 to 8. This study shows that to increase physical activity, children aged 6 to 8 should be encouraged to perform activities in large spatial areas, such as natural environments, and to interact with user interfaces promoting gross motor skills. Because situations of excitability or fear may increase heart rate values, video game play seems an optimal solution to raise physical activity levels. As mentioned, WBM devices in ACE are not promoting MVPA necessary to benefit children's physical and mental health. Similarly, physical education classes and recess programs (spontaneous physical activity), in elementary schools, are not promoting MVPA [40, 43]. "Cratus" may help children increase their daily PA and contribute to a healthy lifestyle. This device could be included in physical education classes (outdoors), recess programs or even help children in hospital environments (e.g., diagnosed with metabolic disorders such as obesity, type 2 diabetes).

The BSD "Albert" consists of a wearable suit with wireless sensors communicating with a computer processor. It includes a monocular see-through head-mounted display (aligned with the child's visual system - VSMA) that displays visual information (augmented reality). Motion sensors capture the child's physical action (e.g., acceler-ometer). The system also captures physiological data – e.g., communicates wirelessly with a HR biosensor on the child's chest. Inputs to control virtual information (e.g., put an avatar into motion) are made through whole-body motion, e.g., the child may walk, run, jump, rotate, trot. Virtual information may also be controlled by interacting directly with sensor-based interfaces, e.g., manipulate a "turn button" or "bar" sensor; blow air into an "airflow sensor"; use a "glove sensor". "Albert" includes automatic feedback control mechanisms (software) similar to the mechanisms in "Cratus" (e.g., encouraging MVPA) (see Fig. 1).

In a cross-sectional pilot study ("Whole-body Interaction in Natural Environments Benefits Children's Cognitive Function Compared to Sedentary Interaction Indoors") - presented in [13] - we compared the effects of whole-body interaction in a natural envi-ronment (stimulating the multiple sensory systems in the body) versus sedentary inter-action in an indoor environment (stimulating mostly the visual and auditory senses) on cognitive function in a group of 10 typically developing children aged 7 to 8 (5 male and 5 female). Sustained attention and episodic memory (supporting long-term infor-mation storage - learning) were evaluated while each child interacted with a whole-body motion screen-based computer device ("Albert"), in a natural forested landscape, and a sedentary SBCD (desktop computer), based on hand-eye coordination skills, in a class-room setting (sitting at a desk) - video game play. Children's preferences and opinions regarding the interaction devices were also evaluated. Results indicate a trend for natural environment whole-body interaction to increase sustained attention in children over time, compared to indoor sedentary interaction. In turn, increases in sustained attention were associated with improvements in episodic memory during video game play. Children also preferred to interact with "Albert" in the NPE.

The latter results show that whole-body interaction in NPE is associated with benefits in children's cognitive function - learning through SBCDs seems to benefit from whole-body interaction in NPE. Interaction with sedentary SBCDs indoors may be failing to maximize children's learning in current educational systems.

The previous studies were approved by the Institutional Review Board at The University of Texas at Austin. All children agreed - by completing assent forms - to engage in the research studies; and that pictures and video data would be used targeting scientific purposes (scientific publications and presentations). The studies were judged to be of to minimal risk to children – not associated with psychological trauma, social or legal risks. We followed standard first aid practices. The main researcher was prepared to go through the following procedures in case of dehydration: direct the child to a cool and ventilated spot; apply cold compresses. In case of fatigue: reduce the intensity of the activity slowly; give small amounts of water to the child; move the child to a cool and ventilated spot.

3 Conclusions

We demonstrated that the current Child-Computer Interaction paradigm - interaction with SBCDs in artificially controlled environments - may be failing to optimize children's physical and mental health (including cognitive development and performance). From two initial studies, we observed that whole-body interaction in natural environments tends to benefit children's physical and mental health (including cognitive function). It is possible that modern children are still evolutionary constrained to favoring information processing in multimodal natural environments. We may have to rethink the current educational paradigm associated with child development through computing machines.

One of the main limitations of the first study - "Increasing Children's Physical Activity Levels Through Biosymtic Robotic Devices" - concerns its methodology - the evaluations were performed in a single experimental moment and were not repeated successively in order to validate the results. Hence, it is necessary to develop full-scale research studies (comprising large samples) in order to confirm the obtained results (including long-term spontaneous adherence to the device).

One of the main limitations of the second study - "Whole-body Interaction in Natural Environments Benefits Children's Cognitive Function Compared to Sedentary Interaction Indoors" - concerns its sample size (small sample). Future research is necessary to confirm the results. We also need to compare multimodal interaction indoors, versus natural environments, to understand if the latter represents a benefit for child cognition.

Acknowledgements. ST. Andrew's Episcopal School, UT Austin, FCT/UNL and Advanced Brain Monitoring.

References

1. American Academy of Pediatrics. Policy Statement – Media Education. http://pediatrics.aappublications.org/content/pediatrics/early/2010/09/27/peds.2010-1636.full.pdf
2. Armstrong, N., Welsman, J.: Development of aerobic fitness during childhood and adolescence. Pediatr. Exerc. Sci. **12**, 128–149 (2000)
3. Baranowski, T., Abdelsamad, D., Baranowski, J., O'Connor, T.M., Thompson, D., Barnett, A., Cerin, E., Chen, T.-A.: Impact of an active video game on healthy children's physical activity. Pediatrics **129**, 636–642 (2012)
4. Barsalou, L.W.: Grounded cognition. Annu. Rev. Psychol. **59**, 617–645 (2008)
5. Bronstein, J.L.: Our current understand of mutualism. Q. Rev. Biol. **69**(1), 31–51 (1994)
6. Calvert, G., Spence, C., Stein, B.E.: The Handbook of Multisensory Processing. The MIT Press, Cambridge (2004)
7. Chaddock, L., Erickson, K.I., Prakash, R.S., Kim, J.S., Voss, M.W., Vanpatter, M., Pontifex, M.B., Raine, L.B., Konkel, A., Hillman, C.H., Cohen, N.J., Kramer, A.F.: A neuroimaging investigation of the association between aerobic fitness, hippocampal volume and memory performance in preadolescent children. Brain Res. **1358**, 172–183 (2010)
8. Chang, C.-H., Pan, W.W., Tseng, L.-Y., Stoffregen, T.A.: Postural activity and motion sickness during video game play in children and adults. Exp. Brain Res. **217**, 299–309 (2012)
9. Chemero, A.: Radical Embodied Cognitive Science. The MIT Press, Cambridge (2009)
10. Chipman, G., Druin, A., Beer, D., Fails, J., Guha, M., Simms, S.: A case of study of Tangible Flags: a collaborative technology to enhance field trips. In: Proceedings of the 2006 Conference on Interaction Design and Children, IDC 2006, pp. 1–8. ACM, New York (2006)
11. Cleary, A.G., McKendrick, H., Sills, J.A.: Hand-arm vibration syndrome may be associated with prolonged use of vibrating computer games. Br. Med. J. **324**, 301 (2002)
12. Cordes, C., Miller, E.: Fool's Gold: A Critical Look at Computers in Childhood. Alliance for Childhood (2002)
13. Ferraz, M., Resta, P., O'Neill, A.: Whole-body interaction in natural environments benefits children's cognitive function compared to sedentary interaction indoors (2016). Submitted for publication
14. Ferraz, M., Camara, A., O'Neill, A.: Increasing physical activity levels in children through biosymtic robotic devices. In: Proceedings of the 13th International Conference on Advances in Computer Entertainment Technology, ACE 2016. ACM, New York (2016)
15. Fitzpatrick, G., Fleck R., Harris, E., Muller, H., O'Malley, C., Price, S., Rogers, S., Smith, H., Randell, C., Stanton, D., Thompson, M., Weal, M.: Ambient wood: designing new forms of digital augmentation for learning outdoors. In: Proceedings of the 2004 Conference on Interaction Design and Children: Building a Community, IDC 2004, pp. 3–10 (2004)
16. Gibson, J.J.: The Ecological Approach to Visual Perception. Lawrence Erlbaum Associates Inc., New York and London (1979)
17. Goldin-Meadow, S., Nusbaum, H., Kelly, S.D., Wagner, S.: Explaining math: gesturing lightens the load. Psychol. Sci. **12**, 516–522 (2001)
18. Granic, I., Lobel, A., Engels, R.: The benefits of playing video games. Am. Psychol. **69**(1), 66–78 (2014)
19. Green, C.S., Bavelier, D.: The development of attention skills in action video game players. Neuropsychologia **47**(8–9), 1780–1789 (2009)
20. Hamlen, K.: Children's choices and strategies in video games. Comput. Hum. Behav. **27**, 532–539 (2011)

21. Hillman, C.H., Kamijo, K., Scudder, M.: A review of chronic and acute physical activity participation on neuroelectric measures of brain health and cognition during childhood. Prev. Med. **52**, S21–S28 (2011)
22. Kuo, F.E., Faber, A.: A Potential natural treatment for attention-deficit/hyperactivity disorder: evidence from a national study. Am. J. Pub. Health **94**, 1580–1586 (2004)
23. LeBlanc, A.G., Chaput, J.-P., McFarlane, A., Colley, R.C., Thivel, D., Biddle, J.H., Maddison, R., Leatherdale, S.T., Tremblay, M.S.: Active video games and health indicators in children and youth: a systematic review. PLoS ONE **8**(6), e65351 (2013). doi:10.1371/journal.pone. 0065351
24. Lewkowicz, D., Roder, B.: Development of multisensory processing and the role of early experience. In: Spence, C., Stein, B.E. (eds.) The Handbook of Multisensory Processing, pp. 607–626. The MIT Press, Cambridge (2012)
25. Lieberman, E.D.: The Story Of The Human Body. Evolution, Health and Disease. Penguin Books, London (2013)
26. Liu, T.-C., Lin, Y.-C., Tsai, M.-J., Pass, F.: Split-attention and redundancy effects on mobile learning in physical environments. Comput. Educ. **58**(1), 172–180 (2012)
27. Lou, D.: Sedentary behaviors and youth: current trends and the impact on health, pp. 1–12. Active Living Research, San Diego (2014)
28. Lumley, M.A., Relamed, B.G., Abeles, L.A.: Predicting children's presurgical anxiety and subsequent behavior changes. J. Pediatr. Psicol. **18**, 481–497 (1993)
29. Magerkurth, C., Cheok, A.D., Mandryk, R.L., Nilsen, T.: Pervasive games: bringing computer entertainment back to the real world. Comput. Entertainment (CIE) Theor. Pract. Comput. Appl. Entertainment **3**(3), 4 (2005)
30. Malinverni, L., López, S.B., Parés, N.: Impact of embodied interaction on learning processes: design and analysis of an educational application based on physical activity. In: Proceedings of the 11th International Conference on Interaction Design and Children, IDC 2012, pp. 60–69. ACM, New York (2012)
31. Montagu, A.: Touching: The Human Significance of the Skin, 2nd edn. Harper and Row, New York (1972)
32. Mueller, F., Gibbs, M.R., Vetere, F.: Taxonomy of exertion games. In: Proceedings of the 20th Australasian Conference on Computer-Human Interaction: Designing for Habitus and Habitat, OZCHI 2008, pp. 263–266. ACM, New York (2008)
33. Noble, J.: Programming Interactivity. A Designer's Guide to Processing, Arduino, and OpenFrameworks. O'Reilly, California (2009)
34. Piek, J.P., Dawson, L., Smith, L.M., Gasson, N.: The role of early fine and gross motor development on later motor and cognitive ability. Hum. Mov. Sci. **27**(5), 668–681 (2008)
35. Rajakumar, K.: Vitamin D, cod-liver oil, sunlight, and rickets: a historical perspective. Pediatrics **112**(2), 132–135 (2003)
36. Rideout, V.J., Foehr, U.G., Roberts, D.F.: Generation M^2: Media in the Lives of 8 to 18-Year-Olds. Kaiser Family Foundation, Menlo Park (2010)
37. Rose, K.A., Morgan, I.G., Ip, J., Kifley, A., Huynh, S., Smith, W., Mitchell, P.: Outdoor activity reduces the prevalence of myopia in Children. Ophthalmology **115**(8), 1279–1285 (2008)
38. Rowland, T., Bar-Or, O.: Pediatric Exercise Medicine. Physiologic Principles to Health Care Application. Habitual activity and Energy Expenditure in the Healthy Child. Human Kinetics Pub Inc, Champaign (2004)
39. Small, G., Vorgan, G.: IBrain: Surviving the Technological Alteration of the Modern Mind. Harper Collins Publishers, New York (2008)

40. Stratton, G.: Review articles physical activity levels in middle and high school physical education: a review. Pediatr. Exerc. Sci. **17**, 3 (2005)
41. Sweller, J.: Instructional Design in Technical Areas. ACER Press, Camberwell (1999)
42. Thelen, E., Smith, L.B.: A Dynamical Systems Approach to the Development of Cognition and Action. The MIT Press, Cambridge (1994)
43. UCLA Center to Eliminate Health Disparities and Samuels and Associates: Failing Fitness: Physical Activity and Physical Education in Schools. Policy Brief. The California Endowment, Los Angeles (2007)
44. Verstraete, S.J.M., Cardon, G.M., De Clercq, D.L.R., De Bourdeaudhuil, M.M.: Increasing children's physical activity levels during recess in elementary schools: the effects of providing game equipment. Eur. J. Public Health **16**(4), 415–419 (2006)
45. World Health Organization. Obesity and Overweight. http://www.who.int/dietphysicalactivity/childhood/en/
46. World Health Organization: Physical Activity and Young People (2013). http://www.who.int/dietphysicalactivity/factsheet_young_people/en/

Interactive Content-Based Image Retrieval with Deep Neural Networks

Joel Pyykkö and Dorota Głowacka$^{(\boxtimes)}$

Department of Computer Science, HIIT, University of Helsinki, Helsinki, Finland
{joel.pyykko,dorota.glowacka}@cs.helsinki.fi

Abstract. Recent advances in deep neural networks have given rise to new approaches to content-based image retrieval (CBIR). Their ability to learn universal visual features for any target query makes them a good choice for systems dealing with large and diverse image datasets. However, employing deep neural networks in interactive CBIR systems still poses challenges: either the search target has to be predetermined, such as with hashing, or the computational cost becomes prohibitive for an online setting. In this paper, we present a framework for conducting interactive CBIR that learns a deep, dynamic metric between images. The proposed methodology is not limited to precalculated categories, hashes or clusters of the search space, but rather is formed instantly and interactively based on the user feedback. We use a deep learning framework that utilizes pre-extracted features from Convolutional Neural Networks and learns a new distance representation based on the user's relevance feedback. The experimental results show the potential of applying our framework in an interactive CBIR setting as well as symbiotic interaction, where the system automatically detects what image features might best satisfy the user's needs.

Keywords: Content-based image retrieval (CBIR) · Deep neural networks · Interactive systems · Exploratory search

1 Introduction

In recent years, image retrieval techniques operating on meta-data, such as textual annotations, have become the industry standard for retrieval from large image collections. This approach works well with sufficiently high-quality meta-data. However, with the explosive growth of image collections it has become apparent that tagging new images quickly and efficiently is not always possible. Secondly, even if instantaneous high-quality image tagging was possible, there are still many instances where image search by query is problematic. It might be easy for a user to define their query if they are looking for an image of a cat but how do they specify that the cat should be of a very particular shade of ginger with sad looking eyes. A solution to this is content-based image retrieval (CBIR) [7], especially in combination with relevance feedback [28] that actively

© The Author(s) 2017
L. Gamberini et al. (Eds.): Symbiotic 2016, LNCS 9961, pp. 77–88, 2017.
DOI: 10.1007/978-3-319-57753-1_7

involves the user into the search loop and utilizes his knowledge in the iterative search process [1–3,10,17].

A variety of feature descriptors have been used for image representation in CBIR, such as color, edge, texture. Similarly in use have been local feature representations, such as the bag-of-words models [26] in conjunction with local feature descriptors (e.g. SIFT [20]). However, using such low-level feature representation may not be always optimal for more complex image retrieval tasks due to the semantic gap between such features and high-level human perception. Hence, in recent years there has been an increased interest in developing similarity measures specifically for such low-level feature image representation [5] as well as enhancing the feature representation in distance metric learning [24], which is the approach that we follow in this paper.

Over the past decade deep neural networks have seen many successful applications in various image recognition and classification tasks. These networks use multiple layers of non-linear transformations learning more abstract features from the input data. For example, Convolutional Neural Networks (CNNs) [19] have been shown to work extremely well in image classification tasks, such as the ImageNet competition [22], and they produce features that are highly descriptive for various image recognition tasks, even in tasks for which they were not trained, or higher level concepts, such as scenes [12,21]. However, the interactive nature of CBIR poses additional difficulties with regards to the application of deep neural networks, such as the responsiveness of the system – search engine response time exceeding 4 s already interferes with the user's experience [4]. Additionally, in interactive CBIR, the systems needs to learn what the user is interested in from a very small amount of feedback – at each search iteration users tend to indicate only a few images that they like or do not like [11,13].

Learning deep hierarchies for fast image retrieval was considered before by using autoencoders [18] or creating hash codes based on deep semantic ranking [27]. While both methods are fast, neither is flexible enough to learn the image target based on the small amount of relevance feedback obtained from the user. Wan et al. [24] is the first study to apply deep learning to learn a similarity measure between images in a CBIR setting. Unfortunately, no consideration was given to the time requirements of the learning task, which is an important aspect of an interactive retrieval systems. The reported training procedure uses entire datasets and the training itself can take days. Similarity learning can also be used to find new metrics between faces by maximizing the inter-class difference, while minimizing the inner-class difference [6,14], however, the method was not tested with a broader set of images and features. Two recent studies [8,25] took into consideration the training time requirements. However, their system setting relies on using thousands of images for training, which is too large for a user to tag over the span of a single search session. The system we describe in this paper needs only a small number of images tagged by the user through iterative relevance feedback in order for the system to be trained to find the target image(s).

Our focus in this paper is twofold. Our first goal is to show how to learn a definite representation of the user's target image(s) with only a few training

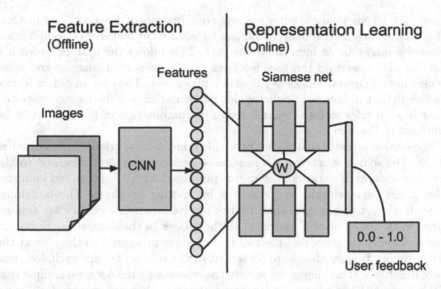

Fig. 1. The siamese architecture with the image feature preprocessing step. The online component accepts two feature vectors, one per image, and user feedback as the label.

examples. This is an important aspect of an interactive CBIR system that can gradually learn from user interaction and adjust to the changes in user's interests as the search progresses. Second, we aim to reduce the training time required for the system to be able to make new suggestions to the user to under 4 s. This will make the proposed system interactive and keep the user engaged in the search loop.

We use a specialized siamese architecture, originally used for face verification [6], that learns the similarity between two example images. This architecture utilizes pre-extracted features from Convolutional Neural Networks (CNNs) and learns a new distance representation based on the user's relevance feedback. Employing ready CNN features as the basis of the similarity learning speeds up the process considerably, while maintaining a broad set of features to prevent the user from getting stuck in a small area of the feature space. The speed of computing the distance metric and the fact that only a small set of examples is needed to learn it makes our framework easily applicable to an interactive retrieval setting, such as CBIR.

2 System Overview

The aim of our system is to assist the user in finding images that cannot be easily described using tags, such as an image of "beautiful sky". Thus, the system needs to learn what the target of the search is through relevance feedback obtained on the small number of images displayed at each iteration. As the user's final search target may be an image containing any combination of features, our method utilizes a distance metric between images to learn what features or combination of features might be of interest to the user. This allows the system to learn a representation based on the user feedback on the presented images, and show the user more relevant images as the search progresses. The system differs from a classifier in that it does not predict which particular classes the user is interested in but instead tries to learn what features or combination of features might be of interest to the user.

The system adheres to a search procedure that can be briefly summarised as follows. The search starts with a random selection of images presented to the user. At each search iteration, the user is presented with k images and indicates which images are relevant to his search by clicking on them. The remaining images in the set of k images that did not receive any user feedback are treated as irrelevant. Based on this feedback, all the images in the dataset are re-ranked using a distance measure and the top k images are presented to the user at the next iteration. Images that were presented to the user so far are excluded from future iterations. If no images are selected as relevant by the user, we assume that all the presented images are irrelevant, and images that are maximally distant from the presented ones are shown to the user at the next iteration. The search continues until the user is satisfied with the presented images.

Below, we describe the feature extraction process and the architecture of the system in more details.

2.1 Feature Extraction

In order to obtain a good base representation, we use CNNs to extract image features. CNNs generate high quality classification results end-to-end from low, pixel-level data to image labels by utilizing deep non-linear architectures. The higher level features from these networks have been successfully used in tasks involving classification of images that were not in the initial training set. This can be achieved by retraining the features extracted from images to represent the area in the image space that corresponds to the user's interests. For our tests, we use features extracted with OverFeat [23] and relearn only the last few fully connected layers for the target representation. OverFeat is a publicly available CNN trained on the ILSVRC13 dataset [22], on which it achieved an error rate of 14.2%. ILVSRC13 contains 1000 object classes from a total of 1.2 million images. OverFeat has been shown to be successful at various image recognition tasks from fine-grained classification to generic visual instance recognition tasks [21]. The chosen features were a set of hidden nodes as the fully connected graph begins from layer 7 (19 within the architecture), totalling 4096 features. The images were shrunk and then cropped from all sides to produce images of equal size of 231×231 pixels. Table 1 shows the composition of the neural architecture used in our system.

Table 1. Composition of the neural architecture used in our system.

Layer	Input size	Output size	
$FC1$	4096	100	Fully connected layer
$ReLU$			Rectified Linear Unit
$FC2$	100	20	Fully connected layer
$ReLU$			Rectified Linear Unit
$Feat$	20	6	Final feature layer
CLF			Contrastive loss function

2.2 System Architecture

Our system employs the siamese architecture [6], which is used for learning similarities between images by labeling pairs of images as similar or dissimilar, and maximizing the distance between different image groups. We employ user relevance feedback to divide the presented images into the two classes, i.e. images with positive feedback (relevant class) and images with negative feedback (non-relevant class). The overview of the system's architecture can be seen in Fig. 2.

The siamese similarity metric aims to find a function that maps the input into a new space, where the target distance measure, such as Euclidean distance, may be used to determine the proximity of two data points. This similarity function, G, is parameterized with weights W, which the system tries to learn to form the similarity metric:

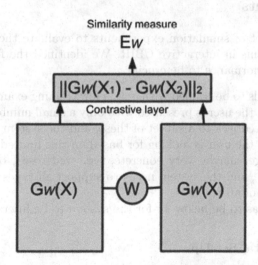

Fig. 2. The siamese architecture: two neural nets G that share the weights W as their parameters. They process the data for the contrastive layer, which outputs the similarity measure E_W.

$$E_W(X_1, X_2) = \|G_W(X_1) - G_W(X_2)\|,$$

where X_1 and X_2 are paired images.

This metric aims to minimize the intra-class similarity, in the case where X_1 and X_2 belong to the same class, and to maximize the inter-class similarity if X_1 and X_2 belong to different classes. The algorithm accepts a pair of observations, which when the loss function is minimized, minimizes or maximizes the similarity metric $E_W(X_1, X_2)$ depending on whether these observations belong to the same class.

The contrastive loss function used in the siamese architecture is:

$$L((W, Y, X_1, X_2)^i) =$$
$$(1 - Y)L_G(E_W(X_1, X_2)^i) + Y L_I(E_W(X, 1, X_2)^i), \tag{1}$$

where $(Y, X_1, X_2)^i$ is the i-th sample, which is composed of a pair of images and a label (inter- or intra-class), L_G is the partial loss function for an intra-class pair, L_I is the partial loss function for an inter-class pair, and P is the number of training samples [6].

The siamese architecture (Fig. 1) can find an angle in the feature space that helps to distinguish between different aspects of the image, such as different position of the face or different facial expressions, making it an ideal choice for our application. An important aspect of this architecture is the fact that it generates a distance metric, which may be used to rank or generate dynamic relevance scores for all the images in a dataset.

3   Experiments

We conducted a set of simulation experiments to evaluate the applicability of the proposed systems in interactive CBIR. We identified the following aspects of the system's performance to be crucial:

1. The system needs to be trained with only a few training examples, i.e. at each search iteration, the user is presented with only a small number of images and often provides feedback to a subset of these, and the system needs to be able to "learn" what the user is looking for based on this limited feedback;
2. The search target maybe very concrete, e.g. "red rose", or very abstract, e.g. "happiness", and the system needs to support all types of searches with varying degrees of abstractness;
3. Training time has to be below 4 s for the system to be interactive.

3.1   Experimental Set-Up

We ran a number of simulations to assess the performance of our system. At each iteration, the system presents 10 images to the simulated user. The target of each search is a class of images with a given label, e.g. "dogs", and the simulated user "clicks" on relevant images from a given target class at each iteration, i.e. the user feedback is 1 for images with a relevant label and 0 for the remaining images in the presented set. The number of relevant images in each iteration can vary from 0 to 10, depending on the number of relevant images in a given dataset and on the accuracy of the user throughout the search session. We assume that the user clicks only on images with the relevant label and that the user clicks on all the relevant images presented in a given iteration. To test whether the system can generalize, we also included as search targets images whose labels were not included in the training set. The search starts with a random selection of 9 images from a given test dataset plus one image with the label of the target class for a specific search – this setting allows us to ensure that all the simulation experiments have a comparable starting point. In summary, our system supports the user in finding an image that best matches their ideal target image(s) in the manner described below. In each iteration, k images from the database $\mathscr{D}$ are presented to the user and the user selects the relevant image(s) from this set, according to the following protocol:

For each iteration $i = 1, 2, \ldots$ of the search:

- Search engine calculates a set of images $\mathbf{x}_{i,1}, \ldots, \mathbf{x}_{i,k} \in \mathscr{D}$ to present to the user.
- If one or more of the presented images are of interest to the user, then the user clicks on them thus providing relevance score of 1 to the clicked images. All the remaining images in the presented set automatically receive relevance feedback of 0.
- If none of the presented images is of interest to the user, then the user proceeds to the next iteration and all the presented images automatically receive relevance feedback of 0.
- The search continues until the user finds their ideal target image.

We used Caffe [16] to produce the live network described above. The simulation experiments were run on a machine with an Intel Core $i5 - 4430$ CPU 3.00 ×4 GHz and a GeForce GTX 660 Ti.

We used three different datasets (Fig. 3):

1. 1096 images from the MIRFlickr dataset [15] with various combination of the following labels: mammals, birds, insects, locomotives. This dataset allowed us to test whether the learned metric is able to generalize to abstract concepts. The arbitrary nature of these classes with regards to the model of the feature extractor is perfect to demonstrate the robustness of our system: the features extracted from the images may be widely different within each label class but as long as each label can be distinguished with a set of features, the system should be able to learn it.

2. Our own collection of 294 images of 6 different dog breeds, of which only four are included in the OverFeat classification list. This dataset allows us to test whether the model is able to learn the target in the presence of semantically related images, some of which are not included in original scope of features used for training. Such a scenario is quite common in a CBIR setting as the search gradually narrows down towards very specific set of image, e.g. the user

Fig. 3. Example images from the three datasets used in our experiments.

starts a search for images of dogs and gradually narrows down the search to images of black dogs with pointy ears and bushy tails.

3. 300 classes from the ImageNet dataset [22], totalling 385412 images. We used this dataset to show that even if the presented images could potentially lead to hundreds of different target images, the learned representation is still able to detect the relevant features and steer the search towards the most relevant images.

In the experiments with the ImageNet and MIRflickr datasets, we simulated 15 search iterations, which is the average number of iterations of a typical CBIR search session [9]. In the experiments with the dog breeds dataset, we simulated only 12 search iterations due to the small size of the dataset. This setting resulted in a gradually increasing training set, starting from 10 images at the beginning of the search session and gradually increasing by 10 images with each search iteration. This setting allowed us to test the robustness of our system with respect to a small number of training examples. All the reported results are averaged over 5 training runs for each of the existing classes in a given dataset.

Before running the simulations, we conducted a number of experiments to configure our system and to learn what effect various networks parameters have on the overall performance. By varying the number of layers between one to three, we noticed smaller gains in the Imagenet dataset, while with the other datasets the accuracy improved when extra layers were added. We varied the number of training iterations and noticed no significant improvement after a thousand iterations. We settled for 1500 iterations for the final simulations. With these results, we chose a structure that takes at most 4 s to train, while maximizing gains from the network structure. For the siamese architecture, the training time was already closer to 4 s with two hidden layers, thus we chose a smaller structure: the incoming 4096 image features are mapped first onto 100 features, then to 20, with the final mapping to 6 output values.

3.2 Experimental Results

The aim of the experiments was to test whether the system is able to find the target image or class of images with a relatively small number of training examples and whether the training time for each iteration is short enough to allow the system to be used interactively. The test results are shown in Figs. 4 and 5. We show the F1 measure and the training time for each dataset. The system is able to retrieve relevant images from all the datasets within the first few iterations. Initially, the confidence intervals are wide, which reflects the uncertainty of the system with regards to the user's search target. However, as the search progresses and the system receives more and more training points and user feedback, the confidence intervals are getting narrower, indicating that the system is gradually zooming in on a specific area of the search space.

In Fig. 5 we show the average training time for each search iteration. For each dataset, the average duration of each search iteration is below the 4 s required to make the system interactive from the usability perspective. This is the case even when the number of the training datapoints grows with each iteration.

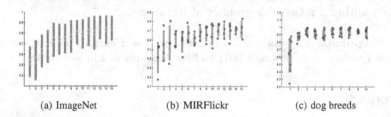

      (a) ImageNet   (b) MIRFlickr   (c) dog breeds

Fig. 4. Test F1-scores (with confidence intervals) for each of the three datasets used in our experiments. The F-1 score increases with the number of iterations and thus more user feedback provided to the system.

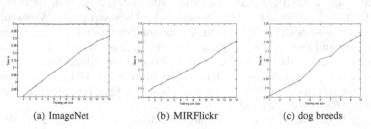

      (a) ImageNet   (b) MIRFlickr   (c) dog breeds

Fig. 5. Training times for the three datasets used in our experiments. For all the three datasets, the training time is less than 4 s

4   Conclusions

We presented a deep neural network framework for learning new representations in an online interactive CBIR setting. The experimental results show that it is possible to build CBIR systems that can dynamically learn the target from very limited user feedback. The system allows users to conduct searches for abstract concepts even though the system may not have been initially trained with abstract image classes. This aspect is also of high importance for symbiotic interactive systems, which can automatically detect what type of images the user might be looking for without the need on the part of the user to specify beforehand what image features would best satisfy their needs. We show that it is possible to produce near-instant image metrics with only a few training examples. Previous studies show that CNNs are able to abstract and discriminate beyond their original use. The descriptive value of the original features was not diminished by the small training set size used in our system, which is a promising step for using these in a CBIR setting.

The average duration of a search iteration with our pipeline is close to the 4 s required in interactive systems, and can be further reduced with more fine tuning of the system and improved hardware. In the future, we are planning to run more extensive simulation experiments as well as conduct extensive user studies to test the system for its applicability in various search scenarios. Additionally, decreasing the sampling size and parallelizing the framework with GPUs are the next steps in our system's development. The goal is to reduce the processing speed to below 3 s in a system that is able to converge to the target image in a user study within a reasonable number of iterations.

Acknowledgments. The work was supported by The Finnish Funding Agency for Innovation (projects Re:Know and D2I) and by Academy of Finland (project COIN).

References

1. Ahukorala, K., Medlar, A., Ilves, K., Glowacka, D.: Balancing exploration and exploitation: empirical parameterization of exploratory search systems. In: Proceedings of the 24th ACM International on Conference on Information and Knowledge Management, CIKM 2015, pp. 1703–1706. ACM, New York (2015)
2. Athukorala, K., Głowacka, D., Jacucci, G., Oulasvirta, A., Vreeken, J.: Is exploratory search different? A comparison of information search behavior for exploratory and lookup tasks. J. Assoc. Inf. Sci. Technol. **67**(11), 2635–2651 (2015)
3. Athukorala, K., Medlar, A., Oulasvirta, A., Jacucci, G., Glowacka, D.: Beyond relevance: adapting exploration/exploitation in information retrieval. In: Proceedings of the 21st International Conference on Intelligent User Interfaces, IUI 2016, pp. 359–369. ACM, New York (2016)
4. Brutlag, J.D., Hutchinson, H., Stone, M.: User preference and search engine latency. In: JSM Proceedings, Qualtiy and Productivity Research Section (2008)
5. Chechik, G., Sharma, V., Shalit, U., Bengio, S.: Large scale online learning of image similarity through ranking. J. Mach. Learn. Res. **11**, 1109–1135 (2010)
6. Chopra, S., Hadsell, R., LeCun, Y.: Learning a similarity metric discriminatively, with application to face verification. In: Proceedings of CVPR (2005)

7. Datta, R., Li, J., Wang, J.: Content-based image retrieval: approaches and trends of the new age. In: Multimedia Information Retrieval, pp. 253–262. ACM (2005)
8. Gao, X., Hoi, S.C., Zhang, Y., Wan, J., Li, J.: SOML: sparse online metric learning with application to image retrieval (2014)
9. Głowacka, D., Hore, S.: Balancing exploration-explotation in image retrieval. In: Proceedings of UMAP (2014)
10. Głowacka, D., Ruotsalo, T., Konuyshkova, K., Athukorala, K., Kaski, S., Jacucci, G.: Directing exploratory search: reinforcement learning from user interactions with keywords. In: Proceedings of the 2013 International Conference on Intelligent User Interfaces, IUI 2013, pp. 117–128. ACM, New York (2013)
11. Głowacka, D., Shawe-Taylor, J.: Content-based image retrieval with multinomial relevance feedback. In: Proceedings of ACML, pp. 111–125 (2010)
12. Gong, Y., Wang, L., Guo, R., Lazebnik, S.: Multi-scale orderless pooling of deep convolutional activation features. CoRR, abs/1403.1840 (2014)
13. Hore, S., Tyrvainen, L., Pyykko, J., Glowacka, D.: A reinforcement learning approach to query-less image retrieval. In: Jacucci, G., Gamberini, L., Freeman, J., Spagnolli, A. (eds.) Symbiotic 2014. LNCS, vol. 8820, pp. 121–126. Springer, Cham (2014). doi:10.1007/978-3-319-13500-7_10
14. Hu, J., Lu, J., Tan, Y.-P.: Discriminative deep metric learning for face verification in the wild. In: Proceedings of CVPR (2014)
15. Huiskes, M.J., Lew, M.S.: The MIR flickr retrieval evaluation. In Proceedings of MIR (2008)
16. Jia, Y., Shelhamer, E., Donahue, J., Karayev, S., Long, J., Girshick, R., Guadarrama, S., Darrell, T.: Caffe: convolutional architecture for fast feature embedding (2014). arXiv:1408.5093
17. Kangasrääsiö, A., Głowacka, D., Kaski, S.: Improving controllability and predictability of interactive recommendation interfaces for exploratory search. In: Proceedings of the 20th International Conference on Intelligent User Interfaces, IUI 2015, pp. 247–251. ACM, New York (2015)
18. Krizhevsky, A., Hinton, G.E.: Using very deep autoencoders for content-based image retrieval. In: Proceedings of ESANN (2011)
19. LeCun, Y., Bottou, L., Bengio, Y., Haffner, P.: Gradient-based learning applied to document recognition. Proc. IEEE 86(11), 2278–2324 (1998)
20. Lowe, D.G.: Object recognition from local scale-invariant features. In: ICCV, pp. 1150–1157 (1999)
21. Razavian, A.S., Azizpour, H., Sullivan, J., Carlsson, S.: CNN features off-the-shelf: an astounding baseline for recognition. CoRR, abs/1403.6382 (2014)
22. Russakovsky, O., Deng, J., Su, H., Krause, J., Satheesh, S., Ma, S., Huang, Z., Karpathy, A., Khosla, A., Bernstein, M., Berg, A.C.: Fei-Fei., L.: Imagenet large scale visual recognition challenge. Int. J. Comput. Vis. 115(3), 211–252 (2014)
23. Sermanet, P., Eigen, D., Zhang, X., Mathieu, M., Fergus, R., LeCun, Y.: Overfeat: integrated recognition, localization and detection using convolutional networks. In: Proceedings of ICLR (2014)
24. Wan, J., Wang, D., Hoi, S.C.H., Wu, P., Zhu, J., Zhang, Y., Li, J.: Deep learning for content-based image retrieval: a comprehensive study. In: Proceedings of MM (2014)
25. Wan, J., Wu, P., Hoi, S.C.H., Zhao, P., Gao, X., Wang, D., Zhang, Y., Li, J.: Online learning to rank for content-based image retrieval. In: Proceedings of the 24th International Conference on Artificial Intelligence, IJCAI 2015, pp. 2284–2290. AAAI Press (2015)

26. Yang, J., Jiang, Y.-G., Hauptmann, A.G., Ngo, C.-W.: Evaluating bag-of-visual-words representations in scene classification. In: Multimedia, Information Retrieval, pp. 197–206 (2007)
27. Zhao, F., Huang, Y., Wang, L., Tan, T.: Deep Semantic ranking based hashing for multi-label image retrieval. ArXiv e-prints, January 2015
28. Zhou, X., Huang, T.: Relevance feedback in image retrieval: a comprehensive review. Multimedia Syst. 8(6), 536–544 (2003)

Finding Kairos: The Influence of Context-Based Timing on Compliance with Well-Being Triggers

Jaap Ham[1]([✉]), Jef van Schendel[1], Saskia Koldijk[2], and Evangelia Demerouti[3]

[1] Human-Technology Interaction, Eindhoven University of Technology,
Eindhoven, The Netherlands
j.r.c.ham@tue.nl
[2] TNO, The Hague, The Netherlands
[3] Human Performance Management, Eindhoven University of Technology,
Eindhoven, The Netherlands
e.demerouti@tue.nl

Abstract. For healthy computer use, frequent, short breaks are crucial. This research investigated whether context-aware persuasive technology can identify opportune and effective moments (of high user motivation and ability to perform target behavior) for triggering short breaks fostering symbiotic interactions between e-Coaching e-Health technology and users. In Study 1, office workers rated their motivation and ability to take a short break (probed at random moments). Simultaneously their computer activity was recorded. Results showed that computer activity (time since last break; change in computer activity level) can predict moments of high and low (perceived) ability (but not motivation) to take a short break. Study 2 showed that when office workers received triggers (to take a short break) at moments of high (vs. low) ability (predicted based on computer activity), compliance increased 70%. These results show that context information can be used to identify opportune moments, at which persuasive triggers are more effective.

Keywords: Persuasive technology · Kairos · Triggers · Well-being · e-Health · e-Coaching

1 Introduction

In modern-day society, a large share of the workload has shifted from physical work to working with information [13]. Many employees gather, processes and produce information as their main task. While computers are useful tools for such knowledge workers, prolonged computer use can also lead to serious health risks [14]. Healthy working behavior is needed to guard the well-being of knowledge workers and reduce health risks. Taking regular short breaks, for instance, can help reduce the risks of repetitive strain injury [15] as well as sedentary behavior [16]. Various studies have investigated the advantages of taking short breaks (also called microbreaks) for computer workers, and characteristics of these breaks (see e.g., [17]). Research [17] shows that 30 s breaks

L. Gamberini et al. (Eds.): Symbiotic 2016, LNCS 9961, pp. 89–101, 2017.
DOI: 10.1007/978-3-319-57753-1_8

from computer work have health benefits while not hampering productivity, and even improving work accuracy [18].

To help computer workers, the smart technology at which they incur risks can also be used to help them prevent it. That is, their systems can also function as e-Health technology [19] by functioning as an eCoach (see e.g., [20]), and help users adapt their behavior. Such technology would be Persuasive Technology [1–3], as it attempts to change user behavior or attitudes without coercion or deception [1, 24].

To influence human behavior, Persuasive Technology must influence determinants of behavior, and in psychological research various theories of behavior determinants have been proposed (e.g., the Theory of Planned Behavior [22], and the Motivation, Opportunity and Ability MOA model [23], see also [5], [6]). Comparable to other models, and directly applied to Persuasive Technology, Fogg's Behavior Model [2] proposed that Motivation and Ability determine the effectiveness of a persuasive trigger. Persuasive triggers (c.f., [2]) can have many different forms (e.g., text message, a sound, a growling stomach), and have in common that they can be successful in changing the user's behavior when noticed by the user, when user associates the trigger with performing the target behavior, and when the user is motivated and able to perform the target behavior.

In support of this model [2], earlier research [21] showed that appropriate localization of triggers (i.e., a manipulation of user ability to act on the trigger), and motivating contents of the trigger message (i.e., a manipulation of user motivation) influence trigger effectiveness. More specifically, in this earlier research, participants visited a virtual supermarket where product images were displayed on posters and in which triggers (to purchase a product) were presented either co-located with products (or not) and these triggers contained a motivating message (or not). Confirming hypotheses, triggers co-located with the target product led to higher sales of that product, especially when the trigger contained a motivating message. This research showed that manipulating ability and motivation (to perform the target behavior) by changing characteristics of the trigger influences trigger effectiveness.

However, trigger characteristics are only one determinant of user's ability and motivation to perform a target behavior. Perhaps even more crucial determinants of user ability and motivation can be found in the context in which behavior takes place. Characteristics of the user him- or herself, the use context, and the behavior, all have a strong influence on user ability and motivation. For example, the physical context of the user (e.g., being in a cold office) will have a dominant influence on user ability and motivation (e.g., to save energy for heating).

Therefore, in the current research we will investigate whether context information can be used to identify moments at which user motivation and ability are high, and triggering (to perform a target behavior) might be especially effective. We will focus on the use context, that is, on the variables that can be detected in the context of computer use by, specifically, computer workers. Context-aware persuasive technology might be able to identify opportune moments (at which a user's motivation and ability to perform the target behavior are high) for triggering, and use those opportune moments for effective influencing a target behavior. Thereby, this kind of technology can foster symbiotic interactions between e-Coaching e-Health technology and users, as it enables adapting output to the user regardless of his/her ability to explicitly refine his/her request (see [30], p. 4).

In two field studies, we investigated (Study 1) computer workers' motivation and ability to take a short break, their computer use context (e.g., mouse movements, keyboard presses), and (Study 2) the effectiveness of persuasive triggers to take a short break.

2 Study 1

Study 1 investigated whether context-aware technology can identify opportune moments (at which a user's motivation and ability to perform the target behavior are high). This question was investigated in the context of knowledge workers at a regular office of a research and consultancy organization. The computer activity of knowledge workers is an important part of their context, and the goal of Study 1 was to explore if this type of context could be used to predict their motivation and ability to take the desired behavior, in this case taking a short break. For this, these office workers rated their motivation and ability to take a short break (probed at random moments in time) during a working week, while simultaneously their computer activity was recorded. Data was collected using an experience sampling method [25], that consisted of two types of measures: (1) The levels of motivation and ability were gathered by asking the participants to periodically report ratings for these two factors. (2) Computer activity was recorded using key and mouse logger software on their computer system.

2.1 Methods

Participants. Six knowledge workers (as defined by [26]) participated in Study 1. All participants were employees or interns at a Dutch research and consultancy organization. The mean age of the participants (4 men and 2 women) was 27.8 years ($SD = 8.47$). All participants participated in the study without receiving any reward.

Materials. To collect the data, two software programs were installed on the participants' work computers. To collect data about the computer activity of the participants, a logger application was installed (uLog, developed by Noldus Information Technology for researchers in user-computer interaction to study computer activity behavior [27]). This software runs in the background and was used to record mouse activity (number of left clicks, right clicks, double clicks, wheel scrolls, drags, hovers; relative and total cursor distance travelled), keyboard activity (number of characters typed, special keys pressed, key combinations made and strings typed) and application activity (applications starts and exits, window switches performed). In light of privacy, no content or personally identifiable information was collected. For instance, keystrokes were recorded, but not which characters were typed.

The dataset collected by this computer activity logger software allowed us to calculate the various variables that were necessary to assess the predictive value of a user's computer activity for that user's self-reported ability and motivation to take a break. Of these variables, two variables showed to be predictors of user ability: A user's change in overall activity, and the time that a user worked since his or her last break. More specifically, to calculate a participant's change in overall computer activity, we divided the total number of events during the last 3 min by the total number of events during the last 30 s. To calculate the time that a user worked since the last break, we used the time passed after ending a period of no activity of at least 5 min.

To collect motivation and ability ratings from the participants, a self-report program was installed. This software (developed in Java) was BabylonA, which periodically administered the self-reports and recorded the responses. To ask users to rate their momentary levels of ability and motivation to take a short break, the software displayed a pop-up windows on the participant's screen (see Fig. 1).

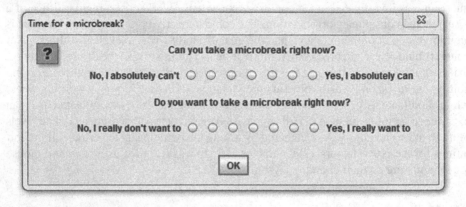

Fig. 1. The self-report pop-up question window.

To assess a user's (self-reported) ability to take a short break, the question "Can you take a microbreak right now?" was posed. Users could answers by clicking an option on a 7-point Likert scale (1 = No, I absolutely can't, to 7 = Yes, I absolutely can). To assess a user's (self-reported) motivation to take a short break, the question "Do you want to take a microbreak right now?"was posed. Users could answers by clicking an option on a 7-point Likert scale (1 = No, I really don't want to, to 7 = Yes, I really want to).

The software (BabylonA) automatically displayed these questions at random moments in time, although between two consequent pop-ups at least 20 min had to pass, and at least one pop-up had to appear every hour (to achieve optimal granularity in the data).

During the 7 workings days, participants answered the questions presented in pop-up windows 219 times (a response rate of 88%), but because (for unknown reasons) sometimes the computer activity logger application had not been running, 148 self-reports (of ability and motivation) were available for analyses. Participants' answers to the motivation and ability questions showed a positive correlation, $r(146) = .48, p < .001$.

Procedure. After agreeing to participate, a participant was asked to sign the informed consent form. Next, the logger application and the BabylonA application were installed on the participant's work computer. During each of seven working days, these two programs gathered data: the logger application recorded computer activity data, and the BabylonA application asked a participant for his or her ability and motivation to take a short break. After these seven days, the computer activity data and self-report response log files were collected from the computers, and the two software applications were de-installed from the participant's computer. Finally, participants were thanked for their participation and debriefed.

2.2   Results and Discussion

Results showed that a *participant's change in overall computer activity* was a significant predictor for that participant's ability rating (at that same moment in time), as indicated by a significant regression equation, $F(1,145) = 8.11$, $p = .005$, with an R^2 of .053 (a correlation of .23).

Also, results showed that the *time that a user had worked since his or her last break* was a significant predictor also for that participant's ability rating (at that same moment in time), as indicated by a significant regression equation, $F(1,137) = 16.981$, $p < .001$, with an R^2 of .110 (a correlation of .33).

A participant's change in overall computer activity and a participant's time worked since last break both are independent predictors of a participant's (self-reported) ability to take a break, as indicated by a multiple regression analysis, in which a participant's change in overall computer activity was a significant predictor (B = .084, SE = .030, Beta = .221, $t = 2.75$, $p = .007$) and also time worked since last break was a significant predictor (B = .008, SE = .002, Beta = .293, $t = 3.65$, $p < .001$).

Results provided no evidence of other relationships between a participant's computer activity and his or her ability, nor any evidence or predictive value of (elements of) a participant's computer activity and his or her motivation to take a break.

Thereby, the current findings show that participants' levels of ability (to take a short break) can be predicted using context-aware technology. That is, these results provide evidence that two context variables have predictive value for an office worker's ability to take a short break: the extent to which the user's overall computer activity has changed (during the last 3 min), and the time that has passed since the last time the user took a break (of more than 5 min).

Based on these findings, that allow identifying opportune moments (at which a user's ability to perform the target behavior is high), Study 2 investigated whether persuasive technology indeed is more effective when triggering user behavior change at such moments. So, Study 2 investigated whether a trigger to take a break would be more effective when it is presented longer after a person took his or her last break, and when it is presented right after a change in that person's overall computer activity level. Thereby, Study 2 investigated Fogg's Behavior Model [2] that proposed that (next to motivation) ability of the user to perform the behavior is a crucial determinant of the effectiveness of a persuasive trigger.

3 Study 2

To study this question, we conducted a field study in which office workers were presented with triggers (pop-up windows on screen) to take a short break. That is, their computer activity was measured, and based on the two variables identified in Study 1 (time since last break and change in overall computer activity), moments of high and low ability to take a break were identified. For each participant, half of the triggers to take a break was presented a such a moment of high (predicted) ability, and half of the triggers to take a break was presented at a moment of low (predicted) ability. We expected that triggers presented at moments of high (predicted) ability would be more effective than triggers presented at moments of low (predicted ability).

3.1 Methods

Participants and Design. Thirty-five knowledge workers (as defined by [26]) participated in the experiment. All participants were employees or interns at a research and consultancy organization (TNO), employees at an engineering consultancy company, or students at Eindhoven University of Technology. The mean age of the participants (27 men and 8 women) was 34.5 years ($SD = 12.3$). For their participation, participants received the chance to win one of three gift vouchers (of €25). All participants were presented with persuasive triggers at moments of high and of low (predicted) ability, as we manipulated this factor within participants.

Materials. As in Study 1, two software applications were used that were installed on each participant's desk computer. The application to record participant's computer activity was completely the same as in Study 1. It ran in the background, and recorded a participant's computer activity making available a dataset that was stored on the computer itself, and such that the other application could immediately use it for calculating the two variables (time since last break and change of computer activity) that are predictors of ability to take a break.

The application to present triggers to take a break to participants was developed in Java and purpose-built for this study. This application was context-aware technology, in the sense that it could read and responded to the logger application dataset in real-time. As described and identical to our procedures for Study 1, the application calculated a participant's change in overall computer activity by dividing the total number of events during the last 3 min by the total number of events during the last 30 s. To calculate the time that a user worked since the last break, it used the time passed after ending a period of no activity of at least 5 min.

To predict whether user ability would be high or low, and thereby whether a trigger to take a break should be presented or not presented, the application used thresholds for both variables. That is, based on analyses of the dataset of Study 1, this application determined that the current moment was a moment of *high* ability to take a break when both the time that had passed since the participant took a break was more than 30 min, or the participant's (current) overall level of computer activity had increased by 25%. Contrarily, this application determined that the current moment was a moment of *low* ability to take a break when both the time that had passed since the participant took a break was less than 18 min, or that the participant's (current) overall level of computer activity had decreased by 25%.

Each hour (but not within 3 min of the previous trigger) the application would present a pop-up window on the participant's screen with a trigger message to take a break (see Fig. 2). This pop-up window presented the text message "Time for a microbreak!" Participants click a button to accept (clicking a button labelled "Start!") or refuse this suggestion (clicking a button labelled "No, I can't right now", or a button labelled "No, I don't want right now"). If a participant clicked the button "Start!", That button disappeared and timer (counting down from 30 s) was shown in its place. This short break duration is the same as used by [28, 29].

Fig. 2. The BabylonB pop-up in its initial state, as it was displayed to the participants (left) and in its state as after clicking the "Start" button (right).

To determine the moment in time at which a trigger would be displayed, at random moments in time, the application determined whether that moment was a moment of high or low ability for the participant to take a break using the two variables and their thresholds as described above. For all participants, half of these triggers (based on these thresholds) were presented at moments of (predicted) low ability, and the other half of these triggers were presented at moments of (predicted) high ability.

Overall, the persuasive trigger was presented to all participants 1007 moments, of which 420 times at a moment of high (predicted) ability and 587 times at a moment of low (predicted) ability. When participants took more than 15 s to respond to a persuasive trigger (i.e., press one of the button, see Fig. 2), we removed this response from the dataset. The reason for this is that we investigated the influence of using contextual information as ability predictor and during these 15 s the use context has changed. Also, some participants barely complied to the triggers (i.e., complied less than 6 times in total over the whole week at moments of both high and low (predicted) ability). As these participants basically had not participated in the study (and produced no data to analyze) we removed them from the dataset. After these two exclusion criteria, data from 29 participants were left to be used in the analysis.

The two dependent variables were reported compliance and actual compliance. We calculated (for each participant) the percentage of reported compliance by counting the number of times that participant clicked the 'Start!' button, and closed the window after the timer had finished, and dividing that number by the total of persuasive triggers that participant was presented with (separately for the high and low ability moment triggers). Likewise, we calculated a participant's percentage of actual compliance by checking for each reported compliance whether the logger data also indicated that the participant had not used his or her computer for 30 s (indicated by no keypresses and no mouse movement). Also this number we then divided by the total number of persuasive triggers that participant was presented with (at low and at high ability moments). Based on this analysis, we removed 52 responses (24 for the high ability condition, and 28 for the low ability condition) for which a participant has reported to start a short break but actually had continued using the computer.

Procedure. After agreeing to participate, participants were asked to sign the informed consent form. Also, each participant received a short document summarizing the procedure and presenting contact information of the researchers. Next, the logger application and the trigger presentation application were installed on the participants' work computer. During each of five working days, the logger application recorded computer activity data, and the trigger presentation application presented triggers to take a break. After these five days, the computer activity data and trigger presentation and response log files were collected from the computers, and two software applications were de-installed from all computers. Finally, participants were thanked for their participation and debriefed. The gift vouchers were randomly distributed after the experiment had finished.

3.2 Results

Confirming expectations, results showed that when a participant received a persuasive trigger at moments of high ability (predicted based on their current computer activity and an algorithm based on analyses of the dataset of Study 1) they showed higher percentages of reported compliance ($M = 47.03\%$, $SD = 29.27$) than when a participant received a persuasive trigger at moments of low (predicted) ability ($M = 28.90\%$, $SD = 27.14$), $t(28) = 4.17$, $p < .001$, *Cohen's d* = .64. The same was found for actual compliance: when a participant received a persuasive trigger at moments of high ability, percentages of actual compliance ($M = 43.72\%$, $SD = 30.16$) were higher than when a participant received a persuasive trigger at moments of low ability ($M = 25.51\%$, $SD = 26.90$), $t(28) = 4.15$, $p < .001$, *Cohen's d* = .64.

In other words, when these office workers received persuasive triggers (during their working week) at moments of high (vs. low) ability (predicted based on their current computer activity and an algorithm based on analyses of the dataset of Study 1), they performed the triggered behavior (taking a short break) about 70% more often (complying in 47.03%/43.72% versus in 28.90%/26.90% of the cases).

4   General Discussion

To investigate whether context-aware technology can identify opportune moments for influencing users using triggers (at which a user's motivation and ability to perform the target behavior are high), in Study 1, office workers rated their motivation and ability to take a short break (probed at random moments in time) during a working week, while simultaneously their computer activity was recorded. Results showed that moments of high and low (perceived) ability to take a short break can be predicted based on computer activity, while motivation could not be predicted. Two factors predicted perceived ability: time since last break, and change in overall computer activity level.

Investigating whether persuasive technology that triggers users is more effective when triggering user behavior change at such opportune moments (as identified by Study 1), Study 2 confirmed that when office workers received persuasive triggers (during a working week) at moments of high (vs. low) ability (predicted based on their current computer activity and an algorithm based on analyses of the dataset of Study 1), they performed the triggered behavior (taking a short break) about 70% more often.

Results of these two studies show that context information can be used to identify opportune moments for triggering specific behavior, and that persuasive triggers are more effective at those moments. Thereby, the current results confirm Fogg's Behavior Model [2] that proposed that (next to motivation) ability of the user to perform the behavior is a crucial determinant of the effectiveness of a persuasive trigger. Specifically, the level of ability can be used to help define what is an opportune moment, or *Kairos* (see [1]). They also confirm the theory by Fogg [2] that triggering at such an opportune moment leads to higher compliance with the target behavior.

This finding is also in line with research evidence that backs up comparable models of behavior determinants, as for example the Motivation and Opportunity as Determinants (MODE) model proposed by Fazio [4], or the Ability-Motivation-Opportunity frameworks (see e.g., [7], and also [23]). Importantly, the current research presents evidence specifically for the effectiveness of triggers by persuasive technology and thereby presents evidence in direct support of Fogg's model.

Future research can study whether use context information may be used to predict motivation to comply too. Although the current research presented evidence for a strong correlation (of .48) between user motivation and ability (to take a short break – see Study 1), future research might also developed new measures to assess user motivation and ability in ways that allow more distinction between the two concepts. Thereby, future research could study both the value of (predicted) ability and motivation for the effectiveness of persuasive triggers, and future studies could even further separate ability and opportunity. Also, future research might investigate the current research question in other and larger populations, studying the importance of interpersonal differences. Another important question is the relationship between a person's inclination to take a break and his or her actual acceptance of the trigger's message. Study 2 could not explicitly assess this inclination as such explicit assessment could have interfered with a participant's naïve motivation (or ability) to take a break. Future research might attempt to tap into this inclination without influencing users (e.g., by measuring bodily signs of tiredness) at the same time as presenting users with persuasive triggers to take a break.

The results of Study 1 and Study 2 also provide evidence for the value of context information for the timing of persuasive technology. This is in line with the expectations of authors such as Munson [7] and IJsselsteijn et al. [8], who described supposed advantages of context awareness for delivering persuasive health messages.

Besides computer activity, many other types of contexts exist. Distinctions might be made between the physical context of a user (e.g., in a hot or a cold office), the social context of a user (e.g., among friends or at the office), the mental context of a user (e.g., busy), and the user's computer use context (e.g., indicated by variables indicating computer use).For example, information about a person's cognitive load, the amount of mental effort needed to perform a task [9], could be of great value for estimating the extent to which users might be influenced, or for understanding how a user should be approached. It is easy for people to see whether their coworkers can be disturbed during a task, and technology can also be improved by being able to determine this. As Hudson et al. [10] put it, "as adults, we can typically assess someone's interruptibility very quickly and with a minimum of effort", yet computers are "almost entirely oblivious to the human context in which they operate and cannot assess whether 'now is a bad time'".

The current research makes clear that software that helps users prevent negative side-effects of repetitive movements (anti-RSI software) could present more effective persuasive triggers when taking into account the opportunity of the moment based on computer use context. Presenting triggers at the wrong moment in time, might not lead to compliance, or lower levels of compliance. Recent research suggested that using the wrong persuasive strategies might even lead to reactance effects causing users to become angry towards the persuasive technology, and even show behavior that opposes the target behavior [11].

As occupational computer use grows, so do the risks of negative health consequences due to repetitive strain injury and sedentary behavior. These risks are already widespread today, but they can be reduced by healthy working behavior. One habit that can decrease the health risks associated with both repetitive strain injury and sedentary behavior, is taking frequent short breaks during work. Encouraging such behavior with persuasive technology has several advantages, such as availability and scalability of such interventions.

The current research showed that (computer use) context information can be used to identify the best moment to present persuasive triggers, and presented evidence for the importance of appropriate timing for the effectiveness of persuasive technology. It shows how persuasive technology can function in symbiotic interaction with its user by combining computation, sensing technology, and interaction design to realize understanding between humans and computers (see [30], p. 11). Next to stimulating healthy working behavior reducing health risks associated with computer use, these insights can also help making persuasive technology (e.g., on-screen triggers) more effective for e-Coaching other kinds of behavior as for example health-related behavior pertaining to diabetes, nutrition, weight loss, and quitting smoking. Context-aware persuasive technology is a form of tailored persuasive technology, just as personalized persuasive technology (see e.g., [12]) is tailored to characteristics of people.

Insights into context-awareness increases understanding of tailoring persuasive technology (to user, user and use context, and even to affordances of the persuasive technology itself, see [21]), and thereby of maximizing the persuasive power of technology.

Aknowledgments. We want to thank the EU for funding the H2020 MAMEM project and the SWELL project (in the contexts of which this research was performed). Also, the TNO research group at The Hague is thanked for important contributions to this research.

References

1. Fogg, B.J.: Persuasive Technology: Using Computers to Change What We Think and Do. Morgan Kaufmann Publishers, Amsterdam (2003)
2. Fogg, B.J.: A behavior model for persuasive design. In: Proceedings of the 4th International Conference on Persuasive Technology, p. 40. ACM (2009)
3. Fogg, B.J., Eckles, D.: The behavior chain for online participation: how successful web services structure persuasion. In: Kort, Y., IJsselsteijn, W., Midden, C., Eggen, B., Fogg, B.J. (eds.) PERSUASIVE 2007. LNCS, vol. 4744, pp. 199–209. Springer, Heidelberg (2007). doi: 10.1007/978-3-540-77006-0_25
4. Reeves, B., Nass, C.: The Media Equation. Cambridge University Press, New York (1996)
5. Fazio, R.H.: Multiple processes by which attitudes guide behavior: the MODE model as an integrative framework. In: Zanna, M.P. (ed.) Advances in experimental social psychology, vol. 23, pp. 75–109. Academic Press, New York (1990)
6. Hughes, J.: The ability-motivation-opportunity framework for behavior research in IS. In: Conference Proceedings of HICSS (2007)
7. Munson, S.A.: Pervasive, persuasive health: some challenges. In: Proceedings of the Sixth International Conference on Pervasive Computing Technologies for Healthcare (Pervasive Health), pp. 241–244. IEEE (2012)
8. IJsselsteijn, W., Kort, Y., Midden, C., Eggen, B., Hoven, E.: Persuasive technology for human well-being: setting the scene. In: IJsselsteijn, Wijnand A., Kort, Yvonne A.W., Midden, C., Eggen, B., Hoven, E. (eds.) PERSUASIVE 2006. LNCS, vol. 3962, pp. 1–5. Springer, Heidelberg (2006). doi:10.1007/11755494_1
9. Sweller, J.: Cognitive load during problem solving: effects on learning. Cogn. Sci. **12**(2), 257–285 (1988)
10. Hudson, S., Fogarty, J., Atkeson, C., Avrahami, D., Forlizzi, J., Kiesler, S., Yang, J.: Predicting human interruptibility with sensors: a wizard of OZ feasibility study. In: Proceedings of the SIGCHI Conference on Human Factors In Computing Systems, pp. 257–264. ACM (2003)
11. Roubroeks, M., Ham, J., Midden, C.: When artificial social agents try to persuade people: the role of social agency on the occurrence of psychological reactance. Int. J. Soc. Robot. **3**, 155–165 (2011)
12. Kaptein, M.C.: Personalized persuasion in ambient intelligence. J. Ambient Intell. Smart Environ. **4**(3), 279–280 (2012)
13. Wolff, E.N.: The growth of information workers in the US economy. Commun. ACM **48**(10), 37–42 (2005)
14. Van Tulder, M., Malmivaara, A., Koes, B.: Repetitive strain injury. Lancet **369**(9575), 1815–1822 (2007)
15. Galinsky, T.L., Swanson, N.G., Sauter, S.L., Dunkin, R., Hurrell, J.J.: Supplementary breaks and stretching exercises for data entry operators: a follow-up field study. Am. J. Ind. Med. **50**(7), 519–527 (2007)

16. Healy, G.N., Wijndaele, K., Dunstan, D.W., Shaw, J.E., Salmon, J., Zimmet, P.Z., Owen, N.: Objectively measured sedentary time, physical activity, and metabolic risk the australian diabetes, obesity and lifestyle study (AusDiab). Diabetes Care **31**(2), 369–371 (2008)
17. Henning, R.A., Sauter, S.L., Salvendy, G., Krieg Jr., E.F.: Microbreak length, performance, and stress in a data entry task. Ergonomics **32**(7), 855–864 (1989)
18. van den Heuvel, S.G., de Looze, M.P., Hildebrandt, V.H., Thé, K.H.: Effects of software programs stimulating regular breaks and exercises on work-related neck and upper-limb disorders. Scand. J. Work, Environ. Health **29**(2), 106–116 (2003)
19. Gaddi, A., Capello, F., Manca, M. (eds.): e-Health, care and quality of life. Springer, Milan (2014)
20. Alpay, L.L., Henkemans, O.B., Otten, W., Rövekamp, T.A., Dumay, A.C.: e-Health applications and services for patient empowerment: directions for best practices in the netherlands. Telemedicine e-Health **16**(7), 787–791 (2010)
21. Basten, F.T.W., Ham, J., Midden, C., Gamberini, L., Spagnolli, A.: Does trigger location matter? The influence of localization and motivation on the persuasiveness of mobile purchase recommendations. In: Conference Proceedings of Persuasive 2015, Chicago, IL (2015)
22. Ajzen, I.: From Intentions to Actions: A Theory of Planned Behavior, pp. 11–39. Springer, Heidelberg (1985)
23. Ölander, F., Thøgersen, J.: Understanding of consumer behavior as a prerequisite for environmental protection. J. Consum. Policy **18**(4), 345–385 (1995)
24. Oinas-Kukkonen, H., Harjumaa, M.: Persuasive systems design: key issues, process model, and system features. Commun. Assoc. Inf. Syst. **24**(1), 28 (2009)
25. Csikszentmihalyi, M., Larson, R.: Validity and reliability of the experience-sampling method. J. Nerv. Ment. Dis. **175**(9), 526–536 (1987)
26. Janssen, J., Van Hall, J.G.: SWELL deliverable 6.3a - CommonSense dashboard v1.0 (2013). http://www.swell-project.net/dynamics//modules/SFIL0100/view.php?fil_Id=87. Accessed 25 Aug 2016
27. Noldus Information Technology: Noldus releases uLogTM: an innovative tool for the automatic logging of user-computer interaction (2006). http://www.noldus.com/news. Accessed 10 Sept 2015
28. Henning, R.A., Jacques, P., Kissel, G.V., Sullivan, A.B., Alteras-Webb, S.M.: Frequent short rest breaks from computer work: effects on productivity and well-being at two field sites. Ergonomics **40**(1), 78–91 (1997)
29. McLean, L., Tingley, M., Scott, R.N., Rickards, J.: Computer terminal work and the benefit of microbreaks. Appl. Ergon. **32**(3), 225–237 (2001)
30. Jacucci, G., Spagnolli, A., Freeman, J., Gamberini, L.: Symbiotic interaction: a critical definition and comparison to other human-computer paradigms. In: Jacucci, G., Gamberini, L., Freeman, J., Spagnolli, A. (eds.) Symbiotic 2014. LNCS, vol. 8820, pp. 3–20. Springer, Cham (2014). doi:10.1007/978-3-319-13500-7_1

Maritime Cognitive Workload Assessment

Daniel Miklody[1]([✉]), Wendie M. Uitterhoeve[2], Dimitri van Heel[2],
Kerstin Klinkenberg[3], and Benjamin Blankertz[1]

[1] Neurotechnology Group, Technische Universität Berlin,
Sekr. MAR 4-3, Marchstr 23, 10587 Berlin, Germany
miklody@tu-berlin.de
[2] MARIN's Nautical Center, Wageningen, The Netherlands
[3] K+S Projects, Rangsdorf, Germany
http://www.neuro.tu-berlin.de/

Abstract. The human factor plays the key role for safety in many indus-
trial and civil every-day operations in our technologized world. Human
failure is more likely to cause accidents than technical failure, e.g. in the
challenging job of tugboat captains. Here, cognitive workload is crucial,
as its excess is a main cause of dangerous situations and accidents while
being highly participant and situation dependent. However, knowing the
captain's level of workload can help to improve man-machine interaction.
The main contributions of this paper is a successful workload indication
and a transfer of cognitive workload knowledge from laboratory to realistic settings.

Keywords: Workload · BCI · EEG

1 Introduction

In the maritime world, as in many other workplaces, working memory, the ability
to process information and to take decision is crucial. The quantification of *cognitive workload* is a measure to study these aspects. The insight can shed light
onto the limitations posed by the *human factor* and point out how to improve
equipment, conditions or training. While there exists no generally accepted definition of cognitive workload, there is a large agreement that it encompasses the
two concepts of *activation* and *resources* or capacity [15].

In the present investigation, we designed a *BCI system* based on spectral
decompositions of electroencephalographic data [17] that is trained to detect
states of high/low *cognitive workload*. The workload was manipulated by the
main task itself within one of the conditions while in the other we employed the
2-back task [8] as a secondary task which is a common tool for the measurement
of workload [14]. The aim of this study was to investigate cognitive workload in
a more realistic environment and set the results into context with those from
experiments obtained in clean laboratory settings. Therefore, professional tugboat captains were observed in a realistic training simulator study, where we
investigated whether and how laboratory based cognitive workload studies are

L. Gamberini et al. (Eds.): Symbiotic 2016, LNCS 9961, pp. 102–114, 2017.
DOI: 10.1007/978-3-319-57753-1_9

transferable to more realistic settings. In particular, we investigated if and how alpha & theta oscillations are modulated by cognitive workload.

1.1 Neurophysilogical Correlates of Cognitive Workload

Cognitive workload is reflected in different components of brain activity. In view of the present target application, modulations of event-related potentials due to workload [11,12,18] are not relevant, since there are no controlled and continuously repeated stimuli. Therefore, we concentrate on workload-induced modulations of spontaneous brain activity.

The power of oscillatory brain activity in the theta frequency range (4 to 7 Hz) in frontal brain regions have been found to positively correlate with the level of workload, see e.g. [5,7,20].

With respect to the more prominent alpha frequency band, most studies report a negative correlation of cognitive workload and alpha power at paritooccipital scalp locations, see e.g. [4,7]. However, these studies used tasks in the visual modality to induce workload, such that one can only derive the implication of alpha reduction for workload in visual resources. In general, the functional role of alpha band oscillations is not yet conclusive. For a memory task in the auditory domain, [6] reports a modulation of theta oscillations only, but no modulations of the alpha rhythm. Some studies using auditory stimulation even found an increase of alpha activity with increasing workload [2,10,13,16]. A possible interpretation is provided by the hypothesis of functional inhibition, which postulates that strong alpha activity reflects active inhibition of task-irrelevant processes [9]: when the critical processing load is in the non-visual, the visual areas are actively deactivated. The idea to build EEG-based workload monitoring systems was presented, e.g. in [3,4,19].

2 Experimental Design

In a 10-participant simulator study, we recorded electroencephalographic data from a realistic tugboat scenario with professional captains (participant 8 excl.: sickness). The participants were recruited along the training network of MARIN and were compensated for their voluntary participation. They were all male with ages ranging from 30 to 65 years and different levels of experience. The experiment consisted of 3 different scenarios (approx. 40 min each), where scenario 1&3 were identical, see Fig. 1.

The simulator was a professional ship simulator bridge optimized for tugboat missions which can be observed in Fig. 2. It consisted of a 360° projected screen around a set of ordinary tugboat controls. This included several additional screens for radar and ship-parameters. The study was approved by the committee of the ethical department of Philips, the Netherlands, as we collaborated with them on this project. An informed written consent was obtained from all participants.

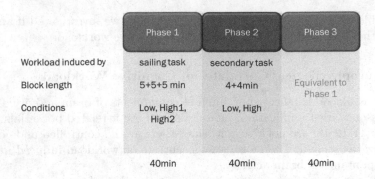

	Phase 1	Phase 2	Phase 3
Workload induced by	sailing task	secondary task	
Block length	5+5+5 min	4+4min	Equivalent to Phase 1
Conditions	Low, High1, High2	Low, High	
	40min	40min	40min

Fig. 1. Experimental design - overview

Fig. 2. Simulator Setting with 360° projections

While in phase 1&3, the cognitive workload was modulated by the sailing task itself in combination with environmental changes (weather, sea), we increased it in phase 2 by an additional task (2-back task [8]) and kept sailing constant.

2.1   Phase 1 and 3: Bow-to-Bow

In this scenario the focus was to keep the experimental conditions as naturalistic as possible while still being able to modulate the workload induced on the captain. Therefore, 3 conditions were generated with different tasks and different weather conditions. An overview about the temporal structure can be found in Fig. 3 on the left. For the later classification, the *high1* and *high2* epochs are combined to a common *high* class.

Condition 1: Free Sailing Condition: *low workload*: The captain was instructed to follow a large container ship astern while the weather was manipulated to have no extra effect on the workload.

Condition 2: Connecting Condition: *high1 workload*: After a transition phase moving to the front of the vessel the tugboat captain got the instruction to get ready for bow-to-bow connection while the weather conditions were changed to

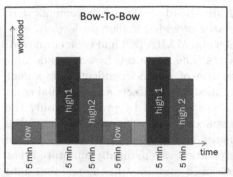 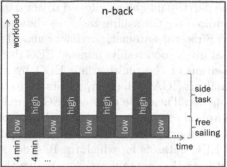

Fig. 3. Experimental design of workload modulation

harsh (wind, waves, fog). Then, the captains were told to wait for connection for 5 min which represents the high1 phase.

Condition 3: Pulling Condition: *high2 workload*: After the rope was connected, a constant tow force and line length was instructed. The weather stayed harsh.

2.2   Phase 2: n-Back

The n-back task is commonly used in neuroscientific research as a manipulation tool for cognitive workload. We used this as a secondary task to have a condition comparable to common research and to see how much our bow-to-bow scenario corresponds to the neural patterns of this commonly known task. We used an auditory 2-back task, where the participant had to follow a stream of spoken numbers. If the last number heard corresponded with the digit 2 back, they had to press a button. The digits 1–9 were used with 3 s interleave randomly (75%) and forced 2-back repetition (25%) to get a reasonable amount of repetitions. The 2-back was played auditorily to keep a realistic behavioral scheme of the captain. There were 2 conditions, 4 min each, which were repeated 5 times, resulting in a total duration of 40 min for the whole phase (see also Fig. 3 on the right):

Condition 1: Free Sailing Condition *low workload*: In this condition, the same low workload task of the bow-to-bow Scenario was induced for comparison.

Condition 2: Free Sailing with 2-Back Condition *high workload*: The 2-back task was used additionally to the Free Sailing to induce a higher workload while keeping the primary task constant.

3   EEG-Analysis

3.1   Dealing with Artifacts

A preliminary analysis of the data's spatio-spectral content showed that the EEG of some participants was heavily affected by artifacts. This was expected due to the participants being allowed to act naturally. Head and trunk movements were required for the sailing tasks, as the simulator provided a 360° projection.

First, the automatic artifact removal method MARA [22] had been employed, that gives good results in usual EEG datasets. The method is based on a decomposition of the multivariate EEG by the use of an Independent Component Analysis (ICA). The components were classified into artifacts and neuronal components. Then, the cleaned EEG signals were obtained by projecting only the neuronal components back into the sensor space. The classifier that distinguishes between artifactual and neuronal components was trained on a large data base of EEG datasets for which the ICA decomposition was manually annotated. For datasets that contain artifacts unlike those ones contained in the training data base, some of the artifactual components may go undetected. This seemed to be the case for the dataset at hand.

Therefore, we went the tedious way of annotating all ICA components (ICs) manually. This decision between artifactual and neuronal components was based on the following plots: the propagation pattern that corresponds to the IC, the time series of the IC and its power spectral density. Examples of those plots are given in Fig. 4.

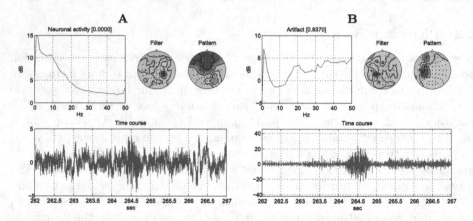

Fig. 4. Inspection of components obtained by ICA: **A** neuronal component: The pattern suggests a left arm motor area origin and shows a smooth dipolar structure. The power spectral density (upper left subplot) has the typical $1/f$ shape with enhanced power around 9.5 Hz, which is the typical frequency of the sensorimotor rhythm. There are no obvious irregularities in the time course. **B** artifactual component: Pattern, spectrum and time course do not look like neuronal activity: the pattern is very focal with no typical spectral $1/f$ shape, has least power in the 10 Hz range and strong power in high frequencies and the time course contains a high frequency burst.

3.2 Results

The grand average (i.e., average across participants) of the spectral analysis of the automatic artifact removal method MARA cleaned signals is shown in

Fig. 5 (2-back task) and Fig. 6 (bow-to-bow task). When comparing the results for individual participants, it became clear that the grand average is only of limited use. The effect of the workload conditions seen in the alpha band varies with respect to the specific frequency range: we observed individual frequencies and topologies at which alpha levels appeared characteristic for the individual participants - also across conditions.

For the *2-back* as a secondary tasks, effects in higher visual alpha can be observed across participants around parietal to occipital electrodes. The effect is contrary to common results in laboratory settings, as the alpha increases with increasing task difficulty. On a single participant level, we find this at an individual frequency of around 10–12 Hz in 6 of 7 participants (subj 1 excluded due to recording error, subj 10 excluded due to obvious task misunderstanding: button press after every stimulus). One participant with seemingly different results shows no effect at these frequencies but contrary signed r^2 at lower alpha (around 9 Hz). A possible explanation to this difference is personal stress we observed on a subjective behavioral level. Unexpectedly, theta is not very relevant except for one participant.

For the *bow-to-bow* condition, the differences are much weaker (note the different scale) and results are more variable in general: the spectra look very noisy and variable across participants. In the grand-average, we find no clearly peaked differences in the spectrum. The lower alpha range shows an increase in power for high workload. For single participants, visual alpha peaks show an effect mostly at lower levels around 7–9 Hz in 6 of 9 while around 10 Hz for 2 participants. These visual alpha peaks are mostly at a frequency 2–3 Hz lower than those of the *2-back* condition and mostly with opposite sign (5 participants). Strong frontal theta is found to be significant in one participant (same as in phase 2), less in others.

4   Classification Analysis

4.1   Aim and Approach

The spectral analysis showed strong artifacts in the data. Apart from noise of the technical devices, there are artifacts from muscle activity (seen in high frequencies, mostly at outer temporal and occipital electrodes) as well as from eye movements (seen in low frequencies at very frontal channels). Furthermore, there may be motion artifacts due to the motion of the electrode cables induced by head and trunk movements.

The muscular and ocular artifacts are indicative of the workload condition for a number of participants and could in principle be used for the workload classifier. However, the goal of this analysis was to estimate the contribution of genuine brain activity to the workload level. Still, we evaluated an approach that works on uncorrected data (R), which can be expected to exploit workload-specific artifacts to some degree, and methods including artifact corrected data which work presumably on brain activity only.

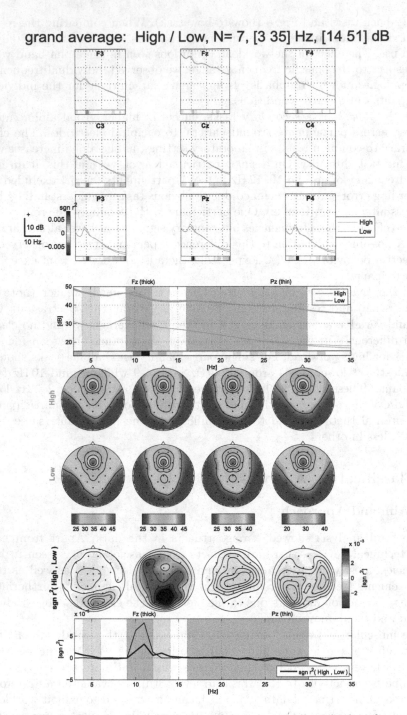

grand average: High / Low, N= 7, [3 35] Hz, [14 51] dB

Fig. 5. Grand average of the spectral analysis of the 2-back task.

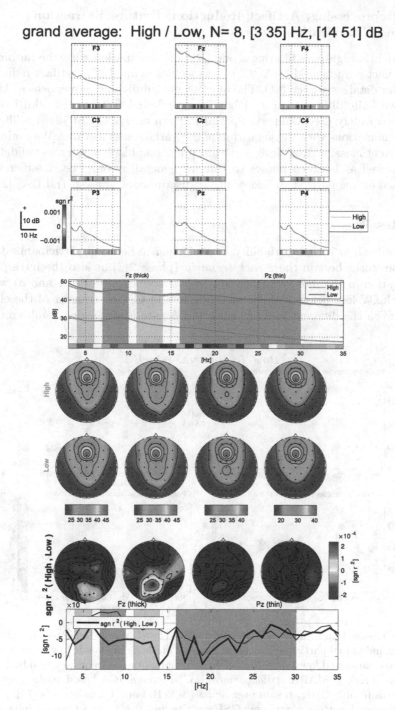

Fig. 6. Grand average of the spectral analysis of the bow-to-bow task.

4.2   Preprocessing, Artifact Reduction, Feature Extraction and Classification

We used 1 Hz high-pass filtering alone (R), in combination with the automatic ICA artifact reduction MARA [22] (C) as well as manual ICA artifact reduction (CM) (for details see Sect. 3.1). The blocks were subdivided into epochs of 1 min. Then, we built different spectral band power based features. In addition, we performed widely used Common Spatial Pattern analysis (CSP) [1] in different band combinations with the logarithm of the variances as features. We evaluated the different classification designs within phases as block-wise cross-validations (CV) as well as between phases to test for generalization. The classifier itself was based on regularized shrinkage linear discriminant analysis (rsLDA) [21].

4.3   Results

The results show a high variability in performance between participants. Classification works best in the *2-back scenario* (phase 2), but also the intra-phase classification in the more complex *bow-to-bow* scenario (phases 1 and 3) works well with CV-loss below 25% for methods **R** and **C**. The transfer of the classifier between the different tasks (*2-back* and *bow-to-bow*) yielded results around

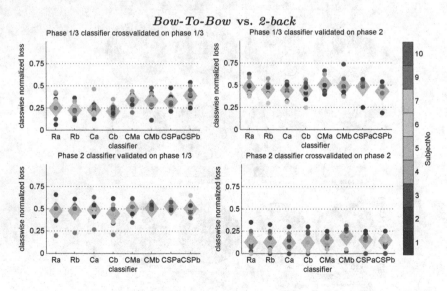

Fig. 7. Classification results: class-wise normalized loss (average indicated by light blue diamond, individual participants colored circles). Methods are labeled by capital letters for preprocessing and lower-case for different combinations of frequency bands: **R** only high-pass (1 Hz), **C** MARA artifact removal, **CM** manual ICA based artifact removal: **a** 1 Hz bins from 1–20 Hz, **b** sum over alpha (8–12 Hz) and theta band (4–7 Hz). CSP common spatial pattern algorithm: **CSPa** alpha and theta band **CSPb** alpha, beta, gamma and theta band. (Color figure online)

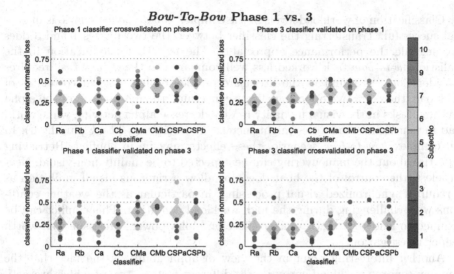

Fig. 8. Classification Results: class-wise normalized loss (average indicated by light blue diamond, individual participants colored circles). Methods are labeled by capital letters for preprocessing and lower-case for different combinations of frequency bands: **R** only high-pass (1 Hz), **C** MARA artifact removal, **CM** manual ICA based artifact removal: **a** 1 Hz bins from 1–20 Hz, **b** sum over alpha (8–12 Hz) and theta band (4–7 Hz). CSP common spatial pattern algorithm: **CSPa** alpha and theta band **CSPb** alpha, beta, gamma and theta band. (Color figure online)

chance level (see Fig. 7), while the transfer of classifiers within the *bow-to-bow* scenario, i.e. between phases 1 and 3, works almost as good as the respective within phase classification (see Fig. 8). On average, the automatically cleaned sums over alpha & theta band (**Cb**) show best results. CSP works comparably in the *2-back* but almost at chance level in the *bow-to-bow* scenario.

5   Discussion

The results of the *2-back* scenario already show the complexity of a physiological index of cognitive workload, when the task is not performed in a constrained laboratory setting, but embedded into a more realistic and complex scenario. The expected increase of the frontal theta oscillation was in general not observed, and the power in the parietal alpha did not decrease as found in most workload studies, but it showed a contrary effect. The alpha effect is consistent with some of the literature on non-visual tasks. The common hypothesis for this ambiguity is that the task-irrelevant visual brain region is actively inhibited in order to focus resources to the relevant non-visual processing. One participant who showed a parieto-occipital alpha decrease might have had a visual strategy to memorize the sequence of numbers - albeit presented auditorily.

Classification of workload levels in the complex *bow-to-bow* scenario is in general successful. Transferring the classifier between the two phases 1 and 3 does not degrade the performance appreciably. The fact that classification in the realistic *bow-to-bow* task worked less well compared to the *2-back* task requires consideration. As found in the literature on electrophysiological correlates of workload, there are two opposing effects concerning the modulation of the alpha rhythm. Tasks in the visual modality mostly decrease alpha activity, while workload in non-visual modalities might increase it (as in our *2-back* paradigm). In the complex *bow-to-bow* scenario, these effects may be in conflict. Retrieving expertise about the maneuvering can be expected to be mainly non-visual. Nevertheless, the control of the boat does not allow a rigorous visual inhibition as it requires synchronized visual processing, in particular as the weather conditions were challenging during the high workload condition. This conflict can be assumed to lead to a much weaker effect on alpha power - an issue well worth deeper investigation.

Another interesting point in the view of applicability is the fact that the complex concept workload encompasses different factors, two of which are *activation* and *resources*. Therefore, a high output of the workload monitor could indicate a strong activation in the sense of an effective focusing of the task at hand (inhibiting task-irrelevant processing). Accordingly, an interpretation of the participant being at the limit of her/his resources might not be adequate.

6   Conclusions

Out-of-the-lab results are not easily transferable to realistic settings, but individual strategy and modality dependent neural activity can be used to adopt the interaction between system and user towards a symbiosis.

Acknowledgments. This research was mainly funded by MARIN, The Netherlands and we want to thank MARIN's Nautical Center, Wageningen for the very kind collaboration. The research leading to these results has also received funding from the European Union Seventh Framework Programme (FP7/2007-2013) under grant agreement no 611570 (MindSee), and by the BMBF (contract 01GQ0850, BFNT).

References

1. Blanchard, G., Blankertz, B.: BCI competition 2003-data set IIa: spatial patterns of self-controlled brain rhythm modulations. IEEE Trans. Biomed. Eng. **51**(6), 1062–1066 (2004)
2. Galin, D., Johnstone, J., Herron, J.: Effects of task difficulty on EEG measures of cerebral engagement. Neuropsychologia **16**(4), 461–472 (1978)
3. Gevins, A., Leong, H., Du, R., Smith, M.E., Le, J., DuRousseau, D., Zhang, J., Libove, J.: Towards measurement of brain function in operational environments. Biol. Psychol. **40**(1–2), 169–186 (1995)
4. Gevins, A., Smith, M.E.: Neurophysiological measures of cognitive workload during human-computer interaction. Theor. Issues Ergon. Sci. **4**(1–2), 113–131 (2003)

5. Gevins, A., Smith, M.E., Leong, H., McEvoy, L., Whitfield, S., Du, R., Rush, G.: Monitoring working memory load during computer-based tasks with EEG pattern recognition methods. Hum. Factors **40**(1), 79–91 (1998)
6. Gundel, A., Wilson, G.F.: Topographical changes in the ongoing EEG related to the difficulty of mental tasks. Brain Topogr. **5**(1), 17–25 (1992)
7. Holm, A., Lukander, K., Korpela, J., Sallinen, M., Muller, K.M.: Estimating brain load from the EEG. Sci. World J. **9**, 639–651 (2009)
8. Kirchner, W.K.: Age differences in short-term retention of rapidly changing information. J. Exp. Psychol. **55**, 352–358 (1958)
9. Klimesch, W., Doppelmayr, M., Schwaiger, J., Auinger, P., Winkler, T.: Paradoxical'alpha synchronization in a memory task. Cogn. Brain Res. **7**(4), 493–501 (1999)
10. Kohlmorgen, J., Dornhege, G., Braun, M., Blankertz, B., Müller, K.-R., Curio, G., Hagemann, K., Bruns, A., Schrauf, M., Kincses, W.: Improving human performance in a real operating environment through real-time mental workload detection. In: Dornhege, G., Millán, J.R., Hinterberger, T., McFarland, D., Müller, K.-R. (eds.) Toward Brain-Computer Interfacing, pp. 409–422. MIT press, Cambridge (2007)
11. Kok, A.: Event-related-potential (ERP) reflections of mental resources: a review and synthesis. Biol. Psychol. **45**(1), 19–56 (1997)
12. Kramer, A.F.: Physiological metrics of mental workload: a review of recent progress. In: Damos, D.L. (ed.) Multiple-Task Performance, pp. 279–328. Taylor & Francis, London (1991)
13. Legewie, H., Simonova, O., Creutzfeldt, O.: EEG changes during performance of various tasks under open-and closed-eyed conditions. Electroencephalogr. Clin. Neurophysiol. **27**(5), 470–479 (1969)
14. Manzey, D.: Determinanten der Aufgabeninterferenz bei Doppeltätigkeiten und ressourcentheoretische Modellvorstellungen in der Kognitiven Psychologie. Deutsche Forschungs- und Versuchsanstalt für Luft- und Raumfahrt (DFVLR), Köln (1988)
15. Manzey, D.: Psychophysiologie mentaler Beanspruchung. In: Rösler, F., (ed.) Ergebnisse und Anwendungen der Psychophysiologie. Enzyklopädie der Psychologie, Göttingen. Hogrefe (1997)
16. Markand, O.N.: Alpha rhythms. J. Clin. Neurophysiol. **7**(2), 163–190 (1990)
17. Pfurtscheller, G., Neuper, C.: Motor imagery and direct brain-computer communication. Proc. IEEE **89**(7), 1123–1134 (2001)
18. Polich, J.: Task difficulty, probability, and inter-stimulus interval as determinants of P300 from auditory stimuli. Electroencephalogr. Clin. Neurophysiol. Evoked Potentials Sect. **68**(4), 311–320 (1987)
19. Pope, A.T., Bogart, E.H., Bartolome, D.S.: Biocybernetic system evaluates indices of operator engagement in automated task. Biol. Psychol. **40**(1), 187–195 (1995)
20. Smith, M.E., Gevins, A., Brown, H., Karnik, A., Du, R., Gevins, A.S.: Monitoring task loading with multivariate EEG measures during complex forms of human-computer interaction. Hum. Factors **43**, 366–380 (2001)
21. Vidaurre, C., Krämer, N., Blankertz, B., Schlögl, A.: Time domain parameters as a feature for EEG-based brain-computer interfaces. Neural Netw. **22**(9), 1313–1319 (2009). Brain-Machine Interface
22. Winkler, I., Haufe, S., Tangermann, M.: Automatic classification of artifactual ICA-components for artifact removal in EEG signals. Behav. Brain Funct. **7**(1), 1–15 (2011)

How Human-Mouse Interaction can Accurately Detect Faked Responses About Identity

Merylin Monaro[1], Francesca Ileana Fugazza[2], Luciano Gamberini[1,2],
and Giuseppe Sartori[1,2(✉)]

[1] Human Inspired Technology Research Centre, University of Padova,
via Luzzati 4, 35122 Padua, Italy
merylin.monaro@phd.unipd.it,
{luciano.gamberini,giuseppe.sartori}@unipd.it
[2] Department of General Psychology, University of Padova,
via Venezia 4, 35131 Padua, Italy
francescaileana.fugazza@studenti.unipd.it

Abstract. Identity verification is nowadays a very sensible issue. In this paper, we proposed a new tool focused on human-mouse interaction to detect fake responses about identity. Experimental results showed that this technique is able to detect fake responses about identities with an accuracy higher than 95%. In addition to a high sensitivity, the described methodology exceeds the limits of the biometric measures currently available for identity verification and the constraints of the traditional lie detection cognitive paradigms. Thanks to the many advantages offered by this technique, its application looks promising especially in field of national and global security as anti-terrorist measure. This paper represents an advancement in the knowledge of symbiotic systems demonstrating that human-machine interaction may be well integrated into security systems.

Keywords: Identity verification · Lie detection · Mouse tracking

1 Introduction

In the last twenty years, the Global terrorism database (Gtd), the most comprehensive and reliable database on terrorism edited by the University of Maryland, has recorded 70.433 acts of terrorism in the world. Considering the frequency of terrorist attacks from 1994, a rapid growth starting from 2007 to date can be noticed [1]. Due to this alarming increment, a great attention has been paid to the measures currently available to improve the security of nations against terrorist threats.

The report of the National Commission on Terrorist Attacks Upon the United States, also known as 9/11 Commission, suggested the introduction of biometric measures within national borders to prevent the entry of people traveling under false identities [2]. In fact, the use of fake identities is an important means for terrorists because they used false passports to facilitate travel in other countries, such as Europe and US countries. Given this direct link between identity theft and terrorism, the identity verification is a very strong issue directly related to both national and global security [3].

L. Gamberini et al. (Eds.): Symbiotic 2016, LNCS 9961, pp. 115–124, 2017.
DOI: 10.1007/978-3-319-57753-1_10

However, the recognition of terrorists using false identities to move from a country to another is not the only practical context in which identity verification is crucial. The identity verification is a key issue for a large number of application domains, such as the security issue for online authentication (e.g., online banking, ecommerce websites) and the use of fake profiles in social networks.

Biometric measures currently available for identity verification exploit physiological or behavioural characteristics such as fingerprints, hand geometry, and retinas to check identity [4]. More recent approaches developed biometric identification systems based on user-pc interaction characteristics, such as keystroke dynamics and mouse dynamics [5, 6].

Nevertheless in the context of terrorism and in other practical domains, these identity check tools are not useful because many of the suspects are unknown and their biometrical characteristics are not included in databases and, therefore, unidentifiable [7]. For this reason, one actual open challenge is to implement a reliable instrument for identity verification that does not require any prior information about the suspect. In other words, an instrument that recognizes the specific user is not helpful to identify terrorists, thus a tool that detects the deception about identity in a more generic way is necessary.

The deception production is a complex psychological process in which cognition plays an important role [8]. During the generation of a false response, the cognitive system does not simply elaborate a statement, but it carries out several executive tasks: it inhibits the *true* statement and, subsequently, it produces a *false* statement [9]. Moreover, the generation of a lie requires to monitor the reaction of the interlocutor and to adjust the behavior congruently to the lie [10]. All these mental operations cause an increase in cognitive load and, generally, a greater cognitive load produces a bad performance in the task the participant is carrying out, in terms of timing and errors [11]. In particular, participants manifest a lengthening of reaction times (RTs) and an increasing in error rate. This phenomenon has been observed by studying the RTs in double choice tasks: the choice between two alternatives becomes slower in the deceptive response than the truthful one [12].

According to the functioning of our cognitive system, behavior-based lie detection tools have been proposed. The most cited are RT-based Concealed Information Test (RT-CIT) [13] and the autobiographical Implicit Association Test (aIAT) [14] that are two memory detection techniques. Based on RT recording, these instruments can detect between two alternative memories presented to the participant in form of words or sentences which is true and which one is false. These techniques have been used also for identity verification, to reveal which of two identities is the real identity of the examinee [15]. However, both RT-CIT and aIAT require that the true identity information is available, while in the real application only the information provided by suspected is obtainable.

As well as RTs are considered reliable behavioral indices of deception, kinematic analysis of hand movements may provide a clue for recognizing deceits [16]. In fact, recently researchers described as a simple hand movement can be used to study the continuous evolution of the mind processes underlying a behavioural response during a computer task [17].

Applying this evidence to the study of lie, Duran, Dale and McNamara published the results of the first work in which hand movements were used to distinguish deceptive responses to the truthful ones [16]. During the task, participants were instruct to answer *yes* or *no* questions about autobiographical information appearing on a screen using the Nintendo Wii controller. Half of the trials required to response truthfully and the other half required a false response. Results interdicted that deceptive responses could be distinguished from truthful ones based on several dynamic indices, such as the overall response time, the motor onset time, the arm movement trajectory, the velocity and the acceleration of the motion.

Hibbeln and colleagues analysed mouse dynamics in an insurance fraud online context, showing that crafty participants had a different mouse usage pattern in comparison to the honest [18]. The same results have been obtained by Valacich et al. that monitored the mouse activity of fair and guilty people while they were compiling an online survey similar to the Concealed Information Test (CIT) [19].

Based on these pioneering studies, in this paper we propose a new method focused on human-mouse interaction to detect fake responses about identity. The described methodology exceeds the limits both of the traditional RT-lie detection paradigms (e.g., RT-CIT and aIAT) and the biometric measures because any previous information about identity is needed. In fact, the lie detection tool is simply built on the information that an unknown suspect declares. In other words, in this paper we demonstrate how human-machine interaction can improve security, creating a symbiotic system between user and security systems.

2 Method

2.1 Participants

40 participants between students and employees of the Department of General Psychology in Padova University volunteered for this experiment. Participants did not receive any compensation from taking part in the study. All participants agreed on the informed consent. The two experimental group were balanced by gender, age and education (truth-tellers: 10 males and 10 females, mean age = 23.4, mean education = 16.9; liars: 10 males and 10 females, mean age = 25.1, mean education = 16.3).

2.2 Experimental Procedure

The experimental task consisted in 50 double-choice questions about identity in which participants answered clicking with the mouse on the correct alternative response on the computer screen. Half of the participants were instructed to lie about their identities, whereas the 20 control participants answered truthfully. Before the task, the 20 liars learned a fake identity profile from an Italian Identity Card, where a photo of the participant was attached. In order to verify that the information was stored, the fake profile in the ID card was recalled for two times, interspersed with a mathematical distracting task. Truth tellers performed a mathematical task and revised their real autobiographical data only once before starting the experiment.

The experiment was implemented and run on a laptop (15.6″) using *MouseTracker* software [20]. Six practice questions preceded the experimental task. Questions appeared centrally in the upper part of the computer screen. The response labels were located one on the right and one on the left upper bound of the screen. Response labels appeared at the same time of the question.

Table 1. The table reported some examples of presented questions to the participants and the possible answers.

Type of question	Example of correct response	Example of incorrect response
Control questions		
Are you female?	Yes	No
Are you male?	No	Yes
Do you have any tattoos?	No	Yes
Do you have pierced ears?	Yes	No
What is your shoe size?	36	42
What is your eye color?	Brown	Blue
How tall are you?	160 cm	190 cm
What is your skin color?	White	Black
Expected questions		
Were you born in April?	Yes	No
Were you born in October?	No	Yes
Do you live in Padova?	Yes	No
Do you live in Napoli?	No	Yes
What is your last name?	Moretti	Greco
What is your year of birth?	1987	1984
What is your city of birth?	Verona	Milano
What is your name?	Sara	Anna
Unexpected questions		
Are there any double letters in your last name?	Yes	No
Do you live in the same region where you were born?	No	Yes
Is your residence city near Abano Terme?	Yes	No
Is your residence city near Saturnia Terme?	No	Yes
How old are you?	28	25
Which is your zodiac sign?	Aries	Capricorn
What is your zip code?	35142	36125
What is the chief town of your born region?	Venezia	Firenze

The half of the questions requested a *yes* or *no* response, while the other requested a response to different labels (e.g., to the question *"Which is your gender?"* possible response labels might be "*male*" "*female*"). Within the entire task, the correct responses, that are the answers congruent with the suspect declarations, were presented for the 50% of trials on right position and for the other 50% on the left. Some examples of the 50 questions included in the experimental task are reported in Table 1.

During the experiment, three different kinds of questions were randomly presented to participants. *Expected questions* were information that has been learned by liars from the fake ID card and explicitly trained during the learning phase (e.g., "*Were you born in 1987?*"), whereas *unexpected questions* derived from this information but were not explicitly rehearsed before the experiment (e.g., "*Are you 29 years old?*"). Finally, *control questions* required a true response both for liars and for truth-tellers because they concerned physical information, which is not possible to hide (e.g., "*Are you female?*"). As reported in literature, the presence of *unexpected questions* has the effect to increase the cognitive load in liars [21]. Whereas for truth-tellers the unexpected information is quickly and easily available even if they are not prepared to those specific questions, liars have to fabricate a new response congruently with the other ones. Because this mental operation requires a greater cognitive effort, liars show in *unexpected questions* a bad performance compared with truth-tellers.

2.3   Collected Measures

During each response, the *MouseTracker* software recorded the following kinematic features:

- *X,Y coordinates over the time* (X_n, Y_n): position of the mouse along the axis over the time. Because each trajectory has a different length, in order to permit averaging and comparison across multiple trials, the *MouseTracker* normalizes each motor response in 101 time frames [20].
- *Velocity over the time* (vX_n, vY_n): velocity of the mouse along the axis over the time.
- *Acceleration over the time* (aX_n, aY_n): acceleration of the mouse along the axis over the time.
- *Initiation time* (IT): time between the appearance of the question and the beginning of the response.
- *Reaction time* (RT): time between the appearance of the question and the end of the response.
- *Maximum deviation* (MD): largest perpendicular distance between the actual trajectory and the ideal trajectory.
- *Area under the curve* (AUC): geometric area between the actual trajectory and the ideal trajectory.
- *Maximum deviation time* (MD-time): time to reach the point of maximum deviation.
- *x-flip*: number of direction reversals along the *x*-axis.
- *y-flip*: number of direction reversals along the *y*-axis.
- *Number of errors*: number of incorrect responses.

For each feature we calculated the mean value within participants for all trials. Finally, we used these values to perform statistical analysis and to build a machine learning classification model.

3   Analysis and Results

3.1   Graphical Observations and Statistics

We graphically compared the performance of the two experimental groups (liars vs truth-tellers), separately for *control*, *expected* and *unexpected questions*. Figure 1 reports the average trajectories for liars and truth-tellers, respectively for *control*, *expected* and *unexpected* questions. Furthermore, the figures below represent the average position of the mouse on *x* and *y*-axis over the time. As it can be noticed, the trajectories of the two experimental groups visually differ especially for the *unexpected questions*, whereas for the *control* and the *expected questions* this difference is not so evident. Considering *unexpected questions*, the truth-teller response shows a more direct trajectory, connecting the starting point with the end-response point. By contrast, liars spend more time moving on *y*-axis in the initial phase of the response and deviate to the selected response with a certain delay compared to truth-tellers.

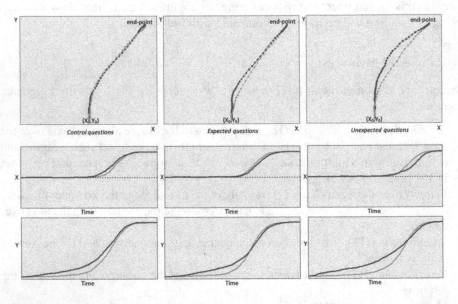

Fig. 1. The panels displayed in the first row report, separately for *control*, *expected* and *unexpected questions*, the average trajectories for liars (red line) and truth-tellers (green line). The panels in second and third row show the average position of the mouse on *x* (second row) and *y*-axis (third row) over the time for liars (red line) and for truth-tellers (green line), respectively for *control* (left panel), *expected* (central panel) and *unexpected questions* (right panel). In other words, these panels represent how the mouse moves along the *x* and *y*-axis during the 101 response time frames. (Color figure online)

In order to confirm whether the difference between liars and truth-tellers trajectories in *unexpected questions* is statistically significant, we run an independent t-test on the collected measures (see Subsect. 2.3). Results showed that liars' responses significantly differ from truth-tellers' ones in AUC ($t = 3.13$, $p < 0.0042$), RT ($t = 3.61$, $p < 0.0042$), and mean velocity along x-axis ($t = -7.62$, $p < 0.0042$). Finally, liars make a higher number of errors compared to truth-tellers ($t = 9.70$, $p < 0.0042$) (to avoid the multiple testing problem the correction of Bonferroni has been apply and the p-value has been set to 0.0042).

Finally, we tested the difference between liars and truth-tellers also for *expected* and *control questions*, confirming that none of the measures considered (see Subsect. 2.3) reach the statistical significance in the independent t-test.

3.2 Machine Learning Models

According to the results, obtained by graphical and statistics observations, we used only *unexpected questions* data to train different machine learning classifiers. The goal is to create a model that is able to predict whether the participant is a liar or a truth-teller, based on the mouse response features. To optimize the accuracy of our model, we perform a feature selection, according to the attribute selection function that is implemented in WEKA software [22]. In particular, we run a ranker analysis [23]: this function uses an attribute/subset evaluator to rank all attributes inserted in the model as predictors. The ranked list of the 12 features considered (see Subsect. 2.3) is the following: errors = 0.83, mean velocity along x-axis = 0.62, AUC = 0.24, RT = 0.23, MD = 0.2, all the other features = 0.00. It can be noticed that the features that show a greater weight for the model, according to the ranker analysis, are the same that reached a significant t-value in the independent t-test (see above). For this reason, we decided to select these four features to implement the classification models.

The classification procedure has been performed using WEKA software [22].

Classification models have been built using a 10-fold cross-validation procedure as implemented in WEKA. Table 2 reports the percentage accuracy values of the different classifiers. It can be noticed that the classification accuracy remains stable across the different classifiers, ranging from 90% to 95%.

Table 2. The table reports the accuracy values in the 10-fold cross-validation for four different ML classifiers: Simple Logistic [24], Support Vector Machine (SVM) [25], Random forest [26] and Naive Bayes [27]. The classification accuracy is reported considering all *unexpected questions*, questions requiring a *yes* or *no* response and questions requiring a response to *different* labels.

Classifier	Accuracy in 10-fold cross validation for all *unexpected questions*	Accuracy in 10-fold cross validation for *unexpected questions* requiring a *yes* or *no* response	Accuracy in 10-fold cross validation for *unexpected questions* requiring a response to *different* labels
Simple Logistic	90%	80%	100%
SVM	95%	77.5%	97.5%
Random Forest	90%	75%	100%
Naive Bayes	95%	67.5%	97.5%

Finally, we separately repeated the classification procedure for the *unexpected questions* that required a *yes* or *no* response and for questions that requested a response to different categories labels (e.g., *"male" "female"*). The percentages of accuracy are reported in Table 2. Results show that, considering only the questions that require a response to different labels, the classification accuracy improves from 2.5% to 10%. In other words, we reach the best classification performance in distinguishing liars from truth-tellers on *unexpected questions* that requested a response to different categories labels.

4   Discussion and Conclusions

In this work, we described a new tool to detect liars about identity. The technique exploits the user-mouse interaction when the suspect is engaged in a computerize task requiring identity information. We tested the method through an experiment involving 40 participants. Half of participants was instructed to declare a fake identity according to a false ID card previously learned. Then, questions about identity information (e.g., name, surname, date of birth, etc.) were presented. Participants clicked with the mouse on the correct response between the two alternatives, according to the identity information that they declared. *Unexpected questions* were introduced to increase the cognitive load in liars. Moreover, we introduced a variability in response labels. In other words, participants did not answer only to fixed *yes* or *no* questions but to different categories questions (e.g., to the question *"How old are you?"* possible response labels might be *"25" "28"*).

The kinematic features of the motor response were collected and used to train different machine learning classifiers.

Responses to unexpected questions are those in which, according both with graphical and statistical observations, liars and truth-tellers show the main difference.

The accuracy, obtained by the classification models in correctly predicting the veracity of the declared identity, is very high, around 95%. Nevertheless, we point out that to confirm the stability of our model and in order to ensure the reproducibility of the data, it will be needed to extend the number of observations included in the training set and to collect a further sample of naïve participants to test the model with an out-of-sample procedure [28].

Results also showed that, considering only *unexpected questions* that required a response to different categories labels, the accuracy improves to 97.5–100%.

Our hypothesis is that the continuous change of the response label categories results in a further increase in cognitive load for liars. In fact, it is possible that using only *yes* or *no* fixed labels, after some trials the label processing becomes partially automated and does not require any mental effort. Conversely, in a task where label categories change away, the true label is often very familiar for truth-tellers. However, the true and the false label are unfamiliar for liars, especially in the case of unexpected questions. For this reason, the liars' response requires more cognitive effort to process labels and implement the correct response. This effort causes a deterioration of the liars' performance and the discrimination between the two experimental groups becomes more accurate. Furthermore, it is possible that the classification accuracy in questions requiring a *yes* or *no* response is lower because liars answer falsely to questions requiring a *yes* response, but they are truthful in answering questions required a *no* response.

In conclusion, this paper represents an advancement in the knowledge of symbiotic interaction demonstrating that human-computer interplay may improve security systems, creating a symbiosis between user and security. This methodology seems to be promising in detecting fake responses about identity for several reasons. In addition to the high accuracy, one of the most innovative advantages of this tool is that it does not requires any knowledge about the real identity of the suspect. Secondly, the classification algorithm exploits a large number of kinematic indices to identify liars, so it is difficult to control via efficient countermeasures all these parameters. Finally, it is cheap both in terms of money and in terms of time for testing. This last feature makes it suitable for large-scale applications, as the control of the international migration flow.

References

1. National Consortium for the Study of Terrorism and Responses to Terrorism (START). Global Terrorism Database [Data file] (2015). http://www.start.umd.edu/gtd
2. National Commission on Terrorist Attacks Upon the United States. http://govinfo.library.unt.edu/911/report/index.htm
3. The University of Texas at Austin (2015). http://news.utexas.edu/2015/12/07/the-direct-link-between-identity-theft-and-terrorism
4. Ashbourn, J.: Biometrics: Advanced Identity Verification: The Complete Guide. Springer, Heidelberg (2000)
5. Shen Teh, P., Beng Jin Teoh A., Yue, S.: A survey of keystroke dynamics biometrics. Sci. World J. **24** (2013)
6. Feher, C., Elovici, Y., Moskovitch, R., Rokach, L., Schclar, A.: User identity verification via mouse dynamics. Inf. Sci. **201**, 19–36 (2012)
7. Sabena, F., Dehghantanha, A., Seddon, A.P.: A review of vulnerabilities in identity management using biometrics. In: Second International Conference on Future Networks, ICFN 2010, Sanya, Hainan, pp. 42–49 (2010)
8. Abe, N.: How the brain shapes deception: an integrated review of the literature. Neuroscientist **17**, 560–574 (2011)
9. Debey, E., De Houwer, J., Verschuere, B.: Lying relies on the truth. Cognition **132**, 324–334 (2014)
10. Gombos, V.A.: The cognition of deception: the role of executive processes in producing lies. Genet. Soc. Gen. Psychol. Monograhs **132**, 197–214 (2006)
11. Blandon-Gitlin, I., Fenn, E., Masip, J., Yoo, A.H.: Cognitive-load approaches to detect deception: searching for cognitive mechanisms. Trends Cogn. Sci. **18**(9), 441–444 (2014)
12. Sheridan, M.R., Flowers, K.A.: Reaction times and deception - the lying constant. Int. J. Psychol. Stud. **2**(2), 41–51 (2010)
13. Kleinberg, B., Verschuere, B.: Memory detection 2.0: the first web-based memory detection test. PLoS ONE **10**(4), e0118715 (2015)
14. Sartori, G., Agosta, S., Zogmaister, C., Ferrara, S.D., Castiello, U.: How to accurately detect autobiographical events. Psychol. Sci. **19**(8), 772–780 (2008)
15. Verschuere, B., Kleinberg, B.: ID-check: online concealed information test reveals true identity. J. Forensic Sci. **61**, S237 (2015)

16. Duran, N., Dale, R., McNamara, D.S.: The action dynamics of overcoming the truth. Psychon. Bull. Rev. **17**(4), 486–491 (2010)
17. Freeman, J.B., Dale, R., Farmer, T.A.: Hand in motion reveals mind in motion. Front. Psychol. **2**, 59 (2011)
18. Hibbeln, M., Jenkins, J., Schneider, C., Valacich, J., Weinmann, M.: Investigating the effect of fraud on mouse usage in human-computer interactions. In: International Conference on Information Systems, ICIS 2014 (2014)
19. Valacich, J.S., Jenkins, J.L., Nunamaker, Jr., J.F., Hariri, S., Howie, J.: Identifying insider threats through monitoring mouse movements in concealed information tests. In: Hawaii International Conference on System Sciences. Deception Detection Symposium (2013)
20. Freeman, J.B., Ambady, N.: MouseTracker: software for studying real-time mental processing using a computer mouse-tracking method. Behav. Res. Meth. **42**, 226–241 (2010)
21. Lancaster, G.L.J., Vrij, A., Hope, L., Waller, B.: Sorting the liars from the truth tellers: the benefits of asking unanticipated questions on lie detection. Appl. Cogn. Psychol. **27**, 107–114 (2013)
22. Hall, M., Frank, E., Holmes, G., Pfahringer, B., Reutemann, P., Witten, I.H.: The WEKA data mining software: an update. ACM SIGKDD Explor. Newsl. **11**(1), 10–18 (2009)
23. Hall, M., Holmes, G.: Benchmarking attribute selection techniques for discrete class data mining. IEEE Trans. Knowl. Data Eng. **15**(6), 1437–1447 (2003)
24. Landwehr, N., Hall, M., Frank, E.: Logistic model trees. Mach. Learn. **95**(1–2), 161–205 (2005)
25. Keerthi, S.S., Shevade, S.K., Bhattacharyya, C., Murthy, K.R.K.: Improvements to Platt's SMO algorithm for SVM classifier design. Neural Comput. **13**(3), 637–649 (2001)
26. Breiman, L.: Random forests. Mach. Learn. **45**(1), 5–32 (2001)
27. John, G.H., Langley, P.: Estimating continuous distributions in Bayesian classifiers. In: Eleventh Conference on Uncertainty in Artificial Intelligence, San Mateo, pp. 338–345 (1995)
28. Dwork, C., et al.: The reusable holdout: preserving validity in adaptive data analysis. Science **349**, 636–638 (2015)

Prediction of Difficulty Levels in Video Games from Ongoing EEG

Laura Naumann[1,2(✉)], Matthias Schultze-Kraft[3,4], Sven Dähne[2,5],
and Benjamin Blankertz[3,4]

[1] Bernstein Center for Computational Neuroscience Berlin, Berlin, Germany
laura-bella.naumann@bccn-berlin.de
[2] Berlin Big Data Center, Berlin, Germany
[3] Bernstein Focus: Neurotechnology, Berlin, Germany
[4] Neurotechnology Group, Technische Universität Berlin, Berlin, Germany
[5] Machine Learning Group, Technische Universität Berlin, Berlin, Germany

Abstract. Real-time assessment of mental workload from EEG plays an important role in enhancing symbiotic interaction of human operators in immersive environments. In this study we thus aimed at predicting the difficulty level of a video game a person is playing at a particular moment from the ongoing EEG activity. Therefore, we made use of power modulations in the theta (4–7 Hz) and alpha (8–13 Hz) frequency bands of the EEG which are known to reflect cognitive workload. Since the goal was to predict from multiple difficulty levels, established binary classification approaches are futile. Here, we employ a novel spatial filtering method (SPoC) that finds spatial filters such that their corresponding bandpower dynamics maximally covary with a given target variable, in this case the difficulty level. EEG was recorded from 6 participants playing a modified Tetris game at 10 different difficulty levels. We found that our approach predicted the levels with high accuracy, yielding a mean prediction error of less than one level.

Keywords: BCI · Cognitive workload · Video games · EEG · Machine learning · Spatial filtering

1 Introduction

While the original and predominant goal of brain-computer interfaces (BCIs) has been to provide a channel for communication and control [1], in recent years BCI research has expanded towards applications that aim for the detection of covert mental states [2], with one focus lying on the assessment of *cognitive workload*. A reliable assessment of cognitive workload from EEG has been suggested as a means for enhancing human-machine interaction in everyday environments [3] and is thus an endeavor that fosters the development of future symbiotic systems.

Typical EEG estimators of workload are based on the fact that changes in workload are associated with modulations in the power of oscillatory activity in particular frequency bands of the EEG, the most prominent ones being theta

© The Author(s) 2017
L. Gamberini et al. (Eds.): Symbiotic 2016, LNCS 9961, pp. 125–136, 2017.
DOI: 10.1007/978-3-319-57753-1_11

(4–7 Hz) and alpha (8–13 Hz). Theta power has been shown to be positively correlated with workload, most notably over frontal regions, whereas alpha power is typically found to be negatively correlated with workload, in particular over parietal regions [4,5]. In typical BCI studies that aim for workload assessment, the experimental paradigm introduces two conditions which induce two levels of workload, e.g. low and high [6,7]. This represents a classical classification setting where common practice is to train a linear classifier on EEG features using the binary labels. A well-established approach for the extraction of EEG features in this setting is the Common Spatial Patterns (CSP) analysis [8] which finds spatial filters that maximize the power contrast between the two classes and has become one of the corner stones of sensorimotor rhythm based BCIs.

In this study, we aimed at predicting the difficulty level of a video game that participants were playing from the ongoing EEG. In a typical video game that requires continuous mental and visuomotor effort, an increase of difficulty is expected to increase the player's cognitive workload. Therefore, it seems obvious to employ a BCI that uses workload induced power modulations of the theta and alpha frequency band as neurophysiological markers for prediction. However, if the goal is to predict from multiple difficulty levels, we leave the regime of binary classification, thus foiling the use of CSP as a method for extracting workload induced power modulations. Here, we employ a novel method called the Source Power Co-Modulation (SPoC) analysis that finds spatial filters such that their corresponding bandpower dynamics maximally covary with a given target variable [9], in this case the difficulty level. A recent study that employed a computer game-like experimental task, demonstrated that SPoC can be used to detect workload states from the EEG with high accuracy [10]. In that study, the task induced two levels of workload and the participant's error rate was considered an indirect measure of workload und thus used as a continuous target variable for SPoC. In this study, we decided to directly use multiple difficulty levels in a video game from a predefined continuum as target. A suitable candidate game for the proposed experiment is the classic Tetris, because the game's difficulty can be easily adjusted by changing the falling velocity of the items. In the conducted experiment, participants played the game several times while EEG data were recorded. In a subsequent analysis, we first selected two crucial model parameters for SPoC and finally evaluated our approach for the prediction of difficulty levels in a cross-validation.

2   Methods

2.1   The Experiment

Six healthy participants (4 female) were engaged in the experiment. Recruited participants were lab members or friends, who gave their informed oral and written consent and did not receive monetary compensation. The average age of the participants was 24 years with a standard deviation of 1.5 years, all of them had normal or corrected to normal vision and previous experience with EEG recordings. Participants were seated in front of a computer monitor and asked to play a Tetris clone[1] with their right hand using the arrow keys of a keyboard (Fig. 1a). The game was implemented in the Python package pygame and modified as follows:

1. The current score, the options to restart, pause or quit and the preview of the next item were removed
2. If the blocks reached the top of the field, all blocks from the top half of the field were removed, as shown in Fig. 1b
3. The fast-drop function of the classic Tetris was disabled

Modification 1 aimed to minimize eye movements caused by distracting objects on the screen. The purpose of modification 2 was to prevent the premature end of the game that normally occurs when the top of the field is reached, and modification 3 was implemented to compensate differences in the players performance and strategies, thus keeping the difficulty within one level constant across participants.

The experiment was structured as follows: Each participant played a total of 9 games with 10 min each. Every game consisted of 10 consecutive 60-second blocks, of which each was assigned one of 10 predefined difficulty levels. In games 1, 4 and 7 the levels increased gradually with every block, while in the remaining games the assignment was randomly permuted. The difficulty of a level was defined by the items' falling velocity: In level 1 the velocity was such that it required falling objects 10 s to reach the bottom of the game screen, while in level 10 this time was 2.5 s. The speed increase across levels was linear. A scoring system was implemented where the points for canceling a line are proportional to the level number and getting the field reduced takes points away. The score was presented to the player at the end of each game (Fig. 1c).

To motivate an active participation in the game, the player with the highest score was rewarded a small price. Apart from that, participation in the experiment was voluntary and participants received no further compensation.

2.2 Data Acqusition and Preprocessing

EEG data was recorded at 1000 Hz using BrainAmp amplifiers and a 32 electrode Fast'n'Easy Cap (Brain Products GmbH, Gilching, Germany) and referenced to an electrode positioned at the FCz electrode location. Furthermore, an electrooculogram (EOG) electrode was placed under the right eye. During recording, markers were sent via a parallel port to record the change to a different level of difficulty.

Before the analysis, the continuous EEG data was high-pass filtered at 1 Hz and subsequently segmented into epochs of 50 s length, starting 10 s after the onset of a new level indicated by the level markers. By discarding the first 10 s of each difficulty level, we aimed at mitigating possible transition effects. The experimental tasks involved persistent movement of the eyes and thus the recorded data was expected to contain ocular artifacts. Therefore, horizontal and vertical

---

[1] http://pygame.org/project-yayatc-1647-.html.

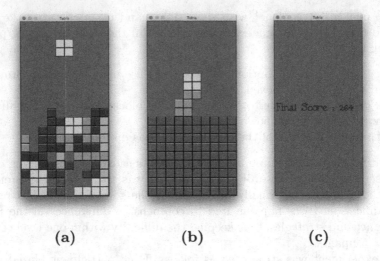

(a)   **(b)**   **(c)**

Fig. 1. Snapshots from the modified Tetris game used as a task. (a) Ongoing game with random items falling from the top. (b) Reduction of the field after reaching the top. (c) The score is displayed at the end of every game.

eye movements were estimated by means of the difference of electrodes *F7* and *F8* and the difference between electrode *Fp2* and the EOG electrode, respectively. The estimated contribution of these combined signals to all remaining channels was removed using linear regression. The four electrodes were excluded from all further analyses. For symmetry reasons, electrode *Fp1* was also removed since it showed very high synchronization with *Fp2*. Remaining artifacts were eliminated by rejecting single epochs based on an excess variance criterion. Finally, the epochs were band-pass filtered in different frequency bands within the theta and alpha frequency range (see Fig. 2).

2.3 Source Power Co-modulation (SPoC) Analysis

The preprocessed data was analysed using the SPoC analysis proposed by Dähne et al. [9]. SPoC optimizes a set of spatial filters **w** based on a presumed covariation between band power dynamics and an external target signal, which in the present study corresponds to the level of difficulty. Let the variable z denote the mean-free target signal and let $\mathbf{x}_f(t)$ denote the EEG signal band-pass filtered in the frequency f. Then the time-resolved component bandpower can be expressed in terms of the spatial filter **w** by computing the variance in consecutive time epochs, indexed by e, as

$$\phi_f(e) \approx \mathrm{Var}[\mathbf{w}^\top \mathbf{x}_f(t)] = \mathbf{w}^\top \mathbf{C}_f(e)\mathbf{w}\,, \tag{1}$$

where $\mathbf{C}_f(e)$ denotes the covariance matrix of the bandpass filtered data within the eth epoch. SPoC then extracts the K best spatial filters solving the optimization problem

$$\min_{\mathbf{w}} \mathrm{Cov}[\phi_f(e), z(e)] = \min_{\mathbf{w}} \mathbf{w}^\top \langle \mathbf{C}_f(e) z(e) \rangle \mathbf{w} \qquad (2)$$

under the constraint that extracted time courses have unit variance and are mutually decorrelated. The optimization problem can be expressed as a generalized eigenvalue problem that can be solved efficiently using standard linear algebra libraries[2].

2.4 Level Prediction via Regression

Having extracted the spatial filters with SPoC, the log-var features corresponding to filters $i \in [1, \ldots, K]$ from frequency bands $f \in [\theta, \alpha]$ are eventually combined by means of *linear regression* into a single predictive variable. Both the specific θ and α frequency bands and the number K of SPoC components used for the prediction are important parameters of the method that have to be determined by means of validation. In order to prevent overfitting, we determined the prediction performance in a cross-validation, where only the training set is used to derive and combine the SPoC components and the correlation to the true levels is calculated subsequently on the test dataset alone. To account for potential non-stationarities in the EEG data, the *leave-one-block-out* procedure was used for validation with every full Tetris game being one block. All preprocessing and analysis steps were conducted using the BBCI toolbox[3] for MATLAB.

3 Results

3.1 Optimal Frequency Bands

As a first step, we aimed to determine the optimal theta and alpha frequency band. Since inter-individual differences in the frequency range of the alpha and theta band are expected, the bands rendering the best performance were determined for every participant individually. For that purpose a sweep over frequency bands ranging from around 3 to 14 Hz using only one SPoC component was performed. The width of the bands scaled logarithmically with the frequency to obtain a higher resolution for lower frequencies. Figure 2 shows the correlation of predicted with the true levels for every participant as a function of frequency band. While for participants 1 and 6 the band that yields the best prediction is in the alpha range, for participants 3 to 5 the best prediction is achieved in the theta range. Interestingly, a decline of correlation can be observed for the 6.7–9.5 Hz band, which comprises the transition between the alpha and theta range. For participant 2, a first analysis showed very poor correlations across all frequencies. A closer inspection of the bandpower of the data projected onto the first three SPoC components over the time revealed that three outliers that were not detected by the artifact rejection procedure during the preprocessing

---

[2] https://github.com/svendaehne/matlab_SPoC/releases/latest.
[3] https://github.com/bbci/bbci_public.

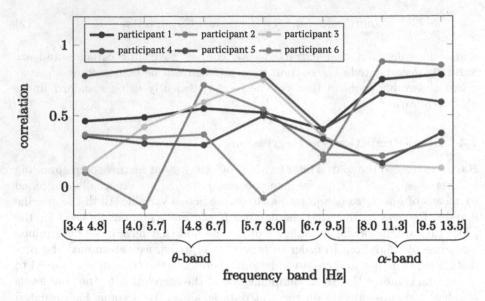

Fig. 2. Frequency sweep with SPoC. Shown is, for each participant individually, the correlation between true levels and predictions as a function of frequency band used for SPoC analysis with one output component. (Color figure online)

strongly dominated the SPoC filters. After removing the epochs corresponding to these outliers, correlations comparable to those of other participants were obtained (Fig. 2, green line). From the results of every participant, the alpha and theta frequency bands with the highest prediction performance were selected for further analyses.

3.2 Number of SPoC Components

For both selected theta and alpha bands, the SPoC method returns a set of components. To determine how many of those are sufficient to yield a high prediction performance for all participants, the cross-validated correlation averaged over all individuals was computed for increasing number of SPoC components used for the prediction. The results on the training and test set are shown in Fig. 3. For one component, the mean correlation is already above 0.8 but shows a high variability. When two components are used, the correlation increases to about 0.85 but stays more or less constant for higher numbers. The mean correlation on the training set indicates overfitting for more then three SPoC features and hence the number of components for the further analysis was set to three.

3.3 Interpretation of Components

We next investigated whether the components found by SPoC are of cortical origin or whether they stem from movement or residual ocular artifacts.

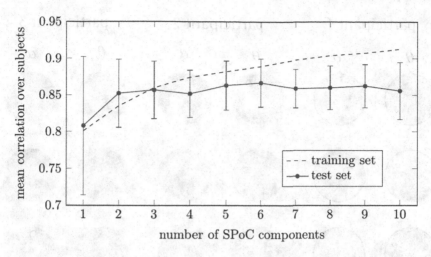

Fig. 3. Crossvalidated correlation as function of the number of SPoC components, averaged over all participants. The standard error is shown with bars for the test set.

For this, the activation patterns corresponding to the spatial filters from the SPoC method were examined (Fig. 4). We found that all investigated patterns are physiologically plausible and show none of the characteristics of patterns related to EOG or electromyogram (EMG) activity. When examining SPoC components in the theta range, for each participant at least one component shows a characteristic theta mid-frontal component (e.g. component 2 for participant 1, and component 1 for participant 2). Regarding the patterns in the alpha range, we find that for many participants SPoC found components with a clear lateralization (e.g. components 1 and 2 for participant 1, and component 1 for participant 6), and components with a centro-parietal topology (e.g. component 2 for both participants 3 and 6).

3.4 Level Predictions

For each participant individually, we evaluated our approach for difficulty level prediction using the optimal, participant-specific theta and alpha frequency bands and three SPoC components. The single and grand average predicted levels as a function of true levels are illustrated in Fig. 5. This qualitative assessment shows that predictions roughly cover the levels from 1 to 10. While the mean across participants indeed shows a monotonic increase with the true levels, for single participants this does not hold in some cases when comparing neighboring levels. Nonetheless, the relationship between the predicted and true levels appears to be clearly linear.

Next, we conducted a quantitative evaluation of prediction performance using three different measures between the predicted and the true levels: (i) The Spearman correlation, (ii) the Pearson correlation, and (iii) the Root Mean Squared Error (RMSE). While the Pearson correlation assumes a linear relation between

participant 1

θ α

participant 2

θ α

participant 3

θ α

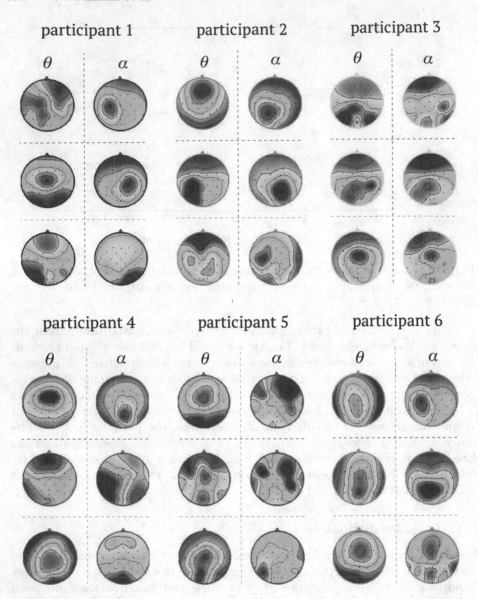

participant 4

θ α

participant 5

θ α

participant 6

θ α

Fig. 4. Spatial activation patterns corresponding to the spatial filters found by SPoC for all six participants. For each person, the left and right columns show the activation patterns for the optimal theta (θ) and alpha (α) band, respectively, and ordered from best to third best, from top to bottom.

the two variables, the Spearman correlation relaxes this assumption and assesses how well their relation is described by any monotonic function. The RMSE allows to estimate how far off a prediction is in units of levels. The mean of the three measures, as well as the grand average are shown in Table 1. Correlations between

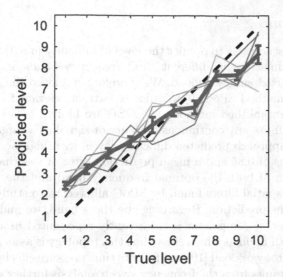

Fig. 5. Prediction of difficulty levels averaged across all games, for single participants (light colors) and grand average and standard error (blue). The dashed line indicates a perfect prediction. (Color figure online)

predicted and true level are statistically significant for all participants as revealed by a permutation analysis with 250 repetitions at a significance level of 0.01. No considerable difference was found between the two correlation measures, corroborating the linearity of the relationship between predicted and true levels. Using the RMSE as a measure finally shows that across all participants and levels, our approach yields predictions that are, on average, about two thirds of a level off the true level.

Table 1. Prediction of difficulty level for single participants, assessed with three measures between predicted and true levels: Pearson correlation, Spearman correlation and RMSE. The last row shows the average across participants and the standard error.

Participant	Pearson correlation	Spearman correlation	RMSE (in levels)
1	0.90	0.90	0.62
2	0.81	0.81	0.78
3	0.84	0.85	0.63
4	0.82	0.83	0.69
5	0.82	0.85	0.75
6	0.89	0.91	0.55
Mean	0.85 ± 0.02	0.86 ± 0.02	0.67 ± 0.04

4   Discussion

The goal of this study was to predict the level of difficulty in a Tetris video game from power modulations in different EEG frequency bands associated with a change in the participants workload. We therefore employed the state-of-the-art spatial filtering method SPoC [9] in order to extract relevant features from the EEG. Whereas established methods like CSP are limited to settings with two classes, SPoC can use any continuous measure or signal as a target variable. We found that our approach predicted difficulty levels with high accuracy, yielding mean correlations of 0.85 and a mean prediction error of less than one level.

An inspection of both the optimal frequency band and the patterns corresponding to the spatial filters found by SPoC allowed us to study which signals contributed to the prediction. Regarding the theta band, we find that the characteristic mid-frontal component is consistently represented in all participants. This is in line with findings which show that this topology is associated both with changes in operator workload [10] and reflects time pressure effects on visuomotor tasks [11]. The results from the frequency sweep analysis further suggest that for participants 1 and 6 alpha power modulations had higher predictive value than in the theta band. Interestingly, for those two participants SPoC found alpha band components that where lateralized over motor regions. Thus, for participants 1 and 2 the contribution to the prediction from the alpha band presumably reflected modulations of the sensorimotor rhythm (SMR) caused by increasing motor demands during high difficulty levels and were thus not directly related to cognitive workload. We therefore repeated our analysis twice, one time using only theta band components and one time using only alpha band components. We found that while in the theta-only analysis a mean correlation of 0.79 ± 0.04 was achieved, which was lower but still comparable to the dual-band case, in the alpha-only analysis the mean correlation dropped considerably to 0.63 ± 0.10 and was not significant for all participants as revealed by a permutation analysis.

A conspicuous observation in the predicted levels in Fig. 5 is that low difficulty levels tend to be overestimated, while high level tend to be underestimated. Thus, the ability of our model to generalize seems to depend on where the levels lie within the continuum of difficulty. Furthermore, it is worth noting that the participants did not practice the Tetris game before the experiment and there was no individual adaptation of the minimal and maximal difficulty level. Such a calibration could ensure a more constant contrast of gaming experience across participants and thus allow for a better comparability.

Our approach allows for a continuous measurement from ongoing EEG activity without intervening with the participants' engagement with the video game. This is in contrast to alternative approaches that rely on the evocation of event-related potentials by means of secondary stimuli [12]. Our approach can furthermore be extended to online application e.g. for adaptive learning systems to adjust progress and presentation of material. With this study we demonstrated the use of novel machine learning techniques for an EEG-based assessment of mental states, thus advancing the endeavor to enhance the symbiotic interaction between human operators and machines.

Acknowledgements. The research leading to these results has received funding from the European Union Seventh Framework Programme (FP7/2007-2013) under grant agreement no 611570 (MindSee), and in part by the BMBF (contract 01GQ0850, BFNT).

References

1. Dornhege, G., del R. Millán, J., Hinterberger, T., McFarland, D.J., Müller, K.-R.: Toward Brain-Computer Interfacing. MIT Press, Cambridge (2007)
2. Blankertz, B., Tangermann, M., Vidaurre, C., Fazli, S., Sannelli, C., Haufe, S., Maeder, C., Ramsey, L.E., Sturm, I., Curio, G., Müller, K.-R.: The Berlin brain-computer interface: non-medical uses of BCI technology. Front. Neurosci. **4**, 198 (2010)
3. Parasuraman, R., Wilson, G.F.: Putting the brain to work: neuroergonomics past, present, and future. Hum. Factors **50**(3), 468–474 (2008)
4. Holm, A., Lukander, K., Korpela, J., Sallinen, M., Müller, K.M.I.: Estimating brain load from the EEG. Sci. World J. **9**, 639–651 (2009)
5. Gevins, A., Smith, M.E.: Neurophysiological measures of cognitive workload during human-computer interaction. Theor. Issues Ergon. Sci. **4**, 113–131 (2003)
6. Kohlmorgen, J., Dornhege, G., Braun, M., Hinterberger, T., McFarland, D., Müller K.-R.: Improving human performance in a real operating environment through real-time mental workload detection. In: Dornhege, G., del R. Millán, J., Hinterberger, T., McFarland, T.D., Müller, K.-R. (eds.), Toward Brain-Computer Interfacing, pp. 409–422. MIT press, Cambridge, MA (2007)
7. Dijksterhuis, C., de Waard, D., Brookhuis, K., Mulder, B., de Jong, R.: Classifying visuomotor workload in a driving simulator using subject specific spatial brain patterns. Front. Neurosci. **7** (2013)
8. Blankertz, B., Tomioka, R., Lemm, S., Kawanabe, M., Müller, K.-R.: Optimizing spatial filters for robust EEG single-trial analysis. IEEE Signal Proc. Mag. **25**, 41–56 (2008)
9. Dähne, S., Meinecke, F.C., Haufe, S., Höhne, J., Tangermann, M., Müller, K.-R., Nikulin, V.V.: SPoC: a novel framework for relating the amplitude of neuronal oscillations to behaviorally relevant parameters. NeuroImage **86**, 111–122 (2014)
10. Schultze-Kraft, M., Dähne, S., Gugler, M., Curio, G., Blankertz, B.: Unsupervised classification of operator workload from brain signals. J. Neural Eng. **13**, 036008 (2016)
11. Slobounov, S.M., Fukada, K., Simon, R., Rearick, M., Ray, W.: Neurophysiological and behavioral indices of time pressure effects on visuomotor task performance. Cognitive Brain Res. **9**, 287–298 (2000)
12. Allison, B.Z., Polich, J.: Workload assessment of computer gaming using a single-stimulus event-related potential paradigm. Biol. Psychol. **77**, 277–283 (2008)

Investigating Tactile Stimulation in Symbiotic Systems

Valeria Orso[1](✉), Renato Mazza[1], Luciano Gamberini[1],
Ann Morrison[2], and Walther Jensen[2]

[1] Human Inspired Technologies Research Centre, Padua University, Padua, Italy
{valeria.orso,luciano.gamberini}@unipd.it,
renatomazza.89@gmail.com
[2] Department of Architecture Design and Media Technology,
Aalborg University, Aalborg, Denmark
{morrison,bwsj}@create.aau.dk

Abstract. The core characteristics of tactile stimuli, i.e., recognition reliability and tolerance to ambient interference, make them an ideal candidate to be integrated into a symbiotic system. The selection of the appropriate stimulation is indeed important in order not to hinder the interaction from the user's perspective. Here we present the process of selecting the most adequate tactile stimulation delivered by a tactile vest while users were engaged in an absorbing activity, namely playing a video-game. A total of 20 participants (mean age 24.78; $SD = 1.57$) were involved. Among the eight tactile stimuli selected, we found that the most frequently chosen stimulus was the one stimulating the back of the participant from the upper to the lower area.

Keywords: Wearable device · Tactile stimulation · Symbiotic system

1 Introduction

Tactile interfaces take advantage of the sense of touch, particularly stimulating mechanoreceptors in the skin, to deliver feedbacks to the user [1, 2]. Tactile displays have proved to be an effective and powerful means for communicating information to users, even when they are already engaged in another activity (e.g., working) users can reliably comprehend messages enclosed in the tactile mode [3, 4]. Given the size of the actuators, tactile displays are usually implemented as wearable computers [5], i.e., fully functional and self-contained electronic devices to be worn and allowing the user to have constant access to information [6]. As already noted by [6], wearable computers are an ideal component of symbiotic systems (i.e., systems that record and interpret a user's cognitive and affective states and respond accordingly), given their ubiquitous and portable nature.

The integration of tactile displays in symbiotic systems could enhance the interaction between the user and the system. Differently from visual or acoustic feedback, tactile stimulations are reliable, because they are tolerant to ambient interference [7]. Furthermore, tactile stimuli require less attentional resources to be processed and lead to natural and fast responses [7, 8]. In sum, a symbiotic system including tactile

© The Author(s) 2017
L. Gamberini et al. (Eds.): Symbiotic 2016, LNCS 9961, pp. 137–142, 2017.
DOI: 10.1007/978-3-319-57753-1_12

stimulations could deliver subtle and unobtrusive feedbacks to the user, thus allowing him/her to keep the interaction focus on the environment [2]. Nevertheless, a proper selection of the tactile stimuli is needed, since the delivery of annoying stimulation could instead disturb and distract the user.

The experiment presented here aimed at identifying the most suitable tactile stimuli delivered through a tactile vest while the user was engaged in an involving activity, namely playing a video-game. In addition, we tested if the preferences emerged were consistent during the entire experimental session. The method employed was devised and comprised both objective data from users' interaction and subjective data from interviews.

2   Equipment

The tactile vest was designed to produce vibrotactile sensations resembling the touch patterns made by kinesiologist-neurophysiologists to activate or calm down a person [9]. The vest is composed of two layers: the inner layer holds 44 actuators and the outer layer keeps the actuators tight to the wearer's skin [9]. All actuators are attached through moveable Velcro patches to adjust their position according to different body sizes (Fig. 1). The vest is connected over Bluetooth with an Android tablet (Nvidia Shield Tablet K1) and a dedicated application was developed to activate the tactile stimuli.

We selected eight of the patterns that prior results [9] had shown either activated or calmed vest wearers. The stimuli were designed with overlapping transitions to create a smooth flowing sensation [9]. Details for each stimulus can be found in Table 1.

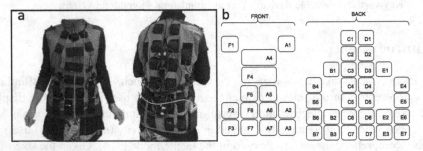

Fig. 1. The tactile vest. (a) A frontal (left) and rear (right) view of the inner layer of the tactile vest. The black male patches hold the actuators tight against the female patches on the vest. (b) A schematic representation of the actuators placement.

3   Experimental Procedure and Metrics

The user was first debriefed on the overall procedure and the goals of the activity. Then s/he signed an informed consent form. The participant wore the tactile vest, sat at the desk and then the training phase started. The experimenter activated all the different tactile

Table 1. A description of the stimuli selected. The pattern sequence of the actuators activated, the duration of activation of each pattern, the duration of the overlapping transition and the amplitude of the vibration.

Stimulus	Pattern sequence	Duration	Overlap	Amplitude
#1	[C7, D7] [C6, D6] [C5, D5] [C4, D4] [C2, D2] [C1, D1]	350	175	100%
#2	[B2, E2] [B2, B3, E2, E3] [B3, E3]	450	175	100%
#3	A3 [F1, A1] [C1, D1, B1, E1] [C2, D2] [C3, D3] [C4, D4] [C5, E5] [C6, D6] [C7, D7] [C6, D6] [C5, D5] [C4, D4] [C3, D3] [C2, D2] [C1, D1]	350	175	85%
#4	[C6, C7, D6, C7] [B6, B7, E6, E7] [F2, F3, A2, A3] [F6, F7, A6, A7] [F6, A6] [F6, F7, A6, A7] [F2, F3, A2, A3] [B6, B7, E6, E7] [B2, B3, E2, E3] [C6, C7, D6, D7]	400	100	100%
#5	A4 [F1, A1] [C1, D1, B1, E1] [C2, D2] [C3, D3] [C4, D4] [C5, D5] [C6, D6] [C7, D7]	500	400	85%
#6	A4 [F1, A1] [C1, D1, B1, E1] [C2, D2] [C3, D3] [C4, D4] [C5, D5] [C4, D4] [C3, D3] [C2, D2] [C1, D1]	500	400	85%
#7	[F1, A1] [F1, A1] [A4] [A4] [] [F1, A1] [A4] [A4]	500	200	85%
#8	[F1, A1] [F1, A1] [A4] [A4] [F1, A1] [F1, A1] [A4] [A4] [F1, A1] [F1, A1]	500	200	85%

stimuli while the user started to play the video game using a desktop PC (21″ monitor) and the computer mouse, in order to make him/her familiar with the task, for an approximate duration of 4 min. After that, the actual experimental session started and lasted about 8 min. During the experimental trail the user was asked to play a popular video-game called Puzzle-Bubble[1] and to activate the tactile stimuli s/he preferred at his/her will by tapping on the tablet paired with the tactile vest. After the experimental session ended, participants answered a brief interview.

A total of 20 people volunteered for the study, 6 of them were male. The mean age of the sample was 24.78 years old (SD = 1.57). Participants were recruited by word of mouth and only one of them had never played Puzzle Bubble before. None of them reported to be a regular video-game player. Participants received no compensation for taking part in the study.

---

[1] The video-game was selected in a preliminary test. The goal of the game is to clear all the bubbles from the board by shooting one colored bubble at a time. Every time the bubble shot hits a group of three or more bubbles of the same color, the group of bubbles hit disappear.

140   V. Orso et al.

4 Results

Users' preferences for the different tactile stimuli can be divided in three temporal intervals, each lasting about 4 min. The first interval corresponded with the training phase; the second interval corresponded to the first half of the experimental session and the third one coincided with the second half of the experimental trail. The data logged during the training were excluded from the analysis. For the first and second temporal intervals of the experimental session, we computed the percentage of times each tactile stimulus was chosen and then compared it against the expected frequency if users chose that stimulus randomly, i.e., 12.5%, through a one-sample t-test.

Considering the first temporal interval, we found that the stimulus participants chose the most was #3, t19 = 2.6 p = .017 (M = 19.81; SD = 12.54). The analysis also showed that there were two stimuli that participants chose significantly less often than the expected frequency. One was #1, t19 = 3.43 p = .003 (M = 6.9; SD = 7.29); while the other one was #5, t19 = 2.9 p = .007 (M = 7.17; SD = 7.94). The rate with which the other stimuli were chosen did not significantly differ form the expected choice rate, detailed values are reported in Table 2.

Regarding the second temporal interval considered, we found that Stimuli #1 and #5 were again chosen to a significantly lower rate than expected, respectively t19 = 3.31 p = .004 (M = 6.51; SD = 8.08) and t19 = 2.30 p = .033 (M = 7.04; SD = 10.58). All the other stimuli were chosen with a selection rate that did not significantly differ from the expected choice rate, see Table 2 for detailed values.

Considering the entire experimental session, Stimuli #1 and #5 confirmed to be the least preferred ones, t19 = 4.58 p < .001 (M = 6.55; SD = 5.47) and t19 = 2.29 p = .009 (M = 7.09; SD = 8.25), respectively. Stimuli #3 confirmed to be the most chosen one, t19 = 3.15 p = .005 (M = 20.15; SD = 10.84). An overview of the results is depicted in Fig. 2.

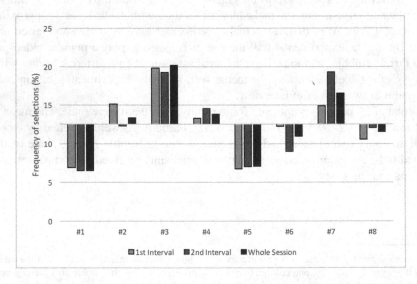

Fig. 2. The choice rate per stimuli throughout the experimental session. The origin of the graph is set at 12.5%, which is the expected casual choice rate. *p < .05

Table 2. The values of the one sample t-test, average selection rate and standard deviations for each of the stimuli participants are reported. *$p < .05$

Stimulus	First interval		Second interval		Whole session	
	t	M(SD)	t	M(SD)	t	M(SD)
#1	3.43*	6.9(7.29)	3.31*	6.51(8.08)	4.85*	6.55(5.47)
#2	.085	15.12(13.71)	0.039	12.3(22.38)	.255	13.31(14.23)
#3	2.60*	19.81(12.54)	1.917	19.21(15.66)	3.15*	20.15(10.84)
#4	.28	13.25(11.62)	0.77	14.56(11.91)	.615	13.8(9.49)
#5	2.99*	7.17(7.94)	2.30*	7.04(10.58)	2.29*	7.09(8.25)
#6	.116	12.21(11.37)	1.78	8.99(8.79)	.847	10.97(8.02)
#7	.952	14.92(11.37)	1.98	19.28(15.26)	1.54	16.53(11.70)
#8	.904	10.59(9.42)	.152	12.09(12.03)	.46	11.56(8.87)

Interview data indicate that half of the sample (n = 10) affirmed that they tended to choose a single stimulus, whilst three of them said they tried different stimuli. Two participants said they activated different stimuli at random and three reported that they first tried different stimuli and then selected their favorite one. When asked to motivate their choice, twelve participants said they selected a particular vibrational pattern because they found it pleasant. One affirmed that the vibration helped him/her to concentrate in the game and one that they were relaxing. Three participants reported the tactile stimuli to be activating. Finally, only one user affirmed that the vibrations were distracting.

5 Conclusions

The experiment presented here aimed at identifying vibrational stimuli that could be integrated into a symbiotic system. By asking participants to freely choose the stimulation they preferred, we found that the stimulus users favored was characterized by a vibrational pattern activated from the upper toward the lower area of the back. Interestingly, the vibration of the same set of actuators, yet activated in the reverse order, which characterized Stimulus #1, was the least chosen stimulus. This finding suggests that besides the basic parameters characterizing a tactile stimulus, i.e., the intensity, the rhythm and the area on the body on which the tactile stimuli are applied [4], developers should also take into account the feeling that a given stimulation produces on the user. As emerged from the interviews, participants' choices were mainly motivated by the pleasantness of the stimuli.

In addition, we found that participants' preferences were overall stable throughout the entire experimental session, suggesting that when a tactile stimulation is perceived as (un)pleasant the feeling persists over time.

The investigation of tactile stimulation embedded into a symbiotic system needs to be extended to other wearable devices integrating a tactile interface, e.g., tactile glove, tactile wrist-band. Finally, in order to build a clear understanding of how tactile stimulations can be successfully employed in a symbiotic system, further experiments are required to understand the impact of tactile stimuli over longer interactions.

Acknowledgments. The present study was partially funded by the EU project CultAR (grant agreement n. 601139).

References

1. O'Malley, M.K., Gupta, A.: Haptic interfaces. In: Kortum, P. (ed.) HCI Beyond the GUI: Design for Haptic, Speech, Olfactory, and Other Nontraditional Interfaces, pp. 25–64. Elsevier Inc., Amsterdam (2008)
2. Jacob, R., Mooney, P., Winstanley, A.C.: Guided by touch: tactile pedestrian navigation. In: Proceedings of the 1st International Workshop on Mobile Location-Based Service, pp. 11–20. ACM (2011)
3. Tsukada, K., Yasumura, M.: ActiveBelt: belt-type wearable tactile display for directional navigation. In: Davies, N., Mynatt, E.D., Siio, I. (eds.) UbiComp 2004. LNCS, vol. 3205, pp. 384–399. Springer, Heidelberg (2004). doi:10.1007/978-3-540-30119-6_23
4. Hoggan, E., Anwar, S., Brewster, S.A.: Mobile multi-actuator tactile displays. In: Oakley, I., Brewster, S. (eds.) HAID 2007. LNCS, vol. 4813, pp. 22–33. Springer, Heidelberg (2007). doi:10.1007/978-3-540-76702-2_4
5. Carton, A., Dunne, L.E.: Tactile distance feedback for firefighters: design and preliminary evaluation of a sensory augmentation glove. In: Proceedings of the 4th Augmented Human International Conference, pp. 58–64. ACM (2013)
6. Spagnolli, A., Guardigli, E., Orso, V., Varotto, A., Gamberini, L.: Measuring user acceptance of wearable symbiotic devices: validation study across application scenarios. In: Jacucci, G., Gamberini, L., Freeman, J., Spagnolli, A. (eds.) Symbiotic 2014. LNCS, vol. 8820, pp. 87–98. Springer, Cham (2014). doi:10.1007/978-3-319-13500-7_7
7. Ahmaniemi, T.T., Lantz, V.T.: Augmented reality target finding based on tactile cues. In: Proceedings of the 2009 International Conference on Multimodal Interfaces, pp. 335–342. ACM (2009)
8. Hornecker, E., Swindells, S., Dunlop, M.: A mobile guide for serendipitous exploration of cities. In: Proceedings of MobileHCI, pp. 557–562. ACM (2011)
9. Morrison, A.J., Manresa-Yee, C., Knoche, H., Jensen, B.W.S., Leegaard, J.: Interactive furniture: bi-directional interaction with a vibrotactile wearable sensate vest in an urban space. In: Recent Advances in Technologies of Inclusive Well-Being (in press)

Towards Interactional Symbiosis: Epistemic Balance and Co-presence in a Quantified Self Experiment

Nicolas Rollet[1(✉)], Varun Jain[2], Christian Licoppe[1], and Laurence Devillers[2,3]

[1] I3 - Telecom ParisTech, Paris, France
{nicolas.rollet,christian.licoppe}@telecom-paristech.fr
[2] LIMSI-CNRS, Paris, France
{varun.jain,devil}@limsi.fr
[3] Paris-Sorbonne 4 University, Paris, France

Abstract. In the frame of an experiment dealing with quantified-self and reflexivity, we collected audio-video data that provide us with material to discuss the ways in which the participants would work out social synergy through co-presence management and epistemic balance – accounting for their orientation towards the familiar symbiotic nature of human interactions. Following a Conversational Analysis perspective, we believe that detailed analysis of interactional behaviors offers opportunities for socially interactive robots design improvements, that is: identify and reproduce human ordinary skills in order to make the machines more adaptable.

Keywords: Quantified self · Conversational analysis · HRI · Epistemics

1 Introduction

Face-to-face conversation between humans implies a moment-by-moment organization of turns at talk, artifacts use and body postures that provide for the accountability of what is going on, what has been done, and what one could expect to be done. By 'accountability' is meant that social practices contain their very intelligibility as they occur in the here-and-now of activities. Analysts can rely on this situated intelligibility to describe and analyze how social activities are organized [17]. Social activity is structured as an emergent product of interrelations between sequential organization of talk, gestures, cognition and objects from the environment [22, 34, 43]. Therefore, social activity *fait système* and becomes a unit for analysts, because it is accountably treated as one by the social actors in the first place. Following Charles Goodwin's definition of symbiosis [22], we will consider that through social interaction, humans are meant to organize some 'wholes' that are both different from, and greater than their parts, and constructed through the mutual interdependence of unlike elements.

There are many ways to describe the social *ballet* that is wound up each time people are co-present – and that would inspire research in Human-Machine Interaction. In this paper we present data collected from an experiment where epistemic balance was at stake. Essentially, in the frame of a musical quiz, we created situations where the robot would at some delimited occasions step into a person's epistemic territory. The intended

L. Gamberini et al. (Eds.): Symbiotic 2016, LNCS 9961, pp. 143–154, 2017.
DOI: 10.1007/978-3-319-57753-1_13

encroachment was triggered through a reflexive utterance produced by the robot during the interaction, that is, a turn-at-talk that would reflect traces of the person's own activity [4]. The emergence of the reflexive turns relied on the participants' physiological measurements that were measured with a connected Empatica E4 wristband [11, 16]. This epistemic encroachment was regularly responded to by the recipients. A close analysis of the following sequential environment 'Reflexive Turn - Response', will lead us to account for a collection of resources used by the participants in order to create a familiar social solidarity/synergy.

2   CA, Quantified-Self and HRI

Leaning on human-human (or animal) interactions to support conversational agents or robots' design, relies on a robust literature [5, 10, 13, 14, 28]. In the light of the development of social robots or socially interactive robots [13], concepts drawn from sociology such as connection, co-presence and cooperation, figure in definitions of engagement as ways to describe commitments or partnership in Human-Machine/Robot interactions [36] (HRI, HCI). However, such concepts are rarely scrutinized in their practical and sequential achievement. For the few researchers in HRI or HCI who have used it, Conversational analysis (CA), as a descriptive and naturalistic approach using interaction itself as a resource for analysis [45], provide analytical and methodological tools either to account for the moment-by-moment accomplishment of Human-Machine situated interactions [40, 41], either to design systems, and therefore anticipate on further interactions [37]. The present work is a contribution to this approach that aims at accounting for the sociality of robots as a practical accomplishment and therefore proposes an interactionist perspective on symbiosis. We assumed that giving access to the robot to something about the personal territory of an individual, like physiological data, could be questionable as something that helps, or somehow has an effect on the relation between this human and that robot.

The concepts of Quantified self and self monitoring are novel ideas to the field of HRI and we (the authors) are not aware of any experiments where this concept has ever been used in human-robot interaction. There are however several studies in the domain of human-computer interaction where the concept of quantified self has been employed. Li, Dey and Forlizzi [31] discuss how we can develop tools for analyzing the data that we collect about ourselves and how we can better perform self-reflection using this data. Human-computer interaction researchers have applied the concept of Quantified Self and self-tracking to diverse domains: to study electricity consumption [39], transportation habits [15], eating habits [46], and exercise habits [6]. While the use of smartphones and wearable devices continues to increase, we are finding new uses for these devices for self-monitoring such as measurement of our physical activity [12, 48], tracking our sleep patterns [1] and even looking at changes in our mood over time [50] among others which have become commercial successes. The E4 sensor and its predecessors have been used in a variety of experiments by researchers. Pieper and Laugero [38] used features collected using the Q sensor (predecessor to E4) in a study on preschool children and their emotional eating habits. Hernandez et al. [27] utilized the E4 to study stress during driving. In our experiment, we utilized only three of these measures: galvanic skin response [3, 7], pulse rate and peripheral skin temperature and two derived measures: slope of the galvanic skin response and change in pulse rate.

3   Experiment's Set up

3.1   Woz Set up

The experiment was carried out at LIMSI-CNRS. Using a Wizard of Oz, the robot Nao (Aldebaran Robotics) is remotely controlled by a human who observes the course of the conversation and reacts accordingly. The Wizard of Oz system used was an adaptation of previous systems developed at LIMSI-CNRS [8, 49]. The content of each scenario is predefined and Nao (that is, the human wizard) follow a conversation tree to perform the next action (uttering a text, give reflexive information, playing a song). The operator of the robot was responsible for making the robot utter turns from a repository available to the operator through a Graphical user interface. The operator also had access to real time physiological parameters measured by the E4 wristband (see Fig. 1). On the basis of the changes in the physiological signals and the chosen profile of the operator discussed in Sect. 3.3, the operator decided to make the robot utter reflexive turns related to changes in physiological states either only at the start and end of the quiz or each time a change was detected.

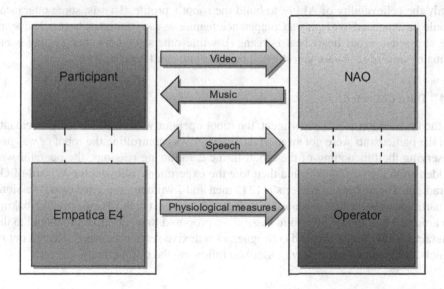

Fig. 1. Woz set up scheme

3.2   Activity's Scenario: The Musical Quiz

The interaction was based on a straightforward musical quiz. After a short greetings sequence, the game started. We asked participants to play at least 3 rounds of the game, so that we could use different profiles (see below). Each round of the quiz contained 4 short extracts of music selected randomly from a music library containing music from various genres. After the extract was played (through the same integrated Nao's speakers), the participant had 30 s to guess the artist and the title of the song. During this search, the participant could be interrupted by the robot producing a reflexive turn if significant physiological variations were detected. Besides, at the beginning of the game as well as at the end of each round, the robot produced a quantitative reflexive turn by uttering the measurements.

3.3   Turn Design and Robot's Profile

The robot's reflexive utterance design relies, first, on an exploration of pragmatic dimensions. That is, we wanted to encompass an occurrences' spectrum from «giving straightforwardly piece of information» to «provide the participant with a warning, a council». Second, we paid attention to the distribution of the turns along an epistemic gradient [24, 30]. That is, some utterances would display a primary knowledge access from the robot's point of view, whereas others would be more balanced towards the participant. Third, we have drawn from the pair Warmth/Competence that is used to study the believability of AI [9], to build the robot's profile. That is, some utterances would be supposed to display a Competence feature (e.g. «your heart beat is X»; «you are stressed»; «your heart beat is rising»), while others would rather display some empathy or care (e.g. «are you stressed because you can't handle it?»).

3.4   Data Collected

In the first session of our experiment, the robot operator was visible to the participants but the participants were not aware if the operator was controlling the robot or was just observing the functioning of the robot. In the 2 following sessions, the operator was hidden from the participants and therefore the experiment followed the Wizard of Oz paradigm. The number of subjects is 12 (5 men and 7 women), recorded over 3 sessions (3 participants in the first session, 5 in the second, and 4 in the third respectively) making up around 3 h of data. In the third session we proposed to a participant to attend to the interaction with her friend and colleague. 97 reflexive sequences were selected out of which 28 have been accurately transcribed following the CA methods.

4   Interactional Symbiosis as a Moment-by-Moment Achievement

Largely, we observed that reflexive turns had recurrently an effect on participants interacting with the robot. That is to say, when the robot claims, one way or another, an access to the participant's personal territory, the latter displays some reaction to it. We intend to show that those reactions account for socio-organic solidarities as proofs of interactional symbiosis. First, there are behaviors that are general to social interactions, namely co-presence management issues and preference for agreement. Second, there are more specific practices related to the epistemic encroachment that participants undergo in the experiment.

4.1 Working Out Social Synergy (1): Co-presence Management

As the robot gives precise measurements, we observed in the data that participants would regularly display body postures, that could be described as 'on-rendering-process faces'. Here is an example with an accurate multimodal transcription[1]:

```
(1) S2_SJ2_EX6
01 N     ton rythme cardiaque est de 56\
your heart beat is 56,
02       #(..) ta #température #est de trente # &
03 p     #looks away#towards Nao#looks away---#towards
Nao------>>
04 N     & virgule trente trois degrés\
your temperature is 30.33 degrees
05 p     ((nod))
```

There are indeed ways to display that one is taking informations into account without disturbing the ongoing accomplishment of the speaker's turn. What is striking here, is that the participant is not only displaying this, but she's also managing a basic co-presence problem [19]: through a meticulous to and fro eye (and head) movement (L03), she operates the possible actions enabled by turn constructional units organization [21, 35, 45] to keep track of both the participation frame and the delivered information on herself. In other words she's considering the robot's turn as a component of a larger organizational process: we can see here how body posture, eyes movements and speech are entangled, in order to structure an intricate event like 'receiving information about oneself'. Moreover, such methods that consist in moving body orientation from the speaker's 'face' to an alternative (imaginary) space where one can accountably think over (i.e. showing a process of thinking), illustrate how treating the robot as a socio-interactional partner could be achieved, in the present of interaction.

This phenomenon can be even more intricate. In the following extracts two participants interact with the robot, P2 is attending to the quiz, P is the one officially 'connected' to the robot:

---

[1] In this paper we use Conversational Analysis transcription convention from ICAR, Lyon 2: http://icar.univ-lyon2.fr/projets/corinte/bandeau_droit/convention_icor.htm.

148   N. Rollet et al.

```
(2) S3_SJ3&part_EX7
(P is one who faces the robot)
01  N    ton rythme cardiaque est de 93\ (..) la
température de
```
your heart beat is of 93, your skin temperature is of 29, 49 degrees
```
02       ta peau est de ¥29 virgule 49 ¥degrés\
03  P2                    ¥draw a seasaw air-curve¥Im1
04  P    ah j'ai diminué en température
```
ah my temperature fell (literally : I've decreased in temperature)
```
05  P2   <((drawing an air-curve)) oui mais tu as
06       augmenté(aussi XX)>
```
yes but but you've raised too [inaudible]

Broadly, as the participants are provided several times with 'their' measures during the game, we observed that one thing they could do is ordering them in a temporal frame. Like in this extract (2), participants can use the new measure to proceed an update/summary. Let's focus on P2's behavior. As P is provided with her measures from N, P2 is drawing in the air a curve (Fig. 2). This curve accounts for an analysis of P's heart rate evolution. This metaphoric gesture [33] is achieved during the stream of N's speech that is directed towards P. Therefore, insofar as the primary exchange is the one between P and N, P2's conduct is configured as a secondary scene or *byplay* [20]. This byplay functions as a co-expressive way to deal both with her friend's reflexive turn, and with the specific participation frame [21].

Fig. 2. Multimodal byplay from the participant's friend

As we've seen that different kinds of semiotic resources are used in order to manage co-presence and to structure 'wholes', we can now turn to other phenomena, more specific to the experiment, for they have to do with epistemic (re)configuration.

4.2 Working Out Social Synergy (2): Epistemic Balance and Preference for Agreement

```
(3) S1_SJ1_EX2
01 N     il semble que tu sois stressée\
it seems that you are stressed
02         (1,3s)
03 P     <((head shaking « no »)) ouais je m'y connais
yeah I don't know much about classical music Nao
04         pas bien en musique classique °Nao° \>

(4) S3_SJ1_EX3
01 N     attention (..) ton rythme cardiaque augmente\
warning, your heart beat is raising
02         <(0,5s) ((she looks away))>
03 P     m/h::\ (0,4s) pas bon ça\
```

We found that participants display more elaborated reactions in face of reflexive turns that, instead of giving a precise measurement, produce other kinds of actions like interpretations, assessments, warnings. Extracts (3), (4) above present two different methods that participants can use to respond.

In extract (3), P couldn't find the name of the music played. N produces a declarative turn that points out the participant's emotional state. This is a kind of turn that call for agreement or disagreement [2, 47, 51]. P in return, displays an affiliation towards the reflexive turn with «ouais», and attaches it with an account that provides an explanation regarding why she may be indeed stressed – namely because she doesn't know much about classical music. As we can see in the transcript this turn is simultaneously accomplished with a «no» head shake (L03). This way P associates a negative valence to her turn. While we can't say for sure what object this valence refers to, this is at least a conduct that contributes to the affiliation of the participant towards the reflexive turn. Moreover, this way of building a turn is congruent with the way two persons preferentially behave in agreement sequences: first you refer to what is projected in the previous turn and then you deliver your position [26, 42, 44]. In extract (4), the participant failed in finding out the song title (and was quite sorry about that). N produces a warning that refers to an analysis of her heart beat increasing. Here again, we can observe an affiliation towards the robot's turn through an assessment – namely that being stressed, is bad news [32].

Informations exchange is not only a matter of input-output mechanism. Informations such as that we're concerned with, lie on a domain, or territory on which social actors have stratified access. That is, they occupy during the interaction an epistemic position on a gradient that extends from knowledgeable to less (or no) knowledgeable [24, 25, 30]. And during social interactions, participants may claim, negotiate, confirm, discard epistemic positions. The ways participants react to Nao's turns, demonstrate that they configure those turns as components of a specific work, and that is: dealing 'together' with epistemic configurations.

Finally, whereas people consider having privileged access to their own experience, and so consider having specific rights to say something about it [2, 26], disagreement or confrontation may be problematic for the participants' face, in a Goffman sense:

```
(5) S3_SJ3&part_EX8
01  N      es tu stressée parce que tu n'y arrives pas/
are you stressed because you can't handle it ?
02         (1s)
03  P      non: pas trop/
no: not that much
04  P2     ((laugh))
05         (2,4s)
06  P      ce n'est pas trop honteux\
this not too shameful
```

In line 01, N produces a polar question that embodies an explanation as a candidate for being stressed. This candidate is rejected by P (L03) but followed with an assessment (L06) that displays an interesting analysis of the very candidate: by showing a moral perspective on the emotional state mentioned in N's turn, she analyzes it as an account of shame. Hence, without denying N's epistemic authority to claim that she might be stressed, P challenges the robot's account candidate in order to justify an epistemic re-balancing [24]. This challenge is allowed by the very format of N's turn – a polar question in which the recipient is entrusted with a knower stance. Moreover, what is striking here is the way the participant manages the juxtaposition of balancing the epistemic configuration with the problem of the preference for agreement: this is in fact not trivial that the «no» on line 03 is followed by a mitigation mark «pas trop», and an account (L06) that justifies the disagreement as a way to preserve both hers and the robot's face [18, 29]. That is to say, P behaves as if the robot was indeed a *ritually delicate object*. Therefore, this peculiar extract, shows that the notion of symbiosis may encompass a moral dimension.

5   Conclusion

In this experiment we used a quantified-self device to provide the robot with the presupposition of a specific epistemic authority vis-à-vis the participant, and we tested this authority through reflexive sequences. Largely, we found (1) that reflexivity taken care of by the robot, has an effect on the participants' behavior, as a step into their personal epistemic territory, and (2) that the persons display practices that show the analogous commitment as in human-human interactions regarding the preferential organization of turns-at-talk in terms of adjacency, agreement, and epistemic balance. Even if they are aware of the robot's limitations, participants display an attention to organize a participation framework (with rights and obligations), in which the robot is treated like a participant in its own right. Organization is what binds elements, events or individuals in a symbiotic relationship, that is, a potential synergy in which different sign systems work together to build relevant action and accomplish consequential meaning. Therefore, the scope of turn-design must not be limited to stream of speech phenomena (grammar, speech acts), but must encompass *structures providing for the organization of the endogenous activity systems within which strips of talk are embedded* [23]: 370.

As Foster [14] put it, detailed analysis of interactional behaviors offers opportunities for socially interactive robots design improvements, that is: identify and reproduce human ordinary skills (perception, practical reasoning, gesture…) in order to make the machines more adaptable regarding interactional situations (assistive robots in the home environment, companion robot). We observed in the data that the participants treat the robot as a body, a presence. It shows that social interaction, as Goffman identified it decades ago, is first, before talking, a matter of hand-to-hand management: entering in a mutual perceptive field, focusing on a common object – depending on the participation footing of the participant. Moreover, we introduced the problem of epistemic balance, and observed some occurrences of plasticity of the epistemic configurations. Epistemic balance phenomena analysis points out that social synergy is a dynamic process: status in the interaction are to be defined and may be negotiated. Epistemic configurations play also a fundamental role in the way higher-order classes of action such as suggestions, proposals, or offers are dealt with in the interaction. We believe this is an entire issue to explore in HRI.

Hence, we observed all sorts of practices that are grist to the interactional mill and accountable arguments for a view of humans working at establishing and maintaining socio-organic solidarities with a robot. This was done in a short term and a quite artificial setting. Prospectively, we would need a larger amount of data to extend the analysis towards (a) more natural interactions, (b) more differentiation in reflexive turn-design impact, (c) better understandings of the usefulness of physiological measurements as resources for Human-Machine situated symbiosis.

References

1. Aura. https://www.withings.com/eu/en/products/aura
2. Bergmann, J.: Veiled morality: notes on discretion in psychiatry. In: Drew, P., Heritage, J. (eds.) Talk at Work, pp. 137–162. CUP, Cambridge (1992)
3. Boucsein, W.: Electrodermal Activity. Plenum, New York (1992)
4. Cahour, B., Licoppe, C.: La confrontation aux traces de son activité. Revue d'Anthropologie des Connaissances 4(2), 243–253 (2010)
5. Cassell, J., Bickmore, T., Campbell, L., Vilhjálmsson, H., Yan, H.: Human conversation as a system framework: designing embodied conversational agents. In: Cassell, J., Sullivan, J., Prevost, S., Churchill, E. (eds.) Embodied Conversational Agents, pp. 29–63. MIT Press, Cambridge (2000)
6. Consolvo, S., Everitt, K., Smith, I., Landay, J.A.: Design requirements for technologies that encourage physical activity. In: Proceedings of the SIGCHI Conference on Human Factors in Computing Systems (CHI 2006), pp. 457–466. ACM, New York (2006)
7. Critchley, H.D.: Electrodermal responses: what happens in the brain. Neuroscientist **8**, 132–142 (2002)
8. Delaborde, A., Tahon, M., Barras, C., Devillers, L.: A wizard-of-Oz game for collecting emotional audio data in a children-robot interaction. In: Proceedings of the International Workshop on Affective-Aware Virtual Agents and Social Robots (Affine 2009), New York (2009)

9. Demeure, V., Niewiadomski, R., Pélachaud, C.: How is believability of a virtual agent related to warmth, competence, personification, and embodiment? Presence Teleoperators Virtual Environ. **20**(5), 431–448 (2011)
10. Dubuisson–Duplessis, G., Devillers L.: Towards the consideration of dialogue activities in engagement measures for human-robot social interaction. In: IROS2015 International Conference on Intelligent Robots and Systems, Designing and Evaluating Social Robots for Public Settings Workshop, pp. 19–24, Hambourg, Germany (2015)
11. Empatica. https://support.empatica.com/
12. Fitbit. https://www.fitbit.com/
13. Fong, T., Nourbakhsh, I., Dautenhahn, K.: A survey of socially interactive robots. Robot. Auton. Syst. **42**(3–4), 143–166 (2003)
14. Foster, M.E.: Natural face-to-face conversation with socially intelligent robots. In: Proceedings of the IROS 2015, Hamburg, Germany (2015)
15. Froehlich, J., Dillahunt, T., Klasnja, P., Mankoff, J., Consolvo, S., Harrison, B., Landay, J.A.: Investigating a mobile tool for tracking and supporting green transportation habits. In: Proceedings of the SIGCHI Conference on Human Factors in Computing Systems (CHI 2009), pp. 1043–1052. ACM, New York (2009)
16. Garbarino, M., Lai, M., Bender, D., Picard, R., Tognetti, S.: Empatica E3: a wearable wireless multi-sensor device for real-time computerized biofeedback and data acquisition. In: EAI 4th International Conference on Wireless Mobile Communication and Healthcare, pp. 39–42. IEEE press, Athens (2014)
17. Garfinkel, H.: Studies in Ethnomethodology. Prentice-Hall, Engelwood Cliffs (1967)
18. Goffman, E.: Interaction Ritual: Essays on Face-to-Face Behaviour. Penguin books, London (1967)
19. Goffman, E.: Behavior in Public Places: Notes on the Social Organization of Gatherings. The Free Press, New York (1963)
20. Goodwin, M.H.: Byplay: participant structure and framing of collaborative collusion. In: Framing Discourse: Public and Private in Language and Society. Meeting of the American Anthropological Association, Washington (1985)
21. Goodwin, C.: Interactive footing. In: Holt, E., Clift, R. (eds.) Reporting Talk: Reported Speech and Footing in Conversation, pp. 16–46. CUP, Cambridge (2007)
22. Goodwin, C.: The semiotic body in its environment. In: Coupland, J., Gwyn, R. (eds.) Discourses of the Body, pp. 19–42. Palgrave Macmillan, New York (2003)
23. Goodwin, C.: Transparent vision. In: Ochs, E., Schegloff, E.A., Thompson, S. (eds.) Interaction and Grammar, pp. 370–404. Cambridge University Press, Cambridge (1996)
24. Heritage, J.: The epistemic engine: sequence organization and territories of knowledge. Res. Lang. Soc. Interact. **45**(1), 30–52 (2012)
25. Heritage, J.: Territories of knowledge, territories of experience: empathic moments in interaction. In: Stivers, T., Mondada, L., Steensig, J. (eds.) The Morality of Knowledge in Conversation, pp. 159–183. CUP, Cambridge (2011)
26. Heritage, J., Raymond, G.: The terms of agreement: indexing epistemic authority and subordination in assessment sequences. Soc. Psychol. Q. **68**(1), 15–38 (2005)
27. Hernandez, J., McDuff, D., Benavides, X., Amores, J., Maes, P., Picard, R.W.: AutoEmotive: bringing empathy to the driving experience to manage stress. In: Proceedings of the Companion Publication on Designing Interactive Systems (DIS 2014), Vancouver, Canada (2014)

28. Janssoone, T., Clavel, C., Bailly, K., Richard, G.: Using temporal association rules for the synthesis of embodied conversational agents with a specific stance. In: Traum, D., Swartout, W., Khooshabeh, P., Kopp, S., Scherer, S., Leuski, A. (eds.) IVA 2016. LNCS (LNAI), vol. 10011, pp. 175–189. Springer, Cham (2016). doi:10.1007/978-3-319-47665-0_16
29. Kerbrat-Orecchioni, C.: Théorie des faces et analyse conversationnelle. In: Colloque de Cerisy, pp. 155–195. Les Editions de Minuit, Paris (1989)
30. Labov, W., Fanshel, D.: Therapeutic Discourse. New York Academic Press, New York (1977)
31. Li, I., Dey, A., Forlizzi, J.: Understanding my data, myself: supporting self-reflection with ubicomp technologies. In: Proceedings of the 13th International Conference on Ubiquitous Computing (UbiComp 2011), pp. 405–414. ACM, New York (2011)
32. Maynard, W.: Bad News, Good News. Conversational Order in Every-Day Talk and Clinical Settings. University of Chicago Press, Chicago & London (2003)
33. McNeill, D.: Gesture and Thought. University of Chicago Press, Chicago (2005)
34. Morin, E.: La Méthode. Tome 1. La Nature de la Nature. Editions du Seuil, Paris (1977)
35. Ochs, E., Schegloff, E.A., Thompson, S. (eds.): Interaction and Grammar. CUP, Cambridge (1996)
36. Pélachaud, C., Glas, N.: Definitions of engagement in human-agent interaction. In: International Workshop on Engagement in Human Computer Interaction (ENHANCE), The Sixth International Conference on Affective Computing and Intelligent Interaction, pp. 944–949, Xi'an, China (2015)
37. Pélachaud, C., Glas, N.: Topic transition strategies for an information-giving agent. In: Proceedings of the 15th European Workshop on natural Language Generation, pp. 146–155, Brighton (2015)
38. Pieper, J.R., Laugero, K.D.: Preschool children with lower executive function may be more vulnerable to emotional-based eating in the absence of hunger. Appetite 62(1), 103–109 (2013)
39. Pierce, J., Paulos, E.: Beyond energy monitors: interaction, energy, and emerging energy systems. In: CHI 2012 Proceedings of the SIGCHI Conference on Human Factors in Computing Systems, pp. 665–674. ACM, Austin (2012)
40. Pitsch, K., Wrede, S.: When a robot orients visitors to an exhibit. Referential practices and interactional dynamics in the real world. In: IEEE ROMAN 23rd International Symposium on Robot and Human Interactive Communication, pp. 36–42. IEEE press, Edinburgh (2014)
41. Pitsch, K., Kuzuoka, H., Suzuki, Y., Süssenbach, L., Luff, P., Heath, C.: The first five seconds: contingent stepwise entry into an interaction as a means to secure sustained engagement in human-robot-interaction. In: IEEE ROMAN 18th International Symposium on Robot and Human Interactive Communication, pp. 985–991, Toyama, Japan (2009)
42. Pomerantz, A.: Agreeing and disagreeing with assessments: some features of preferred dispreferred turn shapes. In: Atkinson, J.M., Heritage, J. (eds.) Structures of Social Action, pp. 57–101. CUP, Cambridge (1984)
43. Rollet, N.: Analyse conversationnelle des pratiques dans les appels au Samu-Centre 15: vers une approche praxéologique d'une forme située «d'accord». Ph.D. Sciences du Langage, Sorbonne Nouvelle Paris 3, Paris (2012)
44. Sacks, H.: On the preferences for agreement and contiguity in sequences in vonversation. In: Button, G., Lee, J.R., (eds.) Talk and Social Organisation, Multilingual Matters, Clevedon, UK (1987)
45. Sacks, H., Schegloff, E.A., Jefferson, G.: A simplest systematics for the organization of turn-taking for conversation. Language 50, 696–731 (1974)

46. Smith, B.K., Frost, J., Albayrak, M., Sudhakar, R.: Integrating glucometers and digital photography as experience capture tools to enhance patient understanding and communication of diabetes self-management practices. Pers. Ubiquit. Comput. **11**(4), 273–286 (2007)
47. Stivers, T., Rossano, F.: Mobilizing response. Res. Lang. Soc. Interact. **43**(1), 3–31 (2010)
48. Swan, M.: Sensor mania! the internet of things, wearable computing, objective metrics, and the quantified self 2.0. J. Sensor Actuator Netw. **1**, 217–253 (2012)
49. Tahon, M., Delaborde, A., Devillers, L.: Corpus of children voices for mid-level social markers and affect bursts analysis. In: LREC 8th International Conference on Language Resources and Evaluation, Istanbul, Turkey (2012)
50. T2 mood tracker. https://play.google.com/store/apps/details?id=com.t2.vas&hl=en
51. Voutilainen, L., Preäkylä, A., Ruusuvuori, J.: Recognition and interpretation: responding to emotional experience in psychotherapy. Res. Lang. Soc. Interact. **43**(1), 85–107 (2010)

Digital Me: Controlling and Making Sense of My Digital Footprint

Mats Sjöberg[1]([⊠]), Hung-Han Chen[2,3], Patrik Floréen[1,2], Markus Koskela[1],
Kai Kuikkaniemi[2], Tuukka Lehtiniemi[2], and Jaakko Peltonen[2,4]

[1] Department of Computer Science, Helsinki Institute
for Information Technology HIIT, University of Helsinki, Helsinki, Finland
mats.sjoberg@helsinki.fi
[2] Department of Computer Science, Helsinki Institute
for Information Technology HIIT, Aalto University, Espoo, Finland
[3] Media Lab Helsinki, Aalto University, Espoo, Finland
[4] School of Information Sciences, University of Tampere, Tampere, Finland

Abstract. Our lives are getting increasingly digital; much of our personal interactions are digitally mediated. A side effect of this is a growing digital footprint, as every action is logged and stored. This data can be very powerful, e.g., a person's actions can be predicted, and deeply personal information mined. Hence, the question of who controls the digital footprint is becoming a pressing technological and social issue. We believe that the solution lies in human-centric personal data, i.e., the individuals themselves should control their own data. We claim that in order for human-centric data management to work, the individual must be supported in understanding their data. This paper introduces a personal data storage system Digital Me (DiMe). We describe the design and implementation of DiMe, and how we use state-of-the-art machine learning for visualisation and interactive modelling of the personal data. We outline several applications that can be built on top of DiMe.

Keywords: Personal data management · Human-centric personal data · Knowledge work · Text analysis · Distributed representations · Interactive machine learning

1 Introduction

Today, much of our daily professional and private lives are mediated through digital technology. This means we are in constant interaction with information systems, sometimes even without realising it. Most – if not all – of this interaction is logged and often stored for a long time. This massive *digital footprint* can be analysed to gain insight into a particular persons behaviour, personal preferences and needs, and even predict future actions. Such knowledge could be used to design a new breed of interactive systems, in which computers would do what they are best at (data processing and statistical modelling) to support humans doing what they are best at (creativity and sense-making).

© The Author(s) 2017
L. Gamberini et al. (Eds.): Symbiotic 2016, LNCS 9961, pp. 155–167, 2017.
DOI: 10.1007/978-3-319-57753-1_14

For example, a proactive computer system could be designed that can anticipate the user's needs based on previous behaviour. A memory expander system
could be designed to help recall previous events, e.g., what was discussed in the
meeting last week or that interesting article you read a few days ago. A tool for
analysing your daily behaviour at work could help you better manage your work
time.

Unfortunately, the collected *personal data* is typically not available for the
individuals themselves, instead it is often collected and stored in a centralised
manner by one of the big Internet companies, such as Google, Apple or Facebook.
The use of this data is restricted by the functions provided by the owners of these
centralised points of collection. In fact, the data may not even be used in the
individual's best interests, as it is controlled by another entity with sometimes
conflicting interests. Furthermore, the user may not even know what data is
being collected and stored about her. Finally, the collected digital footprint is
often not in a single location, but different parts are locked down into several
proprietary silos, which do not share data between each other. In order to get the
full benefits from the data collection, there is a strong incentive for consumers
of these services to use only a single company's tools, as most of the data would
then be collected in a single location. This is obviously detrimental to market
competition and innovation, as the user cannot easily take her data and move to a
competing provider. However, even in this single-vendor scenario, the utilisation
of the personal data is ultimately controlled by the vendor, not the user.

The key to unlock the benefits of personal data for the individual, while
avoiding the pitfalls of vendor lock-in and privacy nightmares, lies in human-
centric *personal data storage (PDS)* systems. The term MyData [21] refers to
this paradigm shift in personal data management and processing that seeks
to transform the current organisation-centric system into a human-centric one.
In this approach, personal data is a resource that the individual controls, and
external services can use this data only to the extent that the user gives them
access. Further driving this development is recent EU legislation [7] according
to which individuals must have machine readable access to all data about them.

In this paper we present our implementation of a PDS system: the *Digital
Me (DiMe)* platform. DiMe is a personal data storage system, which collects
the individual's digital footprint from personal computing devices, and whose
design is focused on enabling different kinds of machine learning and information processing applications to operate in the user-controlled private data repository. The interplay between interactive manipulation and automated analysis
is crucial to enable efficient management of large amounts of personal data, and
DiMe supports both interaction and automated modeling at numerous points
within the system. DiMe was designed especially for knowledge work applications, however, the design is not limited to knowledge work and can be applied
also in other kinds of personal data management scenarios, such as e-commerce,
personal training, well-being, home automation and education. The DiMe platform is available as free and open source software and can be downloaded from
http://reknow.fi/dime/.

2   Related Work

Comprehensive recording of one's personal media and communication has been a long-lasting aspiration. Already in 1945, Vannevar Bush had a vision of a mechanised device, *Memex*, that would store all read books, records, and communications, and enable quick consultation of the recorded material [4]. There have been several projects attempting to fulfill the Memex vision. In *MyLifeBits* [12], the goal is to digitise all personal and professional information, an activity nowadays commonly referred to as *lifelogging* [14]. *Stuff I've Seen* [9] focuses on re-using the recorded information using a single index for all pieces of information (emails, web pages, documents, calendar entries etc.) on the user's computer.

Two main approaches have been proposed to enable human-centric control of personal data. The first approach is to centralise the storage of the data itself. With this approach, the scattering of data is solved by providing individuals with a personal data storage service within which they accumulate data from various sources. The personal data storage system OpenPDS [8] is one such initiative. It is focused on the aggregation and storage of specifically log-type, large-scale behavioural metadata, such as locations or web searches, and it aims to provide its users with the possibility to give fine-grained access to such metadata. Rather than provisioning access to the raw data as such, Open-PDS includes a questions-and-answers feature intended to allow services to ask questions that are responded to based on metadata. Another example of this approach is the digital.me[1] EU project, which focuses in particular on collecting data from social web services. Also commercial developers provide personal data storage services. Digi.me[2] and Meeco[3] are proprietary personal data repositories, whose aim and approach is to become a marketplace for personal data, via which their users would be able to supply personal data to usages they deem beneficial. Cozy Cloud[4] is an open source personal cloud service, whose approach is to bring the services and analytics to the cloud with the aid of an application platform within the cloud service. Its model closely resembles a personal information management system (PIMS) as described in [1]. Another important PDS project is the Hub-of-All things[5], which is especially focused on Internet of Things applications.

The second approach to enabling the control of personal data is to focus not on containing personal data in a centralised storage, but rather on managing the flows of data between data sources and data-users. In this case, the scattering of data with disparate third parties is solved by federation of data sources [18]. The individual controls the uses of personal data by employing tools and infrastructure intended for managing permissions to access data. This is the rationale of the MyData model [21], which also has a reference architecture [10] that describes

---

[1] http://www.dime-project.eu/.
[2] http://www.digi.me/.
[3] http://meeco.me/.
[4] http://www.cozy.io/.
[5] http://hubofallthings.com/.

a MyData consent account system and its functions. Similar frameworks are also UMA [17] and XDI[6]. Another example is Databox [6], which is a personal networked device that contains the index of personal data and the access permissions. An important focus of these models is on delegation or repurposing of data to new uses. While these models are focused on permissioning rather than storing data, they may well include a PDS as one data source.

The Digital Me personal data storage system presented in this paper differs from the other PDS services in two ways. First, its development is focused on integrating with a broad set of loggers that track the digital footprint. These loggers are for example an email logger, a browser logger, a PDF reader, a desktop logger that tracks keyboard and application use, a mobile phone usage logger and a calendar logger. The second difference is that DiMe provides a representation layer to data events that is focused on providing machine learning solutions to annotating, structuring and connecting different data events.

3   Design and Implementation

The Digital Me (DiMe) system has been designed to work as an intelligent database server, which provides a programmatic interface (API) for two types of clients: *loggers* and *applications*. Internally in DiMe vector representations are extracted and tag modelling is performed (see Sect. 4). Figure 1 illustrates this modular architecture.

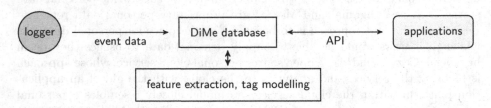

Fig. 1. DiMe architecture with loggers feeding event data into the DiMe database and applications utilising the logged data. Internally in DiMe vector representations are extracted and tag modelling is performed.

Loggers are software (or hardware + software) components that record events related to a person's actions or environment and send them to be stored in the person's own DiMe server. The primary item stored in DiMe is called *event*. Events can be, e.g., reading a document on a computer screen, the mobile phone location or the heart rate measured by a smart watch. Loggers are typically installed by the user, but then run unobtrusively in the background. The user can get an overview of what things are being recorded by checking the *dashboard*, which is the controlling web interface to the system.

---

[6] https://www.oasis-open.org/committees/tc_home.php?wg_abbrev=xdi

DiMe applications are software components, which utilise the events stored in DiMe by the loggers. Applications typically present the user with a graphical user interface, where some part of the DiMe data is visualised and can be manipulated, or the view of the data can be modified. Examples include a time-line viewer of recoded DiMe events over time, a search system that takes into account your previously recorded interests, and a document reader that can highlight sections of the document that you have read before. We distinguish between local applications and connected applications. Local applications run on the user's own machine, while connected applications run on a server and can connect information from many different DiMe instances. In this paper, we focus mainly on local applications. Section 5 lists some potential applications, but there are numerous other possibilities as well. In practice, most applications also act as loggers, for example recording the user's interactions with the user interface.

Through the dashboard, the user can always cease logging to DiMe and also delete already recorded events. In applications relying on sharing information from the user's own DiMe with others, the user can choose what data to share. The dashboard includes a search and a filtering functionality for the data, as well as showing statistics about the data stored in DiMe.

3.1 Data Model

Figure 2 illustrates the basic data model in DiMe. The primary data is composed of events, which occur at a given point in time. The recorded event time should try to approximate the time of the actual real-world event being described, not for example when the event was recorded in the DiMe server. Some events may refer to a file or other time-independent piece of data, such as a PDF document; these we denote *information elements*. Often many events may refer to the same information element: for example the opening and closing of the same document in the computer's user interface constitutes two events referring to the same element. In addition, we define two auxiliary data types, *person* and *tag*. Person refers to an actual person, e.g., the recipient or sender of an email or a participant

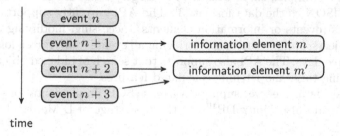

time

Fig. 2. In DiMe, events occur at different times and may refer to information elements.

Table 1. The currently supported DiMe events

DesktopEvent	A desktop event, such as opening a document or web page
ReadingEvent	A detailed reading event (e.g., page, paragraph or sentence)
MessageEvent	An event representing sending or receiving a message
CalendarEvent	An event generated from the user's calendar
BookmarkEvent	An event for adding or removing a bookmark by the user
FeedbackEvent	An event representing user feedback, e.g., ranking a document

Table 2. The currently supported DiMe information elements

Document	A document, e.g., PDF, web page or word-processing file
ScientificDocument	A scientific publication with a bibliographic record
Message	An electronic message, such as an email or instant message

in a meeting. Tags are keywords or key-phrases which allow the user to describe the events or information elements in a way that is personally relevant.

The DiMe data model is based on the OSCAF Ontologies[7], which specify various aspects of personal information access and usage. The most relevant ontologies for our data model are the NEPOMUK User Action Ontology, which defines a vocabulary for describing user events on a device, and the NEPOMUK File Ontology, which provides a vocabulary to express information extracted from various sources (e.g., files, pieces of software, and remote hosts). We have extended the ontologies for our specific purposes as listed in Tables 1 and 2. The two lists are not exhaustive, and new data types can be added as needed.

3.2   Implementation

The current implementation of the DiMe server is written in Java using the Spring framework[8]. The essential components of the core DiMe software are the API interface, database, search engine, and feature extraction framework.

The API is implemented over HTTP, largely following RESTful principles and using JSON as the data format [3]. The API currently supports uploading new objects (events or information elements), accessing, modifying or deleting existing objects, and filtering, e.g., retrieving all events from a given logger during the last three days. The API also supports text search of indexed objects, adding and removing tags, and fetching calculated features.

For the database we support various SQL implementations via Java Hibernate[9], and also MongoDB[10]. As the first stage of DiMe development has

---

[7]   http://www.semanticdesktop.org/ontologies/.

[8]   https://spring.io/.

[9]   http://hibernate.org/.

[10] https://www.mongodb.com/.

focused on running it locally, for example on the person's own laptop, the most commonly used database is the H2 embedded database[11], which makes for easy installation. For the search engine backend we currently use Lucene[12] to index both events and information elements having textual content.

The purpose of the feature extraction framework is to support the extraction of higher level features of the data objects, such as important key-phrases from text documents, visual descriptors from images, and interpretation of a low-level physiological signal (e.g., "person is stressed"). Some of these processes run in the core DiMe server and some outside as external applications, depending on the measure of access needed to the DiMe database. The extracted features are typically used as input for modelling the data, as explained in the next section.

4   Modelling of Personal Data

One of the central principles of the Digital Me design has been to include state-of-the-art machine learning-based modelling capabilities from the start. Some of these algorithms have to run in the core DiMe server, in particular if they need to model the entirety of the personal data or have to reprocess the entire database often (e.g., after model parameters have been updated). Other algorithms may run externally and access DiMe via the API, for example if they only process a small number of objects at a time or simply enhance or rerank the objects returned by DiMe.

There are numerous ways to model personal data that could be implemented in the DiMe platform, but in our research we have focused mainly on two aspects: *automatically generated vector representations*, and *interactive modelling of tags*. The first approach utilises state-of-the-art machine learning techniques to generate highly expressive vector representations in an unsupervised automated manner. The second approach instead attempts to include the human in the loop by using tags for interaction and modelling. After all it is *personal* data, and thus the individual user of DiMe is the one the best positioned to understand the data, and what organisation of the data makes most sense in the personal context. These two approaches are complementary – for example the vector representations can be used as part of the tag modelling mechanism – and will be explained in more detail in the following two sections.

4.1   Vector Representations

The data stored in DiMe is multimodal; it can be of many different types, such as text, images, videos and real-valued vectors representing physical measurements. However, in practice, the vast majority of the data is in textual form, or can be converted into such (e.g., speech-to-text, visual concept detection), and thus analysis and indexing textual data has been our primary focus.

---

[11] http://h2database.com/.
[12] http://lucene.apache.org/.

The traditional approach to vector representation of text documents is to represent the content (in DiMe a single event or information element) as a weighted bag-of-tokens vector, where the vector has a fixed length and whose elements are counts (weights) of individual tokens, such as words (unigrams) or word combinations (bigrams, trigrams, keywords or key-phrases). Standard transformations, such as term frequency-inverse document frequency (TF-IDF) weighting, can be applied to emphasise rare tokens. Once such a representation exists for documents, the same representation becomes available for words: a word is represented by its weight vector across documents, and words are similar if they appear often in the same documents. More advanced transformations involve learning a statistical model that represents the prominent trends in the content, such as principal components across documents or topics of a probabilistic (hierarchical) topic model.

Another approach, which has gained a lot of interest due to recent advances in deep learning, is learning vector representations using neural networks [2,19]. In this approach, each word is represented by a vector and several words from the same context are concatenated or averaged to form the input to a neural network. The neural network then tries to predict other words in the context. After training this results in a vector space mapping, where semantically similar words are mapped to nearby points. For visualising and analysing personal data, we are in particular interested in representing whole documents, i.e., the stored personal information elements and events. For this we use the *Paragraph Vectors* [16] algorithm. Here, in addition to the context word vectors, a paragraph vector is included. The vector tries to capture the topic of the paragraph (or the piece of text to be represented, in our case the entire personal data item). The resulting representation has two advantages over bag-of-words methods: the ordering of the words is retained (without the data sparsity and high dimensionality problems of the n-gram methods), and the semantics of the words is taken into account. A drawback of this approach is that the individual components of the vector do not have any semantic interpretation.

Having highly expressive vector representations that capture the semantic similarity of the content is highly valuable for accessing and analysing personal data, for example for displaying similar events to the one currently being viewed in the user interface, for automatically propagating a tag to similar documents, or for visualising the global structure of the data.

4.2   Interactive Tag Modelling

Our second approach to modelling of personal data is based on using tags. Tags are keywords or key-phrases, which allow the user to describe collected events or documents in a way that is personally relevant. Each user has their own terminology and view on what is relevant. For example, a person could have a tag for a project she is currently working on, and another one for the organisational hierarchy level she belongs to. Another person may instead tag items based on the activities involved, such as programming, writing and meetings. In accordance with the conventional tagging design pattern, the tags label the events as

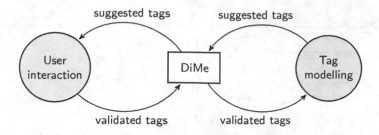

Fig. 3. The interactive tag modelling cycle, where the user validates tags suggested by the tag modelling system. The user can also add new tags manually.

being mapped into possibly several different potentially overlapping categories instead of the traditional hierarchical category system commonly used, e.g., in file systems.

Figure 3 illustrates the interactive tag modelling loop, which involves both a user interaction and a machine learning component. On the left-hand side of the figure, the user interacts with the collected personal data in DiMe, either via the DiMe dashboard or via an external application. With respect to tags, this interaction involves either adding new *user generated* tags or confirming *suggested* tags. Collectively we call these *validated tags*. The validated tags are collected in DiMe together with the events they belong to, and transmitted to the tag modelling system, which is shown on the right-hand side of Fig. 3.

Tags can be modelled by various machine learning algorithms, which can learn from the validated tags and the DiMe events they are assigned to in order to expand those tags to other events in DiMe. In the current DiMe system we are using the KEA [11] algorithm, which uses a naive Bayes classifier to learn an extraction scheme from the validated tags and corresponding documents. In addition to traditional classifiers, also algorithms like TagProp [13] can be used to propagate tags to neighbouring DiMe items in a suitable vector space (such as the ones discussed in Sect. 4.1). Correspondingly, these automatically generated tags have values attached to them related to their likelihood of belonging to that event. The most likely tags are transmitted back to DiMe together with the corresponding events; these are presented to the user as *suggested tags*, which the user, as mentioned, can confirm (or reject). The aim of suggesting tags is to expand the user generated tags, so that the user does not need to annotate all events manually. As more user feedback is gathered, the tag models are successively improved and can provide more accurate suggestions.

The interactive tag modelling approach is closely aligned with previous research on interactive machine learning [15,22]. However, here we focus particularly on personal data, which has its unique challenges. In addition, the proposed system is more generic and could be applied using several different modelling algorithms.

Figure 4 shows two views of the DiMe user interface for displaying the collected events, and highlights several visual elements allowing interaction with

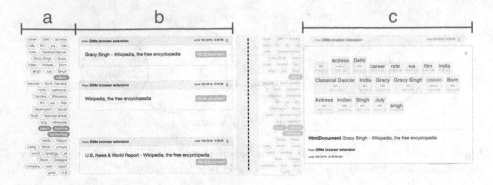

Fig. 4. The interactive tagging interface of DiMe. See text for a detailed explanation. (Color figure online)

tags. First, on the left-hand side is shown the basic event time-line view. The central feature of the interface is a vertical time-line, which consists of card elements representing the individual events collected in DiMe (Fig. 4-b). The associated tags are placed on the left of the event's card element (Fig. 4-a). On the one hand, the tags help users identify events and the information elements they link to. On the other hand, the side-by-side display of the content and the tags enables the user to easily confirm or reject the suggested tags.

Validating a suggested tag is done by mouse-clicking and there is a visual element indicating the tag has been validated (currently the colour green has been used to represent this status, see Fig. 4-a). Rejecting a tag is done by clicking on a red cross that appears when hovering the mouse cursor over the tag label (not shown here). If the user is interested in the details of a particular event, a modal window with detailed information can be opened by clicking on the event. This display is shown on the right-hand side of Fig. 4: the modal information window is displayed as Fig. 4-c. In our design of the tag display we have emphasised visual aesthetics since previous research has found a positive link between aesthetic visualisation and data retrieval tasks [5, 20]. We utilised the styles chosen by the well-accepted Twitter Bootstrap framework[13].

5   Applications

DiMe augments the human with a digital memory of actions undertaken. This memory can provide insight into the person's own behaviour and can be used in different applications building on this personal data. Below are some examples of applications, but generally speaking, all applications relying at least partially on referring to past events are potential DiMe applications.

Time-Line Search. The DiMe information can be displayed on a graphical time-line, helping to recall events and to search for particular pieces of information.

---

[13] http://getbootstrap.com/.

Associative Recall. We may remember some partial information, but not the exact thing we look for. The information gathered in DiMe can provide cues to enable associative recall.

Proactive Search. Instead of explicitly querying for information, information could be automatically provided to the user on the basis of what the user is currently doing. Previously viewed documents in DiMe can be used as a source of search results. Furthermore, the proactive system can learn about the user's interests and search preferences from the user's DiMe history.

Intelligent Meeting Room. Meetings can be consistently recorded on video and audio. The meeting participants gather such information into their personal DiMes. By the participants giving explicitly access to this information, we can for instance recall what a particular person said related to a given topic in a previous meeting.

Quantified Self. The person can follow his own work. As an example, information about working time and the tasks undertaken can be gathered. This can help in allocating the working time more efficiently. Consultants can automatically get information about the time to be charged to different projects.

Profiling and Competence Search. From the work tasks undertaken, a profile can be automatically generated highlighting the particular competences of the person. If the employees so allow, the employer can then use these profiles to optimise the composition of a group of workers, e.g., for a particular project where different complementary competences are needed.

The vector representations of Sect. 4.1 and tags of Sect. 4.2 are resources for the applications. For example in time-line search, associative recall or proactive search, vector representations can be used to find the most relevant previous documents; in competence search vector representations of employee profiles can be used to find complementary competences. Tags can be used to find which parts of the representation is most relevant.

6   Conclusions

The main contribution of this paper is the introduction of the personal data storage system Digital Me (DiMe). This serves as a platform for further research into human-centric personal data, in which individuals are in control of their own digital footprints.

However, simply gathering the data is not enough. Individuals must be supported in understanding their own data with systems that can organise and visualise the data. We propose two ways forward which utilise state-of-the-art machine learning algorithms, while supporting user interaction to modify the learned models and views of the data. Automatically extracted vector representations can be used to learn semantic relationships and visualise the structure of the collected information, or help finding related events or documents. Interactive tag modelling can learn the individual's personal categorisations from a small sample and expand them to organise the whole digital footprint.

The work is ongoing, and this paper both explains our vision and shows some potential ways forward. This paper also represents a call-for-action for interested researchers and organisations to join us in the personal data revolution!

Acknowledgments. This work has been supported by the Finnish Funding Agency for Innovation (project Re:Know) and the Academy of Finland (Finnish Centre of Excellence in Computational Inference Research COIN, 251170).

References

1. Abiteboul, S., André, B., Kaplan, D.: Managing your digital life. Commun. ACM **58**(5), 32–35 (2015)
2. Bengio, Y., Courville, A., Vincent, P.: Representation learning: a review and new perspectives. IEEE Trans. Pattern Anal. Mach. Intell. **35**(8), 1798–1828 (2013)
3. Bray, T.: The JavaScript Object Notation (JSON) data interchange format. RFC 7159 (Proposed Standard), March 2014
4. Bush, V.: As we may think. Atl. Mon. **176**, 101–108 (1945)
5. Cawthon, N., Moere, A.V.: The effect of aesthetic on the usability of data visualization. In Proceedings of the 11th International Conference on Information Visualization, pp. 637–648 (2007)
6. Chaudhry, A., Crowcroft, J., Howard, H., Madhavapeddy, A., Mortier, R., Haddadi, H., McAuley, D., Data, P.: Thinking inside the box. In: Proceedings of the 5th Decennial Aarhus Conference on Critical Alternatives, pp. 29–32 (2015)
7. Council of the European Union: General data protection regulation (2016). http://data.consilium.europa.eu/doc/document/ST-5419-2016-INIT/en/pdf
8. de Montjoye, Y.-A., Shmueli, E., Wang, S.S., Pentland, A.S.: openPDS: protecting the privacy of metadata through SafeAnswers. PLoS ONE **9**(7), e98790 (2014)
9. Dumais, S., Cutrell, E., Cadiz, J., Jancke, G., Sarin, R., Robbins, D.C.: Stuff i've seen: a system for personal information retrieval and re-use. In: Proceedings of the 26th Annual International ACM SIGIR Conference on Research and Development in Information Retrieval, pp. 72–79 (2003)
10. Alén-Savikko, A. et al.: MyData Architecture - Consent Based Approach for Personal Data Management (2016). https://github.com/HIIT/mydata-stack
11. Frank, E., Paynter, G.W., Witten, I.H., Gutwin, C., Nevill-Manning, C.G.: Domain-specific keyphrase extraction. In: Proceedings of the 16th International Joint Conference on Artificial Intelligence, pp. 668–673 (1999)
12. Gemmell, J., Bell, G., Lueder, R.: MyLifeBits: a personal database for everything. Commun. ACM **49**(1), 88–95 (2006)
13. Guillaumin, M., Mensink, T., Verbeek, J., Schmid, C.: Tagprop: discriminative metric learning in nearest neighbor models for image auto-annotation. In: Proceedings of the 12th International Conference on Computer Vision, pp. 309–316 (2009)
14. Gurrin, C., Smeaton, A.F., Doherty, A.R.: Lifelogging: personal big data. Found. Trends Inf. Retr. **8**(1), 1–125 (2014)
15. Kulesza, T., Amershi, S., Caruana, R., Fisher, D., Charles, D.: Structured labeling for facilitating concept evolution in machine learning. In: Proceedings of the SIGCHI Conference on Human Factors in Computing Systems, pp. 3075–3084 (2014)

16. Le, Q., Mikolov, T.: Distributed representations of sentences and documents. In: Proceedings of the 31st International Conference on Machine Learning, pp. 1188–1196 (2014)
17. Machulak, M.P., Maler, E.L., Catalano, D., van Moorsel, A.: User-managed access to web resources. In: Proceedings of the 6th ACM Workshop on Digital Identity Management, pp. 35–44 (2010)
18. McAuley, D., Mortier, R., Goulding, J.: The dataware manifesto. In: Proceedings of the 3rd International Conference on Communication Systems and Networks, pp. 1–6 (2011)
19. Mikolov, T., Chen, K., Corrado, G., Dean, J.: Efficient estimation of word representations in vector space. In: Proceedings of the International Conference on Learning Representations Workshop (2013)
20. Moere, A.V., Purchase, H.: On the role of design in information visualization. Inf. Vis. **10**(4), 356–371 (2011)
21. Poikola, A., Kuikkaniemi, K., Honko, H.: MyData - a nordic model for human-centered personal data management and processing. Finnish Ministry of Transport and Communications (2015)
22. Talbot, J., Lee, B., Kapoor, A., Tan, D.S.: EnsembleMatrix: interactive visualization to support machine learning with multiple classifiers. In: Proceedings of the SIGCHI Conference on Human Factors in Computing Systems, pp. 1283–1292 (2009)

A User-Friendly Dictionary-Supported SSVEP-based BCI Application

Piotr Stawicki, Felix Gembler, and Ivan Volosyak$^{(\boxtimes)}$

Faculty of Technology and Bionics, Rhine-Waal University of Applied Sciences,
Kleve, Germany
ivan.volosyak@hochschule-rhein-waal.de
http://www.hochschule-rhein-waal.de

Abstract. A brain-computer interface (BCI) measures and interprets brain signals enabling people to communicate without the use of peripheral muscles. One of the common BCI paradigms are steady state visual evoked potentials (SSVEPs), brain signals induced by gazing at a constantly flickering target. The choice of stimulation frequencies and the number of simultaneously used stimuli highly influence the performance of such SSVEP-based BCI. In this article, a dictionary-driven four class SSVEP-based spelling application is presented, tested, and evaluated. To enhance classification accuracy, frequencies were determined individually with a calibration software for SSVEP-BCIs, enabling non-experts to set up the system. Forty-one healthy participants used the BCI system to spell English sentences (lengths between 23 and 37 characters). All participants completed the spelling task successfully. A mean accuracy of 97.92% and a mean ITR of 23.84 bits/min were achieved, 18 participants even reached 100% accuracy. On average the number of commands needed to spell the example sentences with four classes, without dictionary support is higher by a factor of 1.92. Thanks to the implemented dictionary the time needed to spell typical everyday sentences can be drastically reduced.

Keywords: Brain-Computer Interface (BCI) · Steady-state visual evoked potential (SSVEP) · Dictionary · Wizard

1 Introduction

Brain-Computer Interfaces (BCIs) translate brain signals, usually acquired non-invasively using electroencephalogram (EEG), in computer commands without using the brain's normal output pathways of peripheral nerves and muscles [24]. Such communication technologies have the potential to help people with physical impairments, as they could provide user interfaces that work independently of the person's limitations.

This article focuses on steady state visual evoked potentials (SSVEPs)-based BCIs [3]; a commonly used BCI paradigm. By looking at a flickering visual stimuli, brain signals are modulated with the corresponding frequency. These signals

© The Author(s) 2017
L. Gamberini et al. (Eds.): Symbiotic 2016, LNCS 9961, pp. 168–180, 2017.
DOI: 10.1007/978-3-319-57753-1_15

are then measured with an EEG and can be classified in real time. An SSVEP-based BCI can be utilized as communication tool and is one of the fastest BCI paradigms [1,20].

A crucial point regarding user friendliness is the design of the graphical user interface (GUI). Four class SSVEP-based BCIs have been proven to grant sufficient control over the system and allow greater freedom in the choice of stimulation frequencies than systems with multiple targets [9,11].

Integrated dictionaries can make spelling applications more efficient [13,23]. However, due to the limited number of commands, implementing a dictionary in a four class BCI is a challenge. As the English alphabet consists of 26 letters, multiple steps are necessary to select a letter. Additional steps are needed to select dictionary suggestions.

Various BCI spelling interfaces with built-in dictionaries have already been developed by different research groups [17].

When designing a communication system with text predictive mechanisms, it is important to take its desired use in lifelike scenarios into consideration. In this regard, the presented dictionary was based on word frequency lists for spoken language. As the 200 most frequently spoken words form 80% of the everyday language [4], the use of such frequency lists can greatly accelerate the communication speed of such systems.

Another way to improve the system speed and accuracy is the careful adjustment of key parameters for SSVEP classification. Auto-calibration procedures allow expert-independent home-use of a BCI as they allow people with no technical knowledge to set up the system. Though such calibration methods are common for other BCI approaches [10,13,15,16], they are rarely used for BCIs based on the SSVEP paradigm. However, in the here presented dictionary supported SSVEP-based BCI, a modified version of our earlier developed calibration methods [9] was integrated to set up user specific stimulation frequencies and other key parameters associated with the utilized classification methods such as frequency dependent classification thresholds.

Our goal was to develop a more user-friendly BCI system suitable for daily communication. To achieve this we improved and consolidated our previous developments [9,23]. The here presented dictionary driven, four class SSVEP-based spelling application was tested with 41 participants. We further

- evaluated the efficiency of the integrated dictionary for daily communication by analyzing results of an online spelling task and
- demonstrate that the modified SSVEP-calibration methods allow expert independent adjustment of BCI key parameters.

The paper is organized as follows: the second section describes the experimental setup, and presents details about the spelling interface. The results are presented in the third section, followed by a discussion and conclusion in the final section.

2   Methods and Materials

2.1   Participants

The study was carried out in accordance with the guidelines of the Rhine-Waal University of Applied Sciences. All participants gave written informed consent in accordance with the Declaration of Helsinki. Information needed for the analysis of the experiments was stored anonymously during the experiment; results cannot be traced back to the participant. All participants had the opportunity to opt-out of the study at any time. Forty-one participants (11 female) with a mean (SD) age 22.31 (2.73) years participated in the study. All participants were students or employees of the Rhine-Waal University of Applied Sciences and had little or no previous experience with BCI systems. The EEG recording took place in a normal laboratory room (area $\approx 36\,\mathrm{m}^2$). Spectacles were worn when appropriate. Participants did not receive any financial reward for participation in this study.

2.2   Hardware

Participants were seated in front of a LCD screen (BenQ XL2420T, resolution: 1920×1080 pixels, vertical refresh rate: $120\,\mathrm{Hz}$) at a distance of about 60 cm. The used computer system operated on Microsoft Windows 7 Enterprise running on an Intel processor (Intel Core i7, 3.40 GHz). Standard Ag/AgCl electrodes were used to acquire the signals from the surface of the scalp. The ground electrode was placed over AF_Z, the reference electrode over C_Z, and the eight signal electrodes were placed at predefined locations on the EEG-cap marked with $P_Z, PO_3, PO_4, O_1, O_2, O_Z, O_9,$ and O_{10} in accordance with the international system of EEG electrode placement. Standard abrasive electrolytic electrode gel was applied between the electrodes and the scalp to bring impedances below $5\,\mathrm{k\Omega}$. An EEG amplifier, g.USBamp (Guger Technologies, Graz, Austria), was utilized. The sampling frequency was set to $128\,\mathrm{Hz}$. During the EEG signal acquisition, an analogue band pass filter (between 2 and $30\,\mathrm{Hz}$) and a notch filter (around $50\,\mathrm{Hz}$) were applied directly in the amplifier.

2.3   Signal Acquisition

Minimum energy combination method (MEC) [7,20] was used for SSVEP signal classification. To detect a frequency in the spatially filtered signals, the SSVEP power estimations for the frequencies were normalized into probabilities:

$$p_i = \frac{\hat{P}_i}{\sum_{j=1}^{N_f} \hat{P}_j} \text{ with } \sum_{i=1}^{N_f} p_i = 1 \tag{1}$$

where N_f is the number of considered frequencies and $\hat{P}_i$ is the ith power estimation, $1 \le i \le N_f$. Note that to increase robustness, three additional frequencies (means between pairs of target frequencies, see e.g. [21]) were also considered, hence $N_f = 7$.

All classifications were performed on the basis of the hardware synchronization of the used EEG amplifier (g.USBamp); the new EEG data were transferred to the PC in blocks of 13 samples (101.5625 ms with the sampling rate of 128 Hz). The classification was performed with a stepwise increasing sliding window (up to 20 s) after receiving the new EEG data block. If non of the p_i exceeded a certain corresponding threshold β_i the classifier output was rejected. The choice of the β_i depended on the corresponding stimulation frequency (in general, lower stimulation frequencies produce higher SSVEP-response) but also on user factors as the quality of the SSVEP-signals differ between participants. The values for the β_i were determined with a calibration software [9]. After each classification the classifier output was rejected for the duration of 914 ms (9 blocks). During this gaze shifting period, the targets did not flicker allowing the user to change his/her focus to another target (see [20] for more details).

2.4 Auto-calibration

Key SSVEP-parameters were determined individually for each participant in a short calibration session with the previously developed BCI wizard software [9]. This wizard ran the user through three phases in order to provide participant-specific stimulation frequencies (phases 1 and 2), classification thresholds, and minimal time segment lengths (phase 3).

The number of stable frequencies on LCD monitors is limited by the vertical refresh rate of 120 Hz since the number of frames in a stimulation cycle needs to be a constant [5]. Therefore, only dividers of the monitor's vertical refresh rate were considered as stimulation frequencies. The four optimal stimulation frequencies were drawn from frequencies obtained with dividers between 6 and 24 of the vertical refresh rate (see x-axis of Fig. 3).

The low frequency band overlaps with the alpha band (8–13 Hz), which can cause false classifications [26]. Therefore, alpha activity was measured in phase 1 and critical frequencies were filtered: If a possible target frequency interfered with the users alpha wave (frequency difference less than 0.3 Hz), this frequency would be neglected as described in [9].

The determination of optimal stimulation frequencies was based on a comparison of the integral value of normalized probabilities (1); more details can be found in [9]. The so called multi-target technique (see [22]) where the user focuses on multiple simultaneously flickering stimuli at once, was used to find optimal target frequencies.

In this respect, the user faced sequentially three circles representing possible stimulation frequencies. Each circle flickered for 10 s while EEG data were recorded and the probabilities of the possible target frequencies were sorted from highest averaged probability to lowest. The first two circles contained seven of the considered frequencies each (see Fig. 1a). In order to avoid mutual influences between stimulating frequencies, the seven frequencies contained in each circle followed the additional restrictions rules (see e.g. [22]):

(a) Phase 2 of the wizard.   (b) Phase 3 of the wizard.

Fig. 1. (a) One of the circles containing seven of the considered stimulation frequencies is displayed on the left. Each tested frequency was represented by the same amount of segments spread randomly across the circle. The random distributed segments representing one specific frequency are shown on the right side. (b) In phase 3 the BCI user had to focus on each of the four determined target frequencies. The recorded data were then analyzed to determine frequency specific classification thresholds. (Color online figure)

$$f_i \neq [f_j + f_k]/2, \ f_i \neq 2f_j - f_k, \ f_i \neq 2f_k - f_j. \tag{2}$$

The considered stimulation frequencies for the first circle were 6.32, 7.50, 8.00, 10.00, 10.91, 13.33, and 6.67, 7.06, 8.57, 9.23, 12.00, 15.00, 12.00 Hz for the second circle.

The third circle contained the seven highest ranked frequencies from the first two recordings. Finally the top four frequencies from the third recording were selected as optimal target frequencies. However, if the highest ranked frequency was more than 20% stronger than the second highest, it was filtered out, as too strong SSVEP responses to a particular frequency could cause classification errors.

In order to find optimal thresholds each of the four determined stimulation frequencies were presented as white boxes on the screen (see Fig. 1b). The boxes contained the numbers 1, 2, 3, and 4. Initially, the box containing the number 1 had a red frame, while the frames of the remaining boxes were white. An audio message instructed the user to focus on the box highlighted by the red frame. Each box flickered for 10 s while EEG data were recorded. The flickering stopped for a two seconds break so that further recordings would not be influenced by the SSVEP-responses from the previous one. Then the second box was highlighted and EEG data were recorded again. This procedure was repeated until data for all four frequencies were collected.

The classification thresholds were then determined as follows. For each frequency the distributions of correct and false classifications were calculated for different threshold sets. Through comparison of these distributions optimal thresholds were determined. Therefore, the classification outputs of the recorded data were analyzed with different threshold sets for each frequency. To determine the threshold for a particular target frequency the distributions of false and correct classifications of those outputs were compared. For further details regarding this procedure please refer to [9].

2.5   Dictionary Driven SSVEP-Based Three-Step Speller

The presented *Dictionary driven SSVEP-based Three-step Speller* resembles previously developed GUI layouts [8,14,23] and allows selection of single letters (*spelling mode*) as well as complete words (*dictionary mode*). In each mode, four frequencies were presented as flickering boxes (175×175 pixels) on the monitor. The size of the boxes varied during the experiment as described in [20]. The output of the *Dictionary driven SSVEP-based Three-step Speller*, the spelled text, was displayed at the bottom of the screen.

Spelling Mode. To select a character in the *spelling mode* three steps were necessary. Initially a matrix of nine boxes, each containing three letters of the alphabet (26 letters plus the command space), was presented (see Fig. 2). The frames of the boxes were colored differently for each row, with each color corresponding to one frequency; green ("A B C", "D E F", "G H I"), red ("J K L", "M N O", "P Q R") and blue ("S T U", "V W X", "Y Z _"), respectively. An additional 10th box with a yellow frame, containing the command "Dict/Del" (delete the last spelled character or switch to *dictionary mode*) was located on the left side of the screen. After first selection, the boxes of the selected row were highlighted with individual colors (green, red and blue), while the other rows were grayed out.

To enhance user friendliness, an animation (in the form of a slow rearrangement of the boxes containing the selected single letters) was presented during the gaze shifting period (between the 2nd and 3rd step of the letter selection - *spelling mode*), while the remaining boxes were faded out (Fig. 2b and c). Next four boxes were presented, three representing a single letter and one for the command "back". The purpose of the animation was to show the user from which box the single letters originated. The animation should ensure that the user did not have to search for the desired letter as he/she witnessed the position change. Based on our previous experience, this should reduce the number of wrong selections in the 3rd step. During the first two steps, no gaze shifting was necessary as only the frequencies (and frame colors) changed, but not the position of the target letter. For example, if the user wanted to select the letter "H", initially the target letter was contained in a green-framed box (first row), then in the blue-framed box, and finally in the red-framed box (see Fig. 2a–c). The role of the yellow-framed box changed depending on the current step of the selection phase. In the 1st step of the *spelling mode* the user could enter the *dictionary mode*, see Fig. 2(a) box "Dict/Del", where he/she could delete the last selected letter or word. In the 2nd and 3rd step of the *spelling mode* the yellow framed box contained the command "back" which gave the user the opportunity to go tho the previous step. In order to increase the user friendliness, every command classification was followed by an audio feedback with the name of the selected command or the letter spelled.

174   P. Stawicki et al.

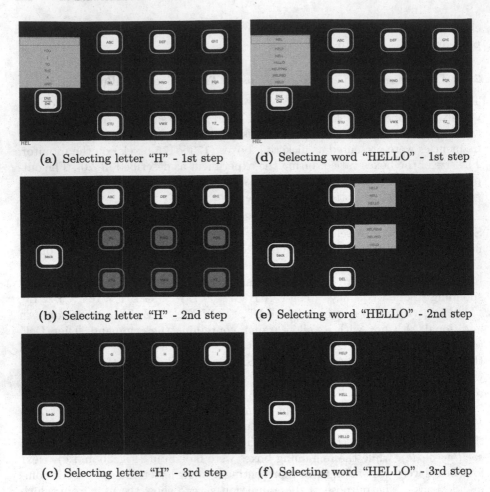

(a) Selecting letter "H" - 1st step   (d) Selecting word "HELLO" - 1st step

(b) Selecting letter "H" - 2nd step   (e) Selecting word "HELLO" - 2nd step

(c) Selecting letter "H" - 3rd step   (f) Selecting word "HELLO" - 3rd step

Fig. 2. Graphical user interface of the *dictionary driven Three-step speller* during the online experiment. At first the participant was selecting the letter "H" (a–c). After the character sequence "HEL" had been selected, the participant entered the *dictionary mode* (d), and selected the word "HELLO" (e, f). In total, twelve correct commands were necessary to select the desired word. (Color figure online)

Dictionary Mode. The *dictionary mode* was used to select from a list of six suggested words which were positioned above the "Dict/Del" button, see Fig. 2(a and d). The presented suggestions were entries from a dictionary containing 39 000 words, ordered by word frequency. This dictionary was derived from a list of the most frequently used words from spoken English (https:// en.wiktionary.org/wiki/Wiktionary:Frequency_lists; accessed on 4th November 2015). Initially, the first six entries of the dictionary were displayed as suggestions. After choosing a single letter in the *spelling mode*, the list of displayed suggestions was updated and contained the first six words from the dictionary list, starting with the selected letter or sequence. If the desired word was displayed as one of the suggestions, the user could switch to the *dictionary mode* and select the whole word directly, or continue to spell the word letter by letter. For example, after entering "HEL" the user was able to choose a word from the suggestion list in three steps: First, the "Dict/Del" button had to be selected to enter the *dictionary mode*. As only four commands were available, the suggestion list was split in two. In a second step, those lists could be selected by gazing at a "select" button located sideways to each list. After selection, the three words from the selected list were displayed in separate boxes and the desired word could be directly selected. Figure 2(d–f), shows the three steps necessary to choose the word "HELLO" after the character chain "HEL" was already selected. When selecting a word from the suggestion list, the system automatically added a white space at the end of the word.

2.6 Experimental Setup

After signing the consent form, each participant completed a brief questionnaire. Thereafter, the participants were prepared for the EEG recording. Participants participated in a brief test run spelling the word "BCI", and a short phrase to get familiar with the application. Next, each participant used the GUI to spell a randomly selected sentence from a list containing 80 sentences from common English conversations. Those sentences were selected from English conversations between two or more people in real life scenarios. Each spelling phase ended automatically when the sentence was spelled correctly. Spelling errors were corrected via the implemented delete button. The entire session took on average about 40 min for each participant.

3 Results

Table 1 summarizes results for all participants. Provided are the time needed to complete the task, the command accuracy and the ITR. It was apparent beforehand that the dictionary support would increase the overall system performance.

BCI performance was evaluated by calculating the commonly used ITR in bits/min (see e.g. [24]):

$$B = \log_2 N + P \log_2 P + (1 - P) \log_2 \left[\frac{1 - P}{N - 1}\right]. \tag{3}$$

In the formula above, B represents the number of bits per trial. The overall number of possible choices was four ($N = 4$), and the accuracy P was calculated based on the number of correct command classifications $\widetilde{C_n}$ divided by the total number of classified commands C_n. To obtain ITR in bits per minute, B is multiplied by the number of command classifications per minute.

Further $\widetilde{C_n^*}$ denotes the number of commands needed to spell the phrase without the implemented dictionary ($\widetilde{C_n^*}$ is three times the sentence length).

Table 1. Results for 41 participants.

Partici-pant	Time [s]	Accuracy [%]	ITR [bits/min]	$\overline{C_n}$	$\overline{C_n^*}$	$\overline{C_n^*}/\overline{C_n}$	Spelling Task
1	343.69	96.72	18.53	59	114	1.93	I_AM_REALLY_LOOKING_FORWARD_TO_SUNDAY
2	227.70	100	23.72	45	96	2.13	I_REMEMBER_NOW_I_MET_HIM_BEFORE
3	236.03	100	21.35	42	72	1.71	WHAT_DO_YOU_DO_FOR_WORK
4	344.70	97.06	20.85	66	111	1.68	REALLY_I_NEED_TO_GO_TO_THE_STORE_TOO
5	164.23	98.00	33.37	49	81	1.65	AT_NIGHT_OR_IN_THE_MORNING
6	192.46	100	20.58	33	84	2.55	SHE_JUST_GOT_HERE_YESTERDAY
7	327.44	98.46	22.17	64	96	1.50	I_WISH_IT_WAS_A_NICER_DAY_TODAY
8	149.60	100	26.47	33	75	2.27	I_THINK_YOU_HAVE_A_VIRUS
9	152.55	100	25.17	32	72	2.25	WHERE_ARE_YOU_GOING_NOW
10	308.34	98.63	26.62	72	108	1.50	I_HAVE_TROUBLE_TAKING_A_DEEP_BREATH
11	150.41	100	**40.69**	51	114	2.24	I_LISTEN_TO_A_DIFFERENT_TYPE_OF_MUSIC
12	245.88	97.92	21.33	47	90	1.91	I_WOULD_LIKE_TO_COME_WITH_YOU
13	310.38	98.21	19.95	55	120	2.18	HOW_LONG_HAVE_YOU_BEEN_STUDYING_ENGLISH
14	418.13	91.18	**6.97**	31	78	2.52	I_WANT_SOMETHING_TO_DRINK
15	195.91	100	33.08	54	117	2.17	I_LIKE_SPAGHETTI_DO_YOU_LIKE_SPAGHETTI
16	109.69	97.30	35.98	36	84	2.33	SHE_JUST_GOT_HERE_YESTERDAY
17	485.37	95.35	8.80	41	75	1.83	WHEN_ARE_YOU_COMING_BACK
18	405.95	96.88	16.55	62	102	1.65	THEY_WERE_NEXT_TO_YOUR_CELL_PHONE
19	859.73	96.00	8.87	72	123	1.71	I_WANT_TO_GO_TO_SEE_A_MOVIE_THIS_WEEKEND
20	180.78	100	35.84	54	90	1.67	AT_NIGHT_YOU_CAN_SEE_THE_STARS
21	212.88	93.75	21.15	45	81	1.80	DID_YOU_GO_TO_SCHOOL_TODAY
22	572.81	100	13.20	63	93	1.48	IT_LOOKS_LIKE_IT_MAY_RAIN_SOON
23	163.31	100	28.66	39	93	2.38	WHEN_ARE_YOU_GOING_ON_VACATION
24	182.91	100	37.39	57	102	1.79	TRAFFIC_IS_NEVER_GOOD_AROUND_HERE
25	240.50	97.37	16.90	37	96	**2.59**	HOW_ABOUT_THE_KOREAN_RESTAURANT
26	549.35	90.12	12.19	73	105	1.44	HOW_LONG_DOES_IT_TAKE_TO_GET_THERE
27	268.02	95.92	18.53	47	93	1.98	WHAT_KIND_OF_MUSIC_DO_YOU_LIKE
28	254.11	96.97	27.37	64	102	1.59	IS_IT_CLOSE_TO_THE_SUBWAY_STATION
29	183.22	98.31	35.73	58	102	1.76	WHAT_ARE_YOU_PLANNING_TO_DO_TODAY
30	405.44	98.28	15.85	57	111	1.95	I_CANNOT_BELIEVE_YOU_REMEMBERED_THAT
31	221.61	94.34	22.91	50	99	1.98	I_KNOW_WHO_YOU_ARE_TALKING_ABOUT
32	496.44	100	10.64	44	105	2.39	HAVE_YOU_BEEN_TO_CALIFORNIA_BEFORE
33	234.41	96.97	29.67	64	120	1.88	HOW_LONG_HAVE_YOU_BEEN_STUDYING_ENGLISH
34	240.50	100	23.95	48	102	2.13	TRAFFIC_IS_NEVER_GOOD_AROUND_HERE
35	197.23	100	34.68	57	90	1.58	AT_NIGHT_YOU_CAN_SEE_THE_STARS
36	160.88	100	40.28	54	123	2.28	DO_YOU_THINK_WE_SHOULD_HAVE_DINNER_FIRST
37	231.97	97.73	20.57	43	99	2.30	I_KNOW_WHO_YOU_ARE_TALKING_ABOUT
38	453.88	100	24.59	93	93	**1.00**	HOW_ABOUT_THE_KOREAN_RESTAURANT
39	188.40	93.10	28.24	54	84	1.56	DID_YOU_LOOK_IN_THE_KITCHEN
40	227.70	100	26.88	51	90	1.76	AT_NIGHT_YOU_CAN_SEE_THE_STARS
41	372.53	100	21.26	66	108	1.64	MY_FATHER_TAUGHT_ME_WHEN_I_WAS_YOUNG
Mean	289.44	97.92	23.84	52.73	97.39	1.92	Mean length of the spelling task: 32.46
SD	112.81	1.95	6.91	10.27	11.67	0.30	characters, Min. 23, Max. 37 characters.

Almost half (18 out of 41) of the participants reached an accuracy of 100% and the rest scored above 93%. The spelling task length varied negligibly from 27 to 37 characters.

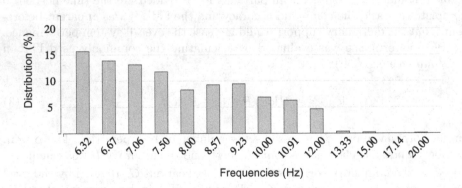

Fig. 3. Frequency power estimations over all participants for the considered frequencies. Probabilities based on the recorded data from the wizard were calculated with the Minimum Energy Combination algorithm.

Figure 3 shows the averaged distribution of the probabilities of the considered frequencies averaged over all participants after the last recording in phase 2 of the wizard. The recorded data were analyzed with the Minimum Energy Combination algorithm to find the frequencies with highest probabilities.

4   Discussion and Conclusion

Though the introduced interface was more complex due to the implementation of the dictionary, neither a drop in accuracy nor speed were observed in comparison to our previous experiments [8,9]. The achieved mean accuracy of 97.92%, as well as the ITR 23.84 bits/min compete with the results from our previous field study where a similar user interface and algorithms were tested (97.02% accuracy and an ITR of 21.58 bits/min were achieved, see [9]).

The dictionary driven speller was implemented as a four-class BCI-system as those systems allow the majority of users to gain control over the system [9,11,19]. Indeed, the accuracies achieved as well as the fact that all participants were able to control the system, confirm that a low number of simultaneously displayed targets might decrease the number of wrong selections, as discussed e.g. in [9]. A further advantage of BCIs with a low number of classes is that they seem to be less stressful for the user (see e.g. [8]). A common drawback of these systems is that due to the used alphabet several steps are necessary to choose a desired target. The time needed to solve the tasks is usually quite large compared to typical input devices or multi-target BCIs (e.g. [12]). However, the accuracy and speed of the system can be increased through mechanisms like this implemented dictionary or other language-based models (see e.g. the review [17]). The number of commands needed to complete the spelling tasks increased on average by a factor of 1.92, if the previously developed three-step spelling application (without dictionary [8]) was used instead (see $\widetilde{C_n^*}/\widetilde{C_n}$ in Table 1).

This factor varied; its maximal value was 2.50. Communication was sped up for almost all participants, however one participant chose purposely not to use the dictionary ($\widetilde{C_n^*}/\widetilde{C_n} = 1.00$). Nevertheless, through the implemented dictionary, the effort to spell typical everyday sentences was reduced immensely for almost all participants. Choosing an appropriate dictionary for everyday use that suits the needs of different users is still a challenging task [4].

Communication interfaces developed for other commonly used BCI approaches yielded similar differences between dictionary driven and conventional spelling. E.g. Akram et al. integrated a word suggestion mechanism in order to reduce typing time into a conventional P300-based speller [2]. With the conventional speller an average word typing time of 2.9 min was achieved. In contrast, with the scheme with word suggestion mechanism the average time was reduced to 1.66 min, which is 1.74 times as fast. D'albis et al. proposed a motor imagery based spelling device adopting natural language processing [6]. The spelling speed with the proposed interface was on average 2.1 times faster (6.15 min compared to 12.93 min with the standard approach).

The automatic calibration procedure integrated in the here presented spelling interface allowed non-experts to setup a functioning SSVEP-BCI with user specific parameters. The experiment was carried out by student assistants with little to no experience in BCI-setup. All necessary parameters were determined automatically. After starting the program no further adjustments by the experimenters were necessary.

The wizard determined a set of target frequencies by comparing SSVEP-responses. As shown in Fig. 3, the lower stimulation frequencies evoked the highest SSVEP-responses, which is inline with previous observations [18]. However, it is known that low frequencies cause more fatigue [25]. A further disadvantage of those frequencies that they overlap with the alpha band (8–13 Hz). If the participant closed the eyes a little too long false classifications might occur. In order to omit this problem the wizard checked the considered frequencies for interference with a participant's alpha wave.

In order to increase user-friendliness of the calibration procedure, we plan to integrate the necessary data recordings for calibration in an online copy spelling task. The dictionary could also be improved. For example, the structure of the already written part of a sentence could also be considered (e.g. through language based spelling correction). Another approach could be the implementation of the detection of error-related potentials that could help the user to correct errors easily. Future work should take those ideas into consideration.

Acknowledgment. This research was supported by the German Federal Ministry of Education and Research (BMBF) under Grants 16SV6364, 01DR14014, and the European Fund for Regional Development (EFRD - or EFRE in German) under Grant GE-1-1-047. We also thank to all the participants of this research study and our student assistants.

References

1. Akce, A., Norton, J., Bretl, T.: An SSVEP-based brain-computer interface for text spelling with adaptive queries that maximize information gain rates. IEEE Trans. Neural Syst. Rehabil. Eng. **23**(5), 857–866 (2015)
2. Akram, F., Metwally, M.K., Han, H.S., Jeon, H.J., Kim, T.S.: A novel p300-based BCI system for words typing. In: 2013 International Winter Workshop on Brain-Computer Interface (BCI), pp. 24–25 (2013)
3. Bin, G., Gao, X., Yan, Z., Hong, B., Gao, S.: An online multi-channel SSVEP-based brain-computer interface using a canonical correlation analysis method. J. Neural Eng. **6**(4), 046002 (2009)
4. Boenisch, J.: Core vocabulary for school-aged students with complex communication needs (Die Bedeutung von Kernvokabular für unterstützt kommunizierende Kinder und Jugendliche). LOGOS Jg. **22**(3), 164–178 (2014)
5. Chen, X., Wang, Y., Nakanishi, M., Jung, T.P., Gao, X.: Hybrid frequency and phase coding for a high-speed SSVEP-based BCI speller. In: 2014 36th Annual International Conference of the IEEE Engineering in Medicine and Biology Society (EMBC), pp. 3993–3996 (2014)

6. D'albis, T., Blatt, R., Tedesco, R., Sbattella, L., Matteucci, M.: A predictive speller controlled by a brain-computer interface based on motor imagery. ACM Trans. Comput. Hum. Interact. **19**(3), 20:1–20:25 (2012)
7. Friman, O., Volosyak, I., Gräser, A.: Multiple channel detection of steady-state visual evoked potentials for brain-computer interfaces. IEEE Trans. Biomed. Eng. **54**(4), 742–750 (2007)
8. Gembler, F., Stawicki, P., Volosyak, I.: Towards a user-friendly BCI for elderly people. In: Proceedings of the 6th International Brain-Computer Interface Conference Graz (2014)
9. Gembler, F., Stawicki, P., Volosyak, I.: Autonomous parameter adjustment for SSVEP-based BCIs with a novel BCI wizard. Front. Neurosci. **9**, 1–12 (2015)
10. Grizou, J., Iturrate, I., Montesano, L., Lopes, M., Oudeyer, P.Y.: Zero-calibration BMIs for sequential tasks using error-related potentials. In: IROS 2013 Workshop on Neuroscience and Robotics (2013)
11. Guger, C., Allison, B.Z., Growindhager, B., Prückl, R., Hintermüller, C., Kapeller, C., Bruckner, M., Krausz, G., Edlinger, G.: How many people could use an SSVEP BCI? Front. Neurosci. **6**, 1–6 (2012)
12. Hwang, H.J., Lim, J.H., Jung, Y.J., Choi, H., Lee, S.W., Im, C.H.: Development of an SSVEP-based BCI spelling system adopting a QWERTY-style LED keyboard. J. Neurosci. Methods **208**(1), 59–65 (2012)
13. Kaufmann, T., Völker, S., Gunesch, L., Kübler, A.: Spelling is just a click away-a user-centered brain-computer interface including auto-calibration and predictive text entry. Front. Neurosci. **6**, 72 (2012)
14. Kick, C., Volosyak, I.: Evaluation of different spelling layouts for SSVEP based BCIs. In: 2014 36th Annual International Conference of the IEEE Engineering in Medicine and Biology Society (EMBC), pp. 1634–1637. IEEE (2014)
15. Kindermans, P.J., Schreuder, M., Schrauwen, B., Müller, K.R., Tangermann, M.: True zero-training brain-computer interfacing-an online study. PLoS ONE (2014)
16. Krauledat, M., Tangermann, M., Blankertz, B., Müller, K.R.: Towards zero training for brain-computer interfacing. PLoS ONE **3**(8), e2967 (2008)
17. Mora-Cortes, A., Manyakov, N.V., Chumerin, N., Van Hulle, M.M.: Language model applications to spelling with brain-computer interfaces. Sensors **14**(4), 5967–5993 (2014)
18. Pastor, M.A., Artieda, J., Arbizu, J., Valencia, M., Masdeu, J.C.: Human cerebral activation during steady-state visual-evoked responses. J. Neurosci. **23**(37), 11621–11627 (2003)
19. Volosyak, I., Valbuena, D., Lüth, T., Malechka, T., Gräser, A.: BCI demographics II: how many (and what kinds of) people can use an SSVEP BCI? IEEE Trans. Neural Syst. Rehabil. Eng. **19**(3), 232–239 (2011)
20. Volosyak, I.: SSVEP-based Bremen-BCI interface - boosting information transfer rates. J. Neural Eng. **8**(3), 036020 (2011)
21. Volosyak, I., Ceçotti, H., Gräser, A.: Steady-state visual evoked potential response - impact of the time segment length. In: Proceedings of the 7th International Conference on Biomedical Engineering BioMed 2010, Innsbruck, 17–19 February, pp. 288–292 (2010)
22. Volosyak, I., Malechka, T., Valbuena, D., Graeser, A.: A novel calibration method for SSVEP based brain-computer interfaces. In: Proceeding 18th European Signal Processing Conference (EUSIPCO 2010), pp. 939–943 (2010)

23. Volosyak, I., Moor, A., Gräser, A.: A dictionary-driven SSVEP speller with a modified graphical user interface. In: Cabestany, J., Rojas, I., Joya, G. (eds.) IWANN 2011. LNCS, vol. 6691, pp. 353–361. Springer, Heidelberg (2011). doi:10.1007/978-3-642-21501-8_44
24. Wolpaw, J., Birbaumer, N., McFarland, D., Pfurtscheller, G., Vaughan, T.: Brain-computer interfaces for communication and control. Clin. Neurophysiol. **113**, 767–791 (2002)
25. Won, D.O., Hwang, H.J., Dähne, S., Müller, K.R., Lee, S.W.: Effect of higher frequency on the classification of steady-state visual evoked potentials. J. Neural Eng. **13**(1), 016014 (2015)
26. Zhu, D., Bieger, J., Molina, G.G., Aarts, R.M.: A survey of stimulation methods used in SSVEP-based BCIs. Comput. Intell. Neurosci. **1**, 702357 (2010)

Author Index

Printed in the United States
By Bookmasters